D0331159

EVERYTHING I NEED TO
KNOW I LEARNED IN THE

TWILIGHT
ZONE

Rod Serling *Courtesy SUNY Broome Community College*

Also by Mark Dawidziak

NONFICTION

The Barter Theatre Story: Love Made Visible

The Columbo Phile: A Casebook

Night Stalking: A 20th Anniversary Kolchak Companion

The Night Stalker Companion: A 25th Anniversary Tribute

Horton Foote's The Shape of the River: The Lost Teleplay About Mark Twain

The Bedside, Bathtub & Armchair Companion to Dracula

Jim Tully: American Writer, Irish Rover, Hollywood Brawler (with Paul J. Bauer)

Mark Twain in Ohio

NOVEL

Grave Secrets

EDITOR

Mark My Words: Mark Twain on Writing

Richard Matheson's Kolchak Scripts

Bloodlines: Richard Matheson's Dracula, I Am Legend, and Other Vampire Stories

Beggars of Life by Jim Tully (with Paul J. Bauer)

Circus Parade by Jim Tully (with Paul J. Bauer)

Shanty Irish by Jim Tully (with Paul J. Bauer)

The Bruiser by Jim Tully (with Paul J. Bauer)

Richard Matheson's Censored and Unproduced I Am Legend Screenplay

Mark Twain's Guide to Diet, Exercise, Beauty, Fashion, Investment, Romance, Health and Happiness

Mark Twain for Cat Lovers: True and Imaginary Adventures with Feline Friends

MARK DAWIDZIAK

EVERYTHING I NEED TO KNOW I LEARNED IN THE

TWILIGHT ZONE

A Fifth-Dimension
Guide to Life

THOMAS DUNNE BOOKS
ST. MARTIN'S PRESS
NEW YORK

THOMAS DUNNE BOOKS.
An imprint of St. Martin's Press.

EVERYTHING I NEED TO KNOW I LEARNED IN THE TWILIGHT ZONE.
Copyright © 2017 by Mark Dawidziak. Foreword copyright © 2017
by Anne Serling. All rights reserved. Printed in the United States
of America. For information, address St. Martin's Press,
175 Fifth Avenue, New York, N.Y. 10010.

www.thomasdunnebooks.com
www.stmartins.com

Library of Congress Cataloging-in-Publication Data

Names: Dawidziak, Mark, 1956– author.
Title: Everything I need to know I learned in the Twilight zone : a
    fifth-dimension guide to life / Mark Dawidziak.
Description: First edition. | New York : Thomas Dunne Books/St. Martin's
    Press, 2017. Includes index.
Identifiers: LCCN 2016038765| ISBN 9781250082374 (hardcover)
    | ISBN 9781250082381 (e-book)
Subjects: LCSH: Conduct of life. | Twilight zone (Television program :
    1959–1964)—Miscellanea. | Dawidziak, Mark, 1956– | BISAC:
    PERFORMING ARTS / Television / History & Criticism. | SELF-HELP
    / General.
Classification: LCC BJ1589 .D39 2017 | DDC 170/.44—dc23
LC record available at https://lccn.loc.gov/2016038765

Our books may be purchased in bulk for promotional, educational,
or business use. Please contact your local bookseller or the Macmillan
Corporate and Premium Sales Department at 1-800-221-7945, extension
5442, or by e-mail at MacmillanSpecialMarkets@macmillan.com.

First Edition: February 2017

10 9 8 7 6 5 4 3 2 1

To Becky,
who shares walks and talks, a sense of wonder
and a sense of humor—with much love

CONTENTS

CONTENTS

Rod Serling's love of dogs (see Lesson 8) is wonderfully evident in this photograph taken by another writer named Serling, his daughter Anne. His friend is the family setter, Michael. *Courtesy Anne Serling*

OVERTURE *for*
ANOTHER DIMENSION

I'm talking about this past season . . . some were dramatic and moving, such as . . . Twilight Zone. . . . When television is good, nothing—not the theater, not the magazines or newspapers— nothing is better.

—Newton N. Minow,
chairman, Federal Communications Commission,
May 9, 1961, speech

He dreamed of much for us, and demanded much of himself, perhaps more than was possible for either in this time and place. But it is that quality of dreams and demands that makes the ones like Rod Serling rare . . . and always irreplaceable.

—Gene Roddenberry,
July 7, 1975, memorial service for Rod Serling

That The Twilight Zone *is damn near immortal is something I will not argue with. . . .*

—Stephen King,
Danse Macabre (1981)

Everybody who does this well, which means fantasy television that has something to say, owes a debt to Rod Serling and The Twilight Zone. *There's TV that kills time and leaves you empty. And then there is TV that is nourishing and nurturing to the soul. That's the type of television Rod Serling did better than anybody else.*

—Frank Spotnitz,
writer-producer, *The X-Files*,
2009 interview with author

It has forever been thus: so long as men write what they think, then all of the other freedoms—all of them—may remain intact. And it is then that writing becomes a weapon of truth, an article of faith, an act of courage.

—Rod Serling,
January 15, 1968, speech

FOREWORD

When Mark asked me to write the foreword to his book, I was both honored and petrified. Honored to be asked and petrified that I had nothing I could add to a book that so clearly articulates the parables of *The Twilight Zone* and pays such heartfelt homage to my dad's work and life. I would like to say that I wrestled with this quandary for days, but, truth be known, it was months. Then, like most ideas, it evolved iteratively until finally the fog lifted and I knew—write about how Mark and I met and one of his very first questions to me: "Why do you think your father wrote what he did?"

Mark and I first connected through Charlotte Gusay, who was representing Mark's proposal for this book. Coincidently, another writer friend, Mark Olshaker, and I were at the same time considering writing a similar book based on my experience with the Fifth Dimension, an elementary school program introducing fifth graders to *The Twilight Zone*. A series of telephone introductions and follow-up calls led to a midpoint meeting at my home to discuss working together on the project. Despite all our good intentions to push the project forward, life happened.

Mark returned to his day job and working on another Mark Twain book; Mark Olshaker succumbed to the pressures of completing a two-book deal on criminal injustice with FBI profiler John Douglas; and I found myself submerged in writing a memoir about my father. But what remained was Mark's question—something I was curious about as I explored both the personal and professional sides of my father's life for the memoir.

So then, what, in fact, do I think about why my father wrote what he did? Before I answer, let me say that I am neither an academic nor a researcher. I am extremely biased; and my thoughts are based on personal experience and comments from those who knew my dad or were fans. That said, let me share with you what I have come to believe by beginning at the beginning.

My father, born on December 25, 1924, often referred to himself as "a Christmas present that was delivered unwrapped," even though he was raised in a Reform Jewish family. Growing up in Binghamton, New York, an enlightened and viable manufacturing hub, my dad was (for the most part) sheltered from the Depression. He was exposed to the industrial philanthropy of George Johnson, who donated Recreation Park (three blocks from my dad's house), along with six carousels to the city and surrounding municipalities. Johnson "felt carousels contributed to a happy life and would help youngsters grow into strong and useful citizens" and "believed carousels should be enjoyed by everyone and insisted that the municipalities never charge money for a magic ride." This enlightened and stable environment, along with the unconditional love of his parents, provided my father an idyllic childhood of riding bikes to the park; Saturday matinees; reading *Amazing Stories,* Poe, and Lovecraft; and forging lifelong friendships.

While the idealism of his childhood may in part explain his propensity for nostalgia, I think other childhood experiences are also important. Although always proud of his Jewish heritage, I suspect that my grandfather's philosophy of taking people "for who they are, not where they go to pray" resonated deeply within my dad. I also think the fact that my father was blackballed from his Jewish fraternity in high school for dating non-Jewish girls hurt him profoundly and was the genesis for his belief that prejudice is the greatest evil of all time.

My dad graduated from high school in January 1943 and within days enlisted, hoping to fight the Nazis in Europe. He ended up a paratrooper in the army (511 Airborne Division) and was dropped onto Leyte in the Philippines, where he witnessed some of the fiercest fighting of World War II. During this time he saw his friend decapitated by an air-dropped supply crate; narrowly escaped death, thanks to a buddy's shooting an enemy soldier whose rifle was aimed directly at my dad; and wrote a short story, "First Squad, First Platoon," which opens with a dedication to his unborn children:

> I'm dedicating my little story to you; doubtless you will be among the very few who will ever read it. It seems war stories aren't very well received at this point. I'm told they're outdated, untimely, and as might be expected—make some unpleasant reading. And, as you have no doubt already perceived, human beings don't like to remember unpleasant things. They gird themselves with the armor of wishful thinking; protect themselves with a shield of impenetrable optimism; and, with a few exceptions, seem to accomplish their "forgetting" quite admirably.
>
> But you, my children, I don't want you to be among those who choose to forget. I want you to read my stories and a lot of others like them. I want you to fill your heads with Remarque and Tolstoy and Ernie Pyle. I want you to know what shrapnel and "88's" and mortar shells and mustard gas mean. I want you to feel, no matter how vicariously, a semblance of the feeling of a torn limb; a burnt patch of flesh;

the crippling, numbing sensation of fear; the hopeless empti-
ness of fatigue. All these things are complimentary to the
province of War and they should be taught and demonstrated
in classrooms along with the more heroic aspects of uniforms,
and flags, and honor and patriotism. I have no idea what
your generation will be like. In mine we were to enjoy "Peace
in our time." A very well-meaning gentleman waved his um-
brella and shouted those very words . . . less than a year before the whole world went to war. But this gentleman was
suffering the worldly disease of insufferable optimism. He
and his fellow humans kept polishing their rose-colored
glasses when actually they should have taken them off. They
were sacrificing reason and reality for a brief and temporal
peace of mind, the same peace of mind that many of my contemporaries derive by steadfastly refraining from remembering the War that came before.

He was nineteen years old when he wrote these words. While
memories of the horrors of war would forever impact my father's
life, I believe the real significance of his story's dedication is his
concern for the future of my generation and those that follow.
Here, in the midst of battle, tired and fearful for his life, he articulates both his hopes for humanity and his understanding of
the human condition. Both foreshadow the writer and the man
my father became.

As scarring as the war was, another horrendous incident occurred while he was in the Pacific theater—the early death of
his father, whom he adored. Despite the war's being over, my
dad was not allowed to return home for the funeral. I am certain that the pain of his father's death, juxtaposed against his
memories of an idyllic childhood, played heavily in the creation of his nostalgic works: "Walking Distance," "A Stop at
Willoughby," and "They're Tearing Down Tim Riley's Bar."

Upon his return to the States, he followed his brother's footsteps to Antioch College. His plan was to major in physical education, because he liked working with kids. However, haunted by unresolved memories of war and the fact that he found writing to be cathartic, he changed his major to language and literature. He once described it as "a kind of compulsion to get some thoughts down, and the desperate sense of a terrible need for some sort of therapy . . . I needed to get it out of my gut, write it down. This was the way it began for me."

Antioch, one of the first colleges to offer work-study programs, proved to be an ideal setting for such a beginning. Philosophically, one of the college's guiding principles were the words of its first president, Horace Mann—"Be ashamed to die until you have won some victory for humanity." This quote resonated deeply with my father and his concern for humanity on one level or another is evident throughout his work. (This quote, in fact, will appear in my dad's *Twilight Zone* episode "The Changing of the Guard.") Additionally, the liberal, freethinking traditions of Antioch honed my father's convictions. His intolerance of racism, impatience with ill-founded opinions, and ability to see many facets of an argument flourished in that environment. By way of example, I recall his classmate, Monroe "Mike" Newman telling me that once

> A group was sitting on the floor in the dorm hallway, discussing the wisdom and ethics of the death penalty. Your dad came out of his room and told us we had overlooked a key. The key was that some part of the executioner died with each execution. Immediately he returned to his room and slammed the door.

The seeds of his strongly felt convictions, understanding of human nature, and ability to see beyond the obvious were nourished at Antioch and would become the trademarks of his work. Beyond its philosophical influence, Antioch provided my father with a unique opportunity in the way of a dilapidated student radio station. With the support of the college, my father upgraded the station and began writing, producing, and acting in programs. I truly believe that writing radio scripts and experiencing the drama with which they could be presented is what led my father to becoming a playwright. Not unlike a painter, he discovered that the use of words and intonation in dialogue could vividly portray images of an evolving story in a listener's mind. This was a skill he worked to perfect and ultimately won second prize in a *Dr. Christian* radio script contest, which included a trip to New York City.

Graduating from Antioch, where they had met as students, my parents moved to Cincinnati, where my dad wrote first for a radio station and then for a television station. It was the late 1940s, television was evolving as a new broadcast medium, and my father envisioned it as a means of bringing theater (à la Broadway) to the masses. My father spent evenings writing and submitting teleplays to the networks in New York City. Despite having worked only in radio, my dad had a knack for setting up the visual aspect of his scripts. After numerous rejections, he sold a couple of scripts; with my mother's blessing they decided to move to Connecticut and he to freelance.

As my father's success grew, his writing became more socially commentative, which was in keeping with the undercurrents of the immense postwar changes that were developing. Contrary to popular opinion, the 1950s was far more than a time of *Ozzie and Harriet* comfort and complacency. It was a time that saw the birth of the Beat Generation, feminism, the sexual revolution, and the civil rights movement. This turbulence jibed with my father's inherent concern for the well-being of humanity, his need to speak out, and it often informed the subject matter of his stories. In both *Patterns* and *Requiem for a Heavyweight,* the hallmark beginnings of my father's career, the protagonists, although influenced by the contexts in which they find themselves, are ultimately free and able to determine their outcomes through acts of will. Of *Requiem* my dad said, "Its basic premise is that every man can and must search for his own dignity."

This arguably existentialist approach to storytelling runs through much of my father's works in the sense that he often portrays subjects in challenging situations in which individual choices decide results, leaving his audience to ponder—"What would I have done in the situation?"

Beyond the influence of existentialism, the murder of fourteen-year-old Emmett Till and the release of those responsible profoundly affected my father. *Noon on Doomsday* was his first attempt to tell the story and it was turned down by the sponsors who were afraid it might offend their southern customers. Subsequently he revised the script by changing the ethnicity and locale to a Jewish immigrant in the northeast and then to a Mexican boy in the southwest, in a script entitled, *A Town Has Turned to Dust*. By the end, as he said, "my script had turned to dust," and he was left frustrated by television's refusal to provide comment on relevant social issues. This was not a new experience. He had battled network executives and their sponsors before, but it was becoming increasingly clear that his conviction that it is "the writer's role to menace the public's conscience" was not something that television as it existed then would consider, let alone welcome. He needed a work-around and, with television evolving from live to prerecorded programs, the opportunity soon presented itself.

With the death of live television and the growth of prerecorded television on the West Coast, we moved to LA in 1958. An expanding industry with an insatiable need for content, coupled with my father's reputation as an established television writer, enabled him to sell a number of teleplays. Among them, a fantasy piece called *The Time Element,* which CBS bought and shelved. That is until a producer convinced them to air it on *Desilu Playhouse,* where it received rave notices and prompted

CBS to approach my dad for a series. This was the break he needed. With his childhood love of fantasy and having at times written in the genre, it dawned on him that this was the work-around. As he said, "An alien can say things that a Democrat or Republican can't." With this in mind, he set up his own production company, Cayuga Productions, Inc., and cut a fifty-fifty deal with CBS—he would be the primary writer and responsible for producing the episodes and they would finance and air the shows. And so *The Twilight Zone* was born with my father having complete creative control without network or sponsor interference. Although he ended up writing 92 of the 156 episodes, he knew he couldn't do it alone and assembled an extraordinary team of talented writers (Charles Beaumont; Earl Hamner Jr.; George Clayton Johnson; Richard Matheson, among others), creative directors, and savvy producers. Once asked what it was like to work at Cayuga Productions, producer Buck Houghton responded, "It was a happy place." I suspect his characterization was spot-on in light of the fact that everyone on the team had recently witnessed the paranoia of the Mc-Carthy era and experienced the censorship of networks and sponsors. To have a platform and the freedom to comment on social issues—such as prejudice, racism, peer pressure, bullying, scapegoating, and any other of the human race's lunacies—had to be an incredible relief for all. I am convinced that one of the reasons that *The Twilight Zone* has survived all these years is because of the synergy of the team, creative individuals who relished the opportunity to focus on their art without the interference of commercial interests. And it is without question the main reason it has survived is its messages about the pitfalls of human nature, which sadly remain relevant and prevalent today.

It has often been said that the episodes of *The Twilight Zone* are parables—short allegorical stories designed to illustrate or teach some truth or moral lesson. My father always said, though, "Whenever you write, whatever you write, *never* make the mistake of assuming the *audience* is any *less intelligent* than you are." Keeping that in mind, he used television as a vehicle to bring awareness of the hypocrisy and disingenuous nature of many of the ills wrought on society by selfishness, apathy, and lack of a moral compass.

Throughout his career my father's deepest concern was for the well-being of humanity. That is evident in all his writings and speeches, but the realm of his concerns culminates in the parables of *The Twilight Zone*. So what exactly are these lessons gathered on *The Twilight Zone* and how are they relevant today? Well, dear reader, you are among the very fortunate in that you are holding the answer in your hands—Mark Dawidziak's book *Everything I Needed to Know I Learned in the Twilight Zone*. It is more than a simple catalog of lessons. It is an in-depth analysis of the multiple lessons to be found in any given episode. Written in a light and entertaining way, the book successfully disguises the profoundness of its analysis and intent, much like the *Twilight Zone* parables themselves. Without question, this book is destined to become the shelf mate to Marc Scott Zicree's *The Twilight Zone Companion*.

In conclusion and in answer to Mark's question, "Why did you father write what he did?" I think the answer is quite simply he truly and deeply cared about all of us.

—ANNE SERLING

ACKNOWLEDGMENTS

Willie Nelson famously proclaimed that his heroes have always been cowboys. That's all well and good for Willie, but I'm singing a slightly different tune. Allow me, if you will, to change one word of that familiar song title. Make it, "My Heroes Have Always Been Writers." The redheaded stranger opts for the riders of the range. I have long been under the spell of writers ranging from Mark Twain and Charles Dickens to John Steinbeck and Dashiell Hammett. Rod Serling has been near the top of that list since my youthful encounters with *The Twilight Zone,* but the more I learn about him, the more wonderfully heroic he gets. So the acknowledgments start there, with Rod Serling, for staking out and cultivating the rich territory where these lessons could take root and blossom for one generation of viewers after another.

I never got the chance to meet Rod Serling, but the universe has rewarded me with the friendship of another gifted writer named Serling: Rod's daughter Anne. She already knows how much her encouragement and support has meant during the writing of this book. This acknowledgment is placed here so everybody else will know how deeply appreciative I am. And would you believe it? I had the chance to introduce my wife and daughter to Anne and her husband, Doug Sutton, in a town called Willoughby (just east of Cleveland . . . look it up). Fans of *The Twilight Zone* will immediately recognize and appreciate the lovely geographic appropriateness of that. Anyone interested in learning about the real Rod Serling needs to read Anne's profoundly moving memoir, *As I Knew Him: My Dad, Rod Serling*.

Another expert guide was the late Richard Matheson, one of the principal writers on *The Twilight Zone*. I am deeply grateful to Richard for the years of conversation, friendship, and insight. There was a lot of talk about many of the titles on his amazing résumé—from *I Am Legend* and *The Shrinking Man* to *Duel* and *The Night Stalker*—and, of course, there was talk about *The Twilight Zone*. Another hero and another gift from the universe. So here is as good a place as any to acknowledge there would be no lessons from *The Twilight Zone* without Serling, Matheson, and the show's other main storytellers: Charles Beaumont, George Clayton Johnson, and Earl Hamner Jr.

It is a complete pleasure to acknowledge my fellow board members at Rod Serling Books: Mark Olshaker, Jim Benson, and Scott Skelton. Each of them has contributed mightily to our understanding of Rod Serling and his work. Jim and Scott are the planet's leading experts on Rod Serling's *Night Gallery,* and Mark was a teenager when he became friends with Rod.

Much has been written on *The Twilight Zone,* but the landmark book that kicked things into high gear was Marc Scott Zicree's *The Twilight Zone Companion*. My well-thumbed first edition has been kept in easy reach since it was published in 1982. I've consulted it often, along with: *Visions from The Twilight Zone* (1990), Arlen Schumer's exploration of the surrealistic and psychological aspects of the series; Peter Wolfe's 1997 study, *In the Zone: The Twilight World of Rod Serling; Dimensions Behind The Twilight Zone: A Backstage Tribute to*

Television's Groundbreaking Series, Stewart T. Stanyard's 2007 collection of interviews and behind-the-scenes pictures; Martin Grams Jr.'s invaluable *The Twilight Zone: Unlocking the Door to a Television Classic* (2008); editors Noël Carroll and Lester Hunt's 2008 collection of essays, *Philosophy in The Twilight Zone;* and the analytical *Rod Serling and The Twilight Zone: A 50th Anniversary Tribute,* the 2011 book by Douglas Brode and Carol Kramer Serling.

During more than thirty-five years as a theater, film, and television critic, I've had the privilege of interviewing many people who worked on *The Twilight Zone* or knew Rod Serling. Each provided some insight into the writer and the writing. They include: Claude Akins, Theodore Bikel, James Coburn, Dan Curtis, Donna Douglas, Howard Duff, Robert Duvall, Peter Falk, Jack Grinnage, Earl Hamner Jr., Jonathan Harris, Mariette Hartley, Sandy Kenyon, Richard Kiley, Jack Klugman, Kevin McCarthy, Roddy McDowell, William F. Nolan, Jack Palance, Cliff Robertston, Carol Kramer Serling, William Shatner, and William Windom.

Over the years, I've been collecting favorite *Twilight Zone* lessons from those involved with the series or influenced by it. You'll find several of these scattered throughout the book, including gems from James Best, Ray Bradbury, Brannon Braga, James L. Brooks, Mel Brooks, Carol Burnett, Chris Carter, David Chase, Joseph Dougherty, Harlan Ellison, Tom Fontana, Mick Garris, James Grady, Martin Grams, Jonathan Harris, George Clayton Johnson, Jack Klugman, Leonard Maltin, Bill Mumy, Greg Nicotero, Robert Redford, Carl Reiner, Frank Spotnitz, Robert J. Thompson, Neil deGrasse Tyson, Dick Van Dyke, Fritz Weaver, and Marc Scott Zicree. A special shout-out to TV critic and historian David Bianculli, who not only provided one of these guest lessons but also solicited others for the book.

And major thanks to:

ACKNOWLEDGMENTS

- Gil Schwartz, Gail Plautz, and David Lombard at CBS for their assistance regarding *Twilight Zone* images. Although this book is not licensed, authorized, endorsed, or sponsored by CBS, which controls the rights to the filmed versions of *Twilight Zone* episodes, their advice, guidance, and encouragement are greatly appreciated.
- Brendan Deneen and Nicole Sohl at Thomas Dunne Books for giving this book a home.
- Tireless champion and agent extraordinaire Charlotte Gusay for her incredible tenacity, belief, and support.
- And Sara and Becky, who are pretty wonderful at being pretty wonderful.

Rod Serling ready to welcome you . . . to the Twilight Zone. *Courtesy CBS Photo Archive*

EVERYTHING I NEED TO
KNOW I LEARNED IN THE

TWILIGHT
ZONE

LESSONS FROM *THE TWILIGHT ZONE*: SUBMITTED FOR YOUR IMPROVEMENT

When the signpost up ahead indicated that my daughter, Becky, was about to turn fifteen, I figured it was time to introduce her to that "wondrous land whose boundaries are that of imagination." Her next stop—*The Twilight Zone*, the classic 1959–1964 fantasy anthology series created by Rod Serling.

This was in the spring of 2011. She had been carefully prepared for this journey into a land of both shadow and substance, of things and ideas. She wasn't quite a child of television, but she was the child of a television critic. She had learned to be her own programmer, breaking open those magical box sets and discovering the black-and-white joys of classic television shows. You might call this a classical education. Becky loved Lucy. She loved spending time with Andy and Barney in Mayberry. She loved hanging with Rob, Buddy, and Sally in the writers' room of *The Alan Brady Show*, the fictional show within *The Dick Van Dyke Show*. The joke around our house was, "Someday, this kid is going to be shocked to find out they're making TV in color."

That joke hit its expiration date when Becky tore through all forty-five of the original *Columbo* mysteries and the box sets for *Night Gallery,* the 1969 TV movie and 1970–1973 horror anthology series that featured *Twilight Zone* creator, host, producer, and principal writer Rod Serling as host and contributing writer. I could sense Rod standing behind me. I could hear his voice. "It is time."

Picture a man sharing the televised delights of his childhood with a delighted child. The flickering images on the screen by any standard cover an enormous amount of territory, touching on the past, the present, and, yes, the future. And they'll soon discover this territory truly is as vast as space and as timeless as infinity—because these images are being beamed directly from the Twilight Zone.

We made this trip in strict chronological order, starting with the first episode aired in 1959 ("Where Is Everybody?"), then letting Rod guide us from story to story. Becky was more than willing to be guided. In addition to being a regular visitor to Rod's *Night Gallery,* she was a great fan of fantasy literature. She was well acquainted with such magical landscapes as Oz, Narnia, Hogwarts, and Ray Bradbury's Martian terrain. A memorable third-season episode penned by Richard Matheson is titled "Little Girl Lost." Becky soon became little girl lost in the Twilight Zone . . . make that happily lost in the Twilight Zone.

It quickly became a family ritual: two episodes a night, two parents, one fascinated teenager. Part of this ritual developed at the conclusion of the sixth episode, "Escape Clause," originally aired on November 6, 1959. For those that don't immediately recognize the title, here's the quick rundown. David Wayne plays cranky Walter Bedeker, a hypochondriac afraid of "death, disease, other people, germs, drafts and everything else." A certain Mr. Cadwallader (Thomas Gomez) shows up with a devilishly seductive offer. If Bedeker signs the contract, he'll be granted immortality and indestructibility. The catch? Should Bedeker for some reason choose to leave this mortal plane, he will relinquish his soul to Cadwallader. Before he leaves, Cadwallader tells Bedeker that the contract contains an escape clause. If he should ever tire of life, he need only summon Cadwallader and, uh, give the Devil his due.

Well, this is *The Twilight Zone,* folks, so you know that no good can come from making bargains signed with an unmistakable whiff of brimstone in the air. Cadwallader realizes this. The audience realizes this. The only person who doesn't seem to realize this is the blindly overconfident Walter Bedeker, who does, of course, ultimately exercise the escape clause.

When the episode penned by Serling was over, I turned to Becky and playfully admonished her with a wagging finger: "Let that be a lesson to you. Always read through a contract, looking for loopholes. Never sign anything without considering the consequences. Consider the case of one Walter Bedeker."

She chuckled. I chuckled. Then I thought about the mortgage crisis and about how many people actually signed contracts, not reading them through, not knowing the ramifications of what they'd signed. Would our nation be in such a deep financial hole if we'd all profited from the case of one Walter Bedeker? Talk about your deals with the Devil. So, after a pause, I turned to Becky and added, "No, really."

It became a running gag at our house. When an excursion through *The Twilight Zone* was completed, I'd turn to Becky and say, "Let that be a lesson to you." That lasted for about four months (about how long it took us to get through all five seasons), but, hey, I can run a running gag into the ground with the best of them. Let that be a lesson to you.

Still, from the running gag we'd inevitably stroll into an actual discussion of what was going on behind all the fun fantasy and delicious irony.

This kind of evening lesson became a ritual for us after each episode, until the penny dropped. If that penny had been dropped into the tabletop fortune-telling machine featured in Richard Matheson's second-season episode "Nick of Time," it would have produced a card that read, "You've got a book on your hands, stupid." I realized there truly is a wonderful set of life rules here. Not only could you live your life according to the precepts and parables of *The Twilight Zone,* maybe you *should.*

Most of the original 156 *Twilight Zone* episodes (ninety-two of them written by Serling) were, after all, little morality plays. There was no grand, minutely defined philosophy at work here, but there was a strong social conscience, framed by a deep sense of justice and ethics. There was an ongoing search for self-awareness, as individuals and as a race. And there were the cautionary tales, the wake-up calls, and the words of warning, courtesy of Serling, Matheson, and the other writers.

The characters who took it in the shorts on *The Twilight Zone* usually were asking for it (boy, were they asking for it). The characters who followed their hearts were, at the very least, rewarded with a dose of enlightenment. The characters who irrevocably lost their way typically were undone by greed, prejudice, anger, spite, envy, intolerance, cruelty, ignorance, hate, resentment, and cynicism. The characters who found some measure of contentment shunned these corrosive things that eat you alive from the inside.

Good people tended to get a second chance in *The Twilight Zone.* Mean, petty, bigoted people tended to be on the receiving end of some terrible form of cosmic justice. Make no mistake: the irony cut both ways in the ol' fifth dimension beyond that which is known to man.

Think of the number of times Rod closed his narration with something like, "Tonight's lesson . . . in the Twilight Zone."

When a word to the wise was sufficient, travelers to the Twilight Zone could move on, move up, or move past the problem condemning them to a life of more shadow and less substance. When danger signals failed to be heeded, then, yes, the moral of a *Twilight Zone* story could have quite a nasty sting in its tail.

When you take it all right back down home, it comes to this. You'd be a better person if you took to heart the principles at work in *The Twilight Zone*. It would be a better world if we all lived according to the rules and precepts of *The Twilight Zone*. Perhaps that's because Rod Serling so deeply believed in that better world.

Best of all, the object lesson was camouflaged by a magical sense of wonder. The storytelling was so delectable on *The Twilight Zone,* you didn't even notice the taste of medicine. The show is one of the few that continues to jump generation to generation, and remains seductively entertaining fun. The balance between escapism and morality is what keeps Serling and *The Twilight Zone* alive. Mark Twain observed, "Humor must not professedly teach and it must not professedly preach, but it must do both if it would live forever." The same could be said of fantasy and its close literary cousins, horror and science fiction.

Not to diminish or dismiss anyone else's dose of self-help inspiration, but kindergarten just didn't provide enough basic intel for me. I definitely required a good deal of postgraduate work after moving on from the land of finger-painting and A-B-C blocks. Some of us are just slow learners, I suppose. Some of us need more. Some of us need extended stays in the Twilight Zone. Hence the playful yet absolutely sincere title on the cover of the book you're holding.

One of television's angry young men during the golden age of the live anthology series, Rod Serling made his name with such powerful and profound dramas as *Patterns* and *Requiem for a Heavyweight*. He was thirty-five when he moved lock, stock, and typewriter into *The Twilight Zone* as host, narrator, creator, executive producer, and lead writer. This was widely viewed as abdicating his place as an important writer and taking a spot at the pop-culture equivalent of the children's table. About the time *The Twilight Zone* premiered, Mike Wallace famously remarked to Serling that working on the fantasy show meant, "in essence, for the time being and for the foreseeable future, you've given up on writing anything important for television, right?"

Given the amount of irony that ran through the five seasons of *The Twilight Zone,* it was a marvelously wrongheaded assumption to hang over the program's debut. Wallace would soon discover what Rod already knew from reading such horror masters as Edgar Allan Poe and H. P. Lovecraft. He knew what terror titans Mary Shelley, Robert Louis Stevenson, and Bram Stoker had proved in the nineteenth century—that fantasy stories are the ideal metaphoric vehicles for exploring life-and-death issues, colossal themes, societal woes, or secrets of the human heart.

Getting the message across had been getting tougher and tougher in commercial television. But the sponsors and censors and networks guardians saw only the spaceships and robots on *The Twilight Zone,* not the messages they were delivering. Rod and such key *Twilight Zone* writers as Matheson, Charles Beaumont, George Clayton Johnson, and Earl Hamner Jr. could have their say on almost any subject. Writing fantasy didn't restrain them. It freed them, allowing for extraordinary flexibility in tone and topic.

"Rod was an incredibly nice man—very caring, very dedicated, very solicitous of other writers," Matheson told me during one of many discussions of *The Twilight Zone.* "He was great company, whether you were talking over story ideas or having dinner. Being a writer, he understood writers, and that made *The Twilight Zone* a wonderful place to work. Chuck [Beaumont] and I weren't established as TV writers, but we did have credits in the fantasy field. We were established writers in fantasy and science fiction, and that's what Rod wanted for *The Twilight Zone.* He wanted the top writers in the field, and Chuck and I were the ones that worked out."

It didn't hurt that Beaumont was one of Matheson's dearest friends.

"Chuck Beaumont was the one I was closest to," Matheson said. "He and his wife had four children. We had four children. They were all about the same age. So we saw them quite a bit. Chuck and I also had a bit of a friendly rivalry. One of us would make a sale to a magazine, then the other one would make a sale. One of us would sell a novel, then the other would sell a

Twilight Zone contributor Richard Matheson, *left*, with the writer who learned everything he needed to know in the Twilight Zone. *Courtesy Mark Dawidziak*

7

novel. One of us would sell a TV script, then the other would sell a TV script. We sort of pushed each other."

If Poe and Lovecraft showed the way for Serling, then Serling showed the way for the TV writer-producers who would follow him into the fantasy field: Gene Roddenberry (*Star Trek*), Chris Carter (*The X-Files*), Joss Whedon (*Buffy the Vampire Slayer, Angel*), Ronald D. Moore (*Battlestar Galactica*), J. J. Abrams (*Lost*), and Alan Ball (*True Blood*). In fact, it would be difficult to find a writer on any current fantasy, horror, or science-fiction series who doesn't count himself or herself as a proud descendant of the creator, host, and principal writer of *The Twilight Zone*. Carter, Whedon, Moore, and Abrams are quick to acknowledge this influence, as you might expect, but so are many leading TV writer-producers outside the fantasy genres, including David Chase (*The Sopranos*), Matthew Weiner (*Mad Men*), and Vince Gilligan (*Breaking Bad*). It's a stirring tribute to the heroic influence of Serling that, more than fifty-five years after *The Twilight Zone* debuted, so many television writers of all kinds cite him and his wondrous land as inspirations. They couldn't have better role models. *The Twilight Zone* not only was a series with a strong social conscience, it was television that believed there was intelligent life on the other side of the television screen.

The enduring wisdom of *The Twilight Zone* also has been acknowledged as a profound influence by such directors as Steven Spielberg and Wes Craven and such writers as George R. R. Martin and Neil Gaiman. They are writers of wonder, and they've been touched, each and every one, by this wondrous land.

No wonder. Although it premiered in 1959, *The Twilight Zone* perfectly embodied the spirit of activism and altruism that would fuel so many movements in the 1960s. For all its dark corners, the series relentlessly shed light on all aspects of human nature. And behind the futuristic settings and creepy concepts, the viewer could sense that here was a show illuminated by hope, optimism, and faith.

Let's return for a second to the notion of *The Twilight Zone* jumping from generation to generation. That's important. Since the spring of 2009, I've been teaching two classes each semester at Kent State University. Every few months, I notice more and more movies and television shows slipping out of the pop-culture consciousness. With very few exceptions, my students no longer recognize stars and titles that were almost basic rites of passage for previous generations. They don't know the Marx Brothers, Humphrey Bogart, W. C. Fields, or Laurel and Hardy. On the television front, they don't know *The Honeymooners* or (and this hurts to say it, folks) *The Andy Griffith Show* or any of the shows that introduced archetypal characters as common reference points. They're pretty much all gone. In 2009, I could say someone was a real Barney Fife, and maybe half of the class would get the reference. Today, blank stares. Nobody gets it.

Each semester I show a film with Boris Karloff and ask if anybody knows who that is. Nobody does. They don't know he was the Frankenstein monster. They don't know such classic Karloff films as *The Body Snatcher* and *Isle of the Dead*. It may seem monstrous, but it's the truth. So, rather than wait for the penny to drop halfway through the film, I tell them that, while they don't recognize Karloff's name and won't recognize his face, they will recognize his voice. Count on it. That's completely due to two things they do know quite well: the 1962 novelty hit played endlessly every Halloween, "The Monster Mash" (with Bobby "Boris" Pickett doing a dead-on Karloff impression), and the 1966 animated special repeated every holiday season, *Dr. Seuss' How the Grinch Stole Christmas!* (with Karloff as narrator and the voice of the Grinch). I slip into a quick Karloff impression of my own, and the heads immediately start bobbing with recognition.

Why? Because unlike *The Honeymooners* and *The Andy Griffith Show,* "The Monster Mash" and *How the Grinch Stole Christmas!* are two little items that continue to jump generation to generation. They are constantly reintroduced into the pop culture. There's not much, when you come to keep score. Musically, you've got the Beatles and Elvis. You can be assured of almost every student getting them on some level. With films, you can't go wrong referencing *Star Wars, The Wizard of Oz,* and *E.T. the Extra-Terrestrial* (notice the enduring power of fantasy there). And television? Most of my students have a built-in resistance to anything in black and white. There are only two black-and-white series that keep making the jump, even as so many others are left by the pop-culture roadside: *I Love Lucy* and *The Twilight Zone.* You want proof? For casual evidence, ask my students. I get to test this theory on a semiannual basis. My students no longer know bus driver Ralph Kramden, deputy Barney Fife, or comedy writer Rob Petrie. But they still have spent some time with the Ricardos and in Serling's "middle ground between light and shadow, between science and superstition." The resistance to black and white is there, yet *The Twilight Zone* breaks down that resistance. The magic that worked then, works now. Or, as astrophysicist and author Neil deGrasse Tyson observed in a contribution for this book, "*The Twilight Zone,* as filmed, would not have succeeded in color. Exploiting the mystery and suspense of shifting people and objects in and out of shadows, the directors clearly knew the cinematic value of light and darkness on film."

An even surer sign is how these two shows are used for merchandise targeted to teens and young adults. There even has been a *Twilight Zone* Tower of Terror thrill ride at Disney theme parks in California and Florida, for crying out loud (or should that be, for screaming out loud?). There's also a semiannual holiday marathon of *Twilight Zone* episodes—a New Year's and Fourth of July tradition on cable's Syfy channel. And in April

2016, CBS announced that it was partnering with a video production company to make an interactive live-action version that will be a cross between a video game and a movie.

Still more proof? In 2013, the Writers Guild of America polled its members and came up with a list of the one hundred best-written shows in television history. David Chase's *The Sopranos* was in the top spot, followed by *Seinfeld*. And there was nothing wrong with that. Let's face it, *The Sopranos* always will rank among the best dramas of all time. *Seinfeld* always will be lurking near the top of the great comedies list. There's nothing surprising about that either. Both shows premiered in the 1990s, enjoying long and celebrated runs well within the consciousness and lifetimes of most WGA members. That last item is important, though. Recent series tend to have a formidable edge on these kinds of lists, being far fresher in fickle pop-culture memories. That's the case with these lists, whether they are being assembled by the *Entertainment Weekly* staff or a Yahoo! entertainment writer. Could you argue about it? Well, come on, one of the primary goals of these lists is to start arguments. But now look at the show that was lurking in the number 3 position: *The Twilight Zone*. Let me just say this outright: a black-and-white anthology series that premiered during the Eisenhower administration was number 3. So, when you handicap the top three and adjust for short Hollywood attention spans, that is practically saying *The Twilight Zone* is in a dimension all its own—way far beyond the number 1 spot. And it is. No irony here. No comment. Just a simple acknowledgment of the obvious: this, ladies and gentlemen, is the real winner of that Writers Guild poll. You certainly could read the results that way.

"The reason people liked them and continue to like them, and the reason they go down easily is because you don't have to know who the characters are," David Chase says of *The Twilight Zone*. "You're going to find out. In other words, you've got to know who Rockford is on *The Rockford Files*. And you do find out, but you've got to be into Rockford before you can start watching *The Rockford Files*. You have to know about his father and all these set pieces that are played over and over. *The Twilight Zone* presented little plays or movies. And so you were given all the information you needed in a half hour, so that the whole drama played out perfectly. That's why they were so great. Oh, it's my favorite show. It really is. And I can watch them over and over again."

As *The Twilight Zone* jumps from generation to generation, therefore, so do the morality plays. The lessons get reintroduced, and a millennial in 2016 finds them every bit as compelling and relevant as a baby boomer did in 1959. It's something you discover about Rod Serling's writing before, during, and after *The Twilight Zone*. Turns out, it truly is as "timeless as infinity."

Some writers seem dated because of themes and settings. Some seem dated because of style and vernacular. Very few remain of their time, yet timeless. Very few leave behind stories that speak to us today as forcefully as they did when first written. Very few transcend eras and fashions. Rod Serling is in that select company. It's another parallel with Twain, who so often seems to be talking about the twenty-first century rather than the nineteenth. The lessons first penned for *The Twilight Zone* during the Eisenhower administration were valuable to a generation that didn't know an Internet, home computers, and smart phones. They're valuable today. And they'll be valuable when we're colonizing Mars and wary of aliens dropping by with cookbooks.

What follows, then, is a self-help book courtesy of *The Twilight Zone*. Admittedly, the approach is somewhat lighthearted throughout, following the pattern of the first observed lesson that followed Becky's introduction to Walter Bedeker in "Escape Clause." But as tongue in cheek as many of these chapter headings might seem at first blush, there is a "no, really" element to each. Lurking in almost every episode of *The Twilight*

Zone is at least one guiding rule, one life lesson, one stirring reminder of a basic right or wrong taught to us as children. There are lessons for individuals. There are lessons for our society. There are lessons for our planet.

They also are lessons you can carry through your entire life. When I was about ten years old and sampling *Twilight Zone* episodes for the first time, I positively delighted in that eerie, unnerving feeling that ran through these stories (and me) like an electric charge. Call it the spook-out factor. There's something in the human animal that revels in it. It's what lured me in, no doubt; but, once lured, the magic started to work on me in all kinds of subtle and overt ways. The magic is one of realization: the awareness that you could open a closed door, wander through it, and end up . . . well, anywhere your imagination might take you. What I was thrilling to and submitting to was the power of great storytelling. At first, it *is* just about the spookout. As you get older, and the magic has its way with you, you understand and appreciate the parables.

You gain this understanding and appreciation while grappling with the lessons in that middle ground between light and shadow. Isn't that where most of us live our lives, struggling toward the light while coping with the shadows that threaten to overwhelm us? Influenced by everything from Poe's tales of psychological terror to the light-and-shadow metaphor Robert Louis Stevenson employed so intriguingly in *The Strange Case of Dr. Jekyll and Mr. Hyde, The Twilight Zone* used this middle ground as a kind of existential playing field. The snap endings often invited comparisons with the short stories of O. Henry, but the endings are just a way of getting us started. A *Twilight Zone* tale doesn't suggest O. Henry as much as it suggests a collaboration between O. Henry and Poe. While that's a generalization, it's a useful one when discussing the tone, structure, and mood at play in the middle ground. It's incredibly fertile territory for life lessons, big and small.

Along the way, you'll stumble on quite a bit of information about Rod Serling and *The Twilight Zone*. As Mark Twain said of one of his books: "Yes, take it all around, there is quite a good deal of information in the book. I regret this very much, but really it could not be helped: information appears to stew out of me naturally. . . . The more I caulk up the sources . . . the more I leak wisdom."

And about now, you're probably thinking, "What's with all of the Twain references?" You might as well get used to it. Okay, full disclosure time. In another part of my life, I fall somewhere on the scale between Twain scholar and fanatic (Twainiac is the term we like to use), and this vantage point has allowed me to see the many parallels between these two distinctly American writers. Those parallels will be more clearly delineated in the opening paragraphs of the next item on the table of contents— the profile of Rod Serling.

For all the information contained in the book, it might be instructive to state here and now what it isn't. It isn't an episode guide or a history of the series. There are some mighty good ones out there, including Marc Scott Zicree's *The Twilight Zone Companion*. It was the dream of my youth to write the first major history of *The Twilight Zone*. Marc beat me to it in 1982, and, as I've told him, I couldn't even be angry about it. He did pioneering work—better than I ever would have. Indeed, soon after, when I started writing the history of a television series (*Columbo*, starring Peter Falk as the rumpled detective), my goal was to get somewhere near the lofty standard set by *The Twilight Zone Companion*. Any temptation to add to the historical record was put to rest by the publication of Martin Grams's comprehensive work, *The Twilight Zone: Unlocking the Door to a Television Classic*. I was approached by a publisher in the mid-eighties about writing a biography of Rod Serling, but the contract offer was contingent on the promise to deliver a dark feet-of-clay portrait of a deeply flawed genius tortured by personal failings and murky psychological complexes. Mind you, the acquisitions editor knew next to nothing about Rod Serling. She had just heard about my interest in him and believed that such a biography could be written as ordered . . . about any artist. I was reasonably certain that Serling was human and had failings (thank goodness), but I thought the demand for a certain tone and content was more than a bit presumptuous, particularly before the research got rolling. I turned it down. What was surprising to me was that the editor was surprised. Then, knowing I was writing a book about *Columbo,* she happily chirped, "How about that kind of biography of Peter Falk?" There are moments in your life when you're quite certain you've landed in the Twilight Zone. You've probably guessed that the dark-side-of-genius biography of Peter Falk wasn't written, either.

But, deep down, silly as it may sound, I have always felt I was "owed" a *Twilight Zone* book. That feeling persisted over the decades, even as so many dedicated enthusiasts contributed more worthy volumes to the shelf devoted to Serling's iconic series. And now here we are, you and I. The right door finally presented itself. You open that door with the key of imagination. It was my way into the Twilight Zone. There's another lesson for you, although this one was memorably articulated by Hannibal Lecter: "All good things to those who wait."

Something else you won't find in this book is any of that *The Twilight Zone* versus *The Outer Limits* stuff, or any other such us-versus-them construct. In the first place, it's not in keeping with the spirit of Serling's stories. In the second place, I've rarely been able to take part in these one-versus-the-other arguments. I love both *The Munsters* and *The Addams Family,* for instance, and I never saw any need to side with one family over the other. Similarly, I love *The Twilight Zone* and *The Outer Limits* . . . and *Thriller* . . . and *Alfred Hitchcock Presents.* When fans start splitting up into camps, it's time to gather them in one big room

The moralist in disguise . . . Rod Serling, pictured in his backyard office. *Courtesy* Palisadian Post

and make them watch Rod's "The Monsters Are Due on Maple Street."

Still, for the sake of classification, it's worth pointing out that *The Twilight Zone* was at the forefront of a golden age for black-and-white anthology shows. Serling, therefore, glided from one golden age (the live anthology drama) to another (the filmed anthology). CBS's *The Twilight Zone,* although often mentioned in the genre, wasn't quite science fiction. That was ABC's *The Outer Limits. The Twilight Zone* also wasn't really a horror show. That was NBC's *Thriller* (at least at its frightening best). And *The Twilight Zone* wasn't a mystery program. That was *Alfred Hitchcock Presents.* Laying claim to the more general category of fantasy (or maybe what we today call speculative fiction), *The Twilight Zone* was big enough to encompass science fiction, horror, mystery, and a good deal more. Each of these three elements fits comfortably in the expansive, broadly defined universe of *The Twilight Zone.*

So this isn't a slice of TV history. It isn't a biography. It isn't an analytical scholarly treatise dissecting the philosophical and sociological underpinnings of *The Twilight Zone.* It isn't a pop-culture polemic. It is, however, in its own way, very much a heartfelt tribute to Serling and *The Twilight Zone* . . . wrapped in a self-help book.

On one level, it's intended as a fun celebration of what Rod Serling started more than fifty-five years ago. On another level, though, this is a kind of fifth-dimension inspirational volume, with each life lesson supported by those morality tales, parables, and homilies told so enchantingly by Rod and his writers. Most are presented humorously, but then, in keeping with the show's design, there's that little serious snap at the tail end. Because these are the ground rules . . . in *The Twilight Zone.*

ROD SERLING: "A MORALIST IN DISGUISE"

Everybody has those *Twilight Zone* moments now and then. The show has become so ingrained in our consciousnesses—such a universally recognized pop-culture reference—that we actually call them *Twilight Zone* moments. In fact, I'm having one right now. Really. Imagine, if you will, that you are reading these words in real time—just as they are being written, just as they are appearing on a computer screen, over which hangs a painting of Rod Serling.

All right, then, guess what day it is? Chance, fate or *The Twilight Zone* stage-managed matters so that I am writing this chapter about Rod Serling on the fortieth anniversary of his death. I certainly didn't plan it this way. I wouldn't have planned it this way. But this was the waiting step on the *Twilight* trail, and when precious time finally was available for the next item on the writing docket, the calendar confirmed the coincidence. It is a coincidence, right? Or is it? Whatever the reason, I am, indeed, writing these words on June 28, 2015.

I remember where I was forty years ago. I was driving across upstate New York, starting a cross-country trip. I was eighteen, and I had packed both of Rod Serling's paperback collections of *Night Gallery* stories for reading at stops along the way. It was an extremely hot and bright summer day. The sun was blaring in a manner reminiscent of Serling's 1961 *Twilight Zone* episode "The Midnight Sun." Air-conditioning in that gold Oldsmobile Cutlass meant roll down the windows and let highway speed push the sultry air around the baked interior. The sad news was delivered by the car radio. Somewhere, not too far away, in Rochester, New York, Rod Serling had died. He was fifty years old, and his great heart had given out. How do you respond when a hero dies? I'm not sure what thoughts ran through my head at the time, but I can tell you without equivocation that it is possible to be positively roasted by summer heat and still feel cold.

"I just want them to remember me a hundred years from now" goes the famous quote from Serling's last interview. "I don't care that they're not able to quote a single line that I've written. But just that they can say, 'Oh, he was a writer.' That's sufficiently an honored position for me."

Fifty years from now, they will still remember Rod Serling was a writer and they will remember a good deal more. They will remember the writing. It will live. Why? Well, here we go, but not right to *The Twilight Zone*. Back to Mark Twain. Even after the publication of such books as *Adventures of Huckleberry Finn* and *A Connecticut Yankee in King Arthur's Court*, Twain was widely viewed by many as a humorist and a genial family author. One young French admirer, Helene Picard, noticed something more behind the laughter, and she said so in a 1902 letter to the writer.

"Yes, you are right," Twain wrote to Helene. "I am a moralist in disguise; it gets me into heaps of trouble."

What a marvelous description of Rod Serling, stamped by *The Twilight Zone* as primarily a purveyor of eerie tales with spaceships and supernatural beings, aliens and angels, ghosts on the phone and gremlins on the wing. Although humor and fantasy (in all its many forms) frequently are treated dismissively in literary discussions, they are both powerful metaphoric tools for addressing the human (and inhuman) condition. They are incredibly sly storytelling devices for an incredibly dangerous undertaking: telling people the truth about themselves. George Bernard Shaw thanked Mark Twain for teaching him the primary lesson when it comes to social criticism. If you're going to tell people the truth, you'd better make them laugh, or they'll kill you. You can do this with humor, and you can do this with fantasy. Both lure the unsuspecting readers or viewers into dropping their guard, leaving them wide open for the moral, the message, or the lesson.

Twain died in April 1910. Fifty years later, they still knew he was a writer—a great American writer. More than *one hundred* years after his death, we still know he was a writer, and we still know the writing. For so many similar reasons, the same will be true of this other moralist in disguise.

If you require further proof of this, consider the test suggested by another American literary giant, Walt Whitman. In his preface to *Leaves of Grass,* Whitman decreed: "The proof of a poet is that his country absorbs him as affectionately as he has absorbed it." Can you imagine a better summary of Rod Serling's legacy? Serling absorbed the American experience, in all of its complexities, with the fervor of a patriot, the conscience of a reformer, and the soul of a storyteller. America returned the favor. Look around you. In any given week, you'll see multiple references to *The Twilight Zone* in everything from opinion columns and political cartoons to news reports and television scripts. There is no pause to explain what *The Twilight Zone* was. The expectation is that you know and fully grasp the significance of that title. You have absorbed it. That's why you know what it means when someone says, "I'm having a *Twi-*

light Zone moment." That's why people know what you mean when you say it.

So, that news report in June 1975 only told a small part of the story. The radio reception simply wasn't good enough. If the signal had been coming from the "middle ground between light and shadow," we would have been reminded of the words penned by George Clayton Johnson for that intriguing third-season episode "A Game of Pool": "As long as they talk about you, you're not really dead. As long as they speak your name, you continue. A legend doesn't die just because the man dies."

Exactly. It is a lesson to keep in mind before we get to the lessons.

The story also begins in upstate New York. Rodman Edward Serling was born in Syracuse's Good Shepherd Hospital on December 25, 1924. As his daughter Anne notes, he liked to joke that he was a Christmas present delivered unwrapped. The present was delivered to parents, Sam and Esther, and an older brother, Bob, but little Rodman became the gift that kept on giving.

He grew up in Binghamton, which would be recalled in some of his *Twilight Zone* scripts. The idealized summers of cotton candy, carousels, and bandstands were beloved echoes of his Binghamton childhood.

"Everybody has to have a hometown, Binghamton's mine," Serling famously said. "In the strangely brittle, terribly sensitive makeup of a human being, there is a need for a place to hang a hat or a kind of geographical womb to crawl back into, or maybe just a place that's familiar because that's where you grew up. When I dig back through memory cells, I get one particularly distinctive feeling—and that's one of warmth, comfort, and well-being. For whatever else I may have had, or lost, or will find—I've still got a hometown. This, nobody's gonna take away from me."

Nobody ever did. He was drawn back to Binghamton in his

stories, with tired businessmen yearning for the comfort and peace of a gentler time in "Walking Distance" and "A Stop at Willoughby." *Twilight Zone* historian Marc Scott Zicree has rightly called "Walking Distance" a "fantasy journey to the Binghamton of his youth." But Rod Serling also was drawn to his hometown in a physical sense. In her book *As I Knew Him: My Dad, Rod Serling,* his daughter Anne recalls that every summer he would make the pilgrimage to Binghamton. He told New York *Daily News* TV critic Kay Gardella that he got the idea for "Walking Distance" while walking through the MGM backlot in Culver City and being struck by how much it resembled the Binghamton of his youth. On another occasion, he said the idea occurred to him during one of those visits to Binghamton, "taking a long evening stroll to a place called Recreation Park three blocks from my old house and seeing the merry-go-round and remembering that wondrous, bittersweet time of growing up." Whether it was Culver City or Binghamton, or both, that provided the spark for "Walking Distance," Serling recognized, as he told Gardella, that overwhelming sense of nostalgia that stirs "a deep longing to go back—not to our home as it is today but as we remember it."

He remembered it fondly, and that must be recognized as an exercise in understatement. To understand what Binghamton meant to Rod Serling, emphasize the home part of hometown. He did. The town that businessman Martin Sloan is trying to reach in "Walking Distance" is symbolically called Homewood. If you wish to chart the dimensions of Serling's fifth dimension, you must start with Binghamton.

An imaginative and outgoing child, Rod was doted on by his parents and brother. They were a close family. Sam, who managed one of his father-in-law's wholesale meat markets, delighted in young Rod's animated and extroverted personality. Esther adored her handsome, curly-haired son, and he adored his mother, calling her "Dearest." And Bob, despite being seven years older, was a boon companion and enthusiastic partner in games of make-believe. It was an ideal nurturing environment for a boy brimming with creativity and confidence. What he lacked in height, he made up in drive and personality.

This plaque, honoring favorite son Rod Serling, is in the middle of the bandstand in Recreation Park in Binghamton, New York. The park, with its carousel, was the inspiration for Serling's "Walking Distance," one of his finest scripts for *The Twilight Zone*. *Photograph by Becky Dawidziak*

He enjoyed his days at Alexander Hamilton Elementary School. In high school, he was a class leader—on student council and the debate team, a member of the honor society, editor of the newspaper, and an eager participant in school plays. But although popular with classmates and teachers, the bubbly teenager also encountered disappointment and prejudice at Binghamton Central High School. The athletic, competitive, and sports-loving Rod was judged too short and too light to take the field in a varsity football game. The coach, "the late and beloved Henry Merz," Serling recalled in 1968, tried to explain "he found it difficult to reconcile playing a quarterback who weighed less than the team bulldog" (the Bulldogs' mascot). And while being voted out of the school's Jewish fraternity for dating gentile girls, Rod was blocked from joining a non-Jewish fraternity.

Graduation day was January 15, 1943. "A brief lemonade after the graduation ceremonies," he remembered, and then the eighteen-year-old was boarding a train for an induction center. He enlisted in the army, joining the 11th Airborne Division's 511th Parachute Infantry Regiment, even though, at five foot four, he weighed only 118 pounds. Basic training was in Georgia, where he earned extra money and privileges by boxing as a flyweight. He won his first seventeen bouts. His eighteenth fight was with a professional boxer, who broke Rod's nose and knocked him out in the third round. He decided it was time to hang up the gloves. Yet the boxing ring was another place that lured him back—in such powerful tales as *Requiem for a Heavyweight,* his stunning 1956 *Playhouse 90* drama and the *Twilight Zone* episode "The Big Tall Wish."

In May 1944, the paratroopers of the 511th were sent to New Guinea. Six months later, they were sent into the hellish fighting on Leyte Island. An exploding mortar shell sent shrapnel into Serling's knee and wrist. He was awarded the Purple Heart for his injuries and the Bronze Star for bravery. The knee continued to give him trouble, sometimes spontaneously bleeding, sometimes causing him to fall. He served in the South Pacific until the Japanese surrender in August 1945. With the dream of peace and home so very close, he received the devastating news that his father had died of a heart attack. Sam Serling was fifty-two. Rod put in for emergency leave to attend the funeral. His request was denied. The wound went deeper than any physical injury suffered during the war.

Coping with the psychological impact of his war experiences probably is what turned Rod Serling into a writer. He certainly thought so. Describing himself as "bitter about everything," he "turned to writing to get it off my chest." Yet, when he enrolled at Antioch College in Yellow Springs, Ohio, in 1946, the plan was to be a physical education major. Switching to language and literature, he began writing stories about war. He never really stopped. While proud of having served as a paratrooper, Serling again and again would probe the costs of war, almost always from the soldier's perspective. And two of his *Twilight Zone* scripts, "The Purple Testament" and "A Quality of Mercy," were set in the Philippine Islands during 1945. In each story, we are asked to stare in the faces of young soldiers, and, by doing so, stare into the face of war.

"Keep in mind only this—that province of combat is not the end—it is simply the means," he told students during his 1968 Binghamton Central High School commencement address. "And the most essential part of the challenge is for you to find another means that does not come with the killing of your fellow man."

He met Carolyn Louise Kramer, a seventeen-year-old education major, in the fall of 1946. They were married in June 1948. Serling's true apprenticeship as a writer began five months later when he was named manager of the Antioch Broadcasting System, the grandly named campus radio station. He had already had some experience writing scripts: during the war for Armed Service Radio and as an Antioch intern at New York public radio station WNYC. At the Antioch station, however, he was writing and directing a new show every week, often acting in the productions that were broadcast on Springfield station WJEM.

Greatly influenced by the radio work of Norman Corwin and Orson Welles, Serling later realized it was during this intense period that he developed from a "cheap imitation" into a writer struggling toward a style of his own.

He emerged from this baptism by fire with a script about a boxer dying of leukemia. "To Live a Dream" was good enough to win one of three second prizes awarded in the annual competition held by the long-running CBS Radio program *Dr. Christian*, starring Jean Hersholt. By the late 1940s, most of the *Dr. Christian* scripts were submitted by listeners. It was billed as "the only show on radio where the audience writes the scripts." Second prize included five hundred dollars and an all-expenses-paid trip to New York for Rod and Carol in May 1949. It was during this trip that he met another *Dr. Christian* prize winner, a twenty-five-year-old aspiring writer from Schuyler, Virginia, Earl Hamner Jr. A year later, Serling replaced Hamner as a staff writer at WLW, an AM radio station in Cincinnati. Hamner would become a contributor to *The Twilight Zone* before creating and producing the autobiographical drama *The Waltons*.

Two more scripts were sold in 1949, both to the radio anthology series *Grand Central Station*. The Serlings moved to Cincinnati after graduation in 1950. With an eye on the emerging medium of television, he sold his story about an idealistic lawyer, "Grady for the People," to the NBC anthology series *Stars over Hollywood* for a hundred dollars. But he found the work at WLW frustrating and unrewarding. Worse, it was sapping his energies for the scripts he was trying to work on at night. While at WLW, he started contributing scripts to *The Storm*, a new anthology show on Cincinnati television station WKRC.

"I used to come home at seven o'clock in the evening, gulp down dinner, and set up my antique portable typewriter on the kitchen table," he recalled in his 1957 book, *Patterns: Four Television Plays with the Author's Personal Commentaries*.

"The first hour would then be spent closing all the mental gates and blacking out all the impressions of a previous eight hours of writing. . . . After two years of double-shift writing, I had made approximately six sales to network television. . . . They showed in many ways that they were done on a kitchen table during the eleventh and twelfth and thirteenth hours of a working day. They were always sharpened, but never to their finer points."

It was also during this stretch that he collected forty rejection slips in a row. "Nobody but a beginning writer can imagine how crushing this is to the ego," he said. Something had to give. In late 1951, he made the decision. The WLW job had to go.

"The process of writing cannot be juggled with another occupation," he reasoned. "The job of creating cannot be compartmentalized with certain hours devoted to one kind of creation and other hours set aside for still another. Writing is a demanding profession and a selfish one. And because it is selfish and demanding, because it is compulsive and exacting, I didn't embrace it. I succumbed to it."

He quit the radio station. That night, Serling disclosed the decision to his wife before dinner at a Howard Johnson's restaurant.

"You know, honey, a man could make a lot of money freelancing," he told Carol.

Six years later, looking back on that night, Serling gave shape and size to how gutsy a roll of the dice this was. "Freelance writing would no longer be a kind of errant hope to augment our economy, to be done around the midnight hour on a kitchen table," he recalled. "Freelance writing would now be our bread, our butter, and the now-or-never of our whole existence. My wife was twenty-one, three months pregnant, and a most adept reader of the score. . . . She knew that in my best year I had netted exactly $790. . . . She knew that it was a frustrating, insecure, bleeding business at best, and the guy she was married to could get his pride, his composure, and his confidence eaten away with the acid of disappointment. All this she knew sitting at a table in Howard Johnson's in 1951. And as it turned out, this was a scene with no dialogue at all. All she did was to take my hand. Then she winked at me and picked up a menu and studied it. . . . For lush or lean, good or bad, Sardi's or malnutrition, I'd launched a career."

Indeed, he had. It was an act of faith, but, then, writing is an act of faith—proceeding from the belief that there is something in the human condition worth exploring, examining, criticizing, celebrating, indicting, and improving. It was an act of faith in the power of writing and in the powers of this particular fledgling writer.

"There's no alternative to faith . . . and, God help us, there's no salvation without it," Serling said in a Binghamton Central High School commencement address in 1968.

A few months after leaving WLW, he sold the first of thirteen scripts to the New York–based CBS anthology show *Lux Video Theatre*. That faith was justified to the tune of five thousand dollars, the amount he made during his first season as a freelance television writer. He doubled that the following year. And he doubled those earnings the year after that. In addition to the *Lux* scripts, there were sales to such anthology series as *Kraft Television Theatre, Suspense, Campbell Playhouse, The Philip Morris Playhouse, The Motorola Television Hour, Danger,* and *Armstrong Circle Theatre*. Still, despite the growing résumé, Serling kept Ohio as his home base.

"Between late 1951 and 1954 I lived in Ohio, commuting back and forth to New York to take part in story conferences and the rehearsals of my shows," he wrote in the introduction to his first book, *Patterns*. "This was expensive and time-consuming, but was a concession to my own peculiar hesitancy about all things big, massive, and imposing. New York television and its people were such an entity. For some totally unexplainable reason, every time I walked into a network or agency office I had the strange and persistent feeling that I was wearing overalls and Li'l Abner shoes."

There is a lesson for all of us. No matter how much natural confidence, optimism, and, yes, faith one may possess, the nagging voices of insecurity, inferiority, and self-doubt can't be completely silenced. And maybe that's a good thing. Recognizing and wrestling with those voices will drive the individual toward understanding, into the land of insight, and on to the higher ground of accomplishment. Fixating on and surrendering to those voices will draw one into that dark terrain where feelings of unworthiness play havoc with self-esteem.

Serling once recalled a New York meeting that left him feeling more than a little humiliated. The young writer felt he had overstayed his welcome, so he mumbled something about needing to catch a plane back to Ohio. He turned abruptly, bolted from the room, and promptly crashed into the wall. Trying to regain his balance and his composure, he ran into a secretary and dropped his briefcase. We've all had these moments, right? The briefcase hit the floor and popped open, revealing scripts, writing material, socks, handkerchiefs, and underwear. The wise and sympathetic script editor, Dick McDonagh, followed the flustered Serling out and gripped his hand. "Look, little friend," McDonagh told him, "these people don't give a good healthy damn what you carry in your briefcase or how you leave a room." Then, pointing at Serling's head, he added, "All they care about is what's in there!"

Gradually, Serling's mighty talent overwhelmed thoughts of uncertainty and underwear. The Serlings moved to Westport, Connecticut, in 1954. A daughter, Jodi, had been born in 1952. A second daughter, Anne, arrived in 1955.

Speaking of arrivals, stepping back and looking at the career of an artist, you often can spot that moment of arrival. For Rod Serling, that moment was January 12, 1955. This was the night that NBC's *Kraft Television Theater* aired the live production of *Patterns,* Serling's riveting play about a young executive hired by the hard-driving, hard-hearted president of a major corporation. A record of what happened that night survives, thanks to kinescope, the filming of a television program by setting up a camera in front of a video monitor. The picture quality, as you might imagine, is not the sharpest, but you can plainly see why this drama inspired *New York Times* critic Jack Gould to write: "Nothing in months has excited the television industry as much as the *Kraft Television Theatre*'s production of *Patterns,* an original play by Rod Serling. The enthusiasm is justified. In writing, acting, and direction, *Patterns* will stand as one of the high points in the TV medium's evolution." It was an amazingly prophetic evaluation on Mr. Gould's part. The enthusiasm for *Patterns* was as justified as Serling's faith in himself. The *Times* reviewer added that, "For sheer power of narrative, forcefulness of characterization, and brilliant climax, Mr. Serling's work is a creative triumph. . . ."

Serling's assessment: "It was good, perhaps better than good."

It certainly was. The cast was superb, led by Richard Kiley as idealistic Manhattan newcomer Fred Staples, Ed Begley as aging and vulnerable Andy Sloane, and Everett Sloane as ruthless boss Walter Ramsey. Fiedler Cook was the talented director for this 463rd presentation of the anthology series (which started its illustrious run on May 7, 1947, when Serling was twenty-two and attending Antioch College). But it was Serling's writing that truly caused a sensation.

For Serling, this was one of those overnight successes that took years of struggle and patient attention to bring about. He calculated that he had written seventy-one television scripts before hitting this prime-time home run. He was thirty years old.

Intriguing autobiographical touches can be spotted here and there in *Patterns,* something that would run through *The Twilight Zone* and many of his subsequent writings. Consciously or not, Rod Serling gave his lead character a name that followed the, uh, pattern of his own: same number of syllables, first name ending in a *d*, last name starting with an *s*. Like Fred Staples, Rod Serling had moved from Cincinnati, where he was pegged as a talented young man with great potential. Like Staples, Serling had a wife supportive of his career choices. Like Staples, he was living in Connecticut. Like Staples, he was doing everything in his power to do good work in a competitive business that often challenged principles and demanded compromise.

If Serling's experiences in television didn't shape the plot and themes of *Patterns,* they certainly informed it.

Early in the drama, a secretary played by twenty-one-year-old Elizabeth Montgomery says, "You never know when you're going to hit a nerve." *Patterns* hit a nerve, all right, rocketing Serling to the head of television's star class of writers. The two writers who most came to symbolize the Golden Age were Serling and Paddy Chayefsky, whose tale of a lonely Bronx butcher, *Marty,* aired to great acclaim in May 1953. Small wonder they were the first two writers specializing in drama inducted into the Academy of Television Arts & Sciences' Hall of Fame.

To fully appreciate how and why Rod Serling became a star in the 1950s, you must start with the realization that TV very much needed stars in the 1950s. With this upstart medium sweeping the nation, the major film studios went to war. Television was keeping Americans home with free entertainment, and the studio bosses were fighting to protect their endangered territory. Film stars were told in no uncertain terms that they should not consort with the enemy. Television had little leverage and less money to compete for talent back then, so programmers' answer was to make their own stars. This included writers, and the outgoing, articulate Serling had charisma, drive, and talent to spare.

"I have never ceased liking publicity," Serling admitted in the *Patterns* introduction, even before *The Twilight Zone* shot his recognition factor into the ionosphere. "This isn't ego for its own sake, because I don't drop names and I don't purposely seek it. But I still get a kick when I see my name in the paper, and I probably always will."

Rod and Paddy were in good company. Also contributing distinguished scripts to live dramas were Gore Vidal, Horton Foote, J. P. Miller, Tad Mosel, William Gibson, Helene Hanff, Robert Alan Aurthur, Reginald Rose, Ernest Kinoy, and Ira Levin. Plays by these writers "were stamped with that particular quality that forced recognition," Serling commented. Their stories were compelling reasons for Americans to stay home, anxious to see what this new medium had to offer.

"The medium began to show a cognizance of its own particular fortes," Serling observed. "It had the immediacy of the living theater, some of the flexibility of the motion picture, and the coverage of radio. It utilized all three in developing and improving what was actually a new art form. As indicated previously by the plays on *Kraft, Studio One,* and *Celanese Theatre,* one could see that the television play was beginning to show depth and a preoccupation with character. Its plots and its people were becoming meaningful. Its stories had something to say."

Patterns had a great deal to say about ambition, competition, talent, success, decency, ethics, power, and the misuse of power. Like Arthur Miller's *Death of a Salesman,* a play that had a profound impact on Serling, it spoke eloquently about the value and dignity of each human life, and the need for that dignity to be recognized. It indicted a culture—any culture—that views age and experience as disposable items to be pushed toward the scrap heap. It cautioned the individual to beware of those moments that tempt what Serling called a "minimum set of ethics." The dilemma: "When he refuses to compromise those ethics, his career must suffer; when he does compromise them, his conscience does the suffering." The moralist is not in disguise at this point. He's putting it all right out there. The story established patterns Serling would pursue on *The Twilight Zone.*

These are themes he would revisit again and again, examining them through an ever-changing prism altered by age and experience.

Fred Staples is climbing the corporate ladder in *Patterns*. Andy Sloane is on his way down. Four years later, in one of Serling's best *Twilight Zone* episodes, thirty-six-year-old business executive Martin Sloan (Gig Young) is wearying of the rat race and yearning for a simpler time in "Walking Distance." Martin Sloan is looking backward, but if he could see himself a few years in the future, he might be looking at Andy Sloane.

Already farther down that road is Gart Williams (James Daly), the main character in another of Serling's exceptional *Twilight Zone* excursions, "A Stop at Willoughby." Hounded by a Ramsey-like "what-have-you-done-for-me-lately" boss, Gart Williams already knows the demons haunting Andy Sloane. And, as Marc Scott Zicree points out in his excellent book *The Twilight Zone Companion*, Serling's finest script for *Night Gallery*, "They're Tearing Down Tim Riley's Bar," is pretty much a companion piece to *Patterns* and "Walking Distance" (although I'd add the stop at "Willoughby" to this ongoing journey). At forty-five, Serling told the story of Randy Lane (William Windom), a tired, disillusioned business executive desperately trying to hold on to the ladder rungs but losing his grip nonetheless and slipping down and down. Zicree rightly notes that this *Night Gallery* story "represents Serling at his best, writing with an insight and power the equal of anything he had done before."

Patterns, "Walking Distance," and "They're Tearing Down Tim Riley's Bar" "offer a progression of what is essentially the same character at different points in his life," say Scott Skelton and Jim Benson in their comprehensive book, *Rod Serling's Night Gallery: An After-Hours Tour*. "All three characters hold up a mirror to Serling as he responds to the fortunes of his career."

Unquestionably true, but the other characters and other pieces, like "A Stop at Willoughby," add significant threads to the tapestry. You can follow the path that leads from Fred Staples to Martin Sloan to Randy Lane. You also can trace the thread that takes you from Andy Sloane to Gart Williams to Randy Lane. It's not as clean or direct, perhaps, yet it is no less fascinating. You can just dwell on how the choice of names seem to echo each other: Sloane to Sloan, Andy to Randy . . . patterns, indeed. And, at each stop, from the Manhattan offices of Ramsey and Company to the quaint station in Willoughby to the ruins of Tim Riley's bar, there are lessons to be learned.

So, when we first meet Fred Staples in *Patterns,* he is about to board the elevator that will take him up to the executive offices and into television history.

"You've arrived, Mr. Staples," his wife, Fran, tells him.

It could have been Carol Serling telling her husband, "You've arrived, Mr. Serling."

Yes, he had, and the sensation caused by *Patterns* cleared the way for a presentation of Serling's *The Rack* on *The United States Steel Hour.* Aired three months later, on April 12, 1955. *The Rack* was a provocative drama about a mentally tortured American POW accused of collaborating with his North Korean captors. A former army paratrooper scarred physically and emotionally during World War II, Serling wasn't about to make it easy on himself or his audience. He delved into many sides of a thorny issue, managing to make all the viewpoints sympathetic.

While impressed, some critics griped that *The Rack* wasn't another *Patterns.* It was a complaint that Serling would grow tired of hearing during this typically prolific phase of his career. "By and large I think *The Rack* is one of the most honest things I have ever written," Serling said.

If 1955 was the year of arrival for Rod Serling, the following year was what confirmed his stature as an important new writer. There were film versions of *Patterns* (with Sloane, Begley, and Van Heflin replacing Kiley as Fred) and *The Rack* (with Paul Newman in the role played by Marshall Thompson on television). On March 17, 1956, Serling won the first of his six Emmys (it was, of course, for *Patterns*). And on October 11, 1956, *Playhouse 90* premiered one of the most triumphant dramas ever written (or ever will be written) for television, *Requiem for a Heavyweight*.

This is Serling summoning all his considerable powers and delivering the knockout blow. He worried that his career would always be defined by *Patterns*—measured by it. While *The Rack* was greatly admired by many critics, Serling was still that guy who wrote *Patterns*. *Requiem for a Heavyweight* was stirring proof that the writer could reach back and throw an even more devastating dramatic punch. It was proof, as Serling said, that *Patterns* "was not a happy accident."

Requiem for a Heavyweight is the story of Harlan "Mountain" McClintock, a one-time contender on his way to Punchy Land. The doctor says his fighting days are done, but he only knows boxing. Meanwhile, his manager, Maish, is deep in debt. Absorbing horrific punishment in his last fight, Mountain managed to stay on his feet until the seventh round. Maish bet that his aging fighter wouldn't last three rounds.

Now a desperate Maish is pushing the proud Mountain to become a wrestler. Mountain's loyal handler, an ex-boxer named Army, knows this will hurt more than any punch. As battered as he is, Mountain is holding on to the dignity of a bruiser who never threw a fight and always gave Maish and fight fans everything he had. Now Maish wants to strip away whatever dignity is left.

"You're not a winner anymore, Mountain," Maish tells the washed-up fighter who has left so much of himself behind in smoke-filled arenas. "And that means there's only one thing left—make a little off the losing."

Everything fell into place for this three-act *Playhouse 90* drama. Jack Palance, stunningly convincing as a thick-voiced pug, didn't make a wrong move as Mountain. "There are times in a career of a writer when a single performance in a play can add such a fantastic dimension and moving quality that the role appears to have been molded into the actor's shape," Serling wrote in his book *Patterns*. "This was the case when Jack Palance played Mountain McClintock. His interpretation left nothing to be desired."

Keenan Wynn, so memorable as defense attorney Steve Wasnik in *The Rack*, found all the many levels Serling envisioned in the deeply conflicted Maish. Wynn's father, comedian Ed Wynn, overcame a shaky rehearsal period to deliver a moving performance as the sympathetic Army. And Kim Hunter made the most of every moment on screen as Grace, the social worker trying to help Mountain. While the characteristically self-critical Serling thought Grace could have been better drawn, she couldn't have been better played.

The sets, Ralph Nelson's direction, the pacing—it all clicked. Towering above all, however, was Serling's writing, properly recognized with the Emmy for best teleplay on March 16, 1957. *Requiem for a Heavyweight* also won the Emmys for program of the year, best single performance by an actor (Palance), and best direction. A film version appeared in 1962, with Anthony Quinn, Jackie Gleason, Mickey Rooney, and Julie Harris. Like the film adaptation of *Patterns,* it was good but not as good as what aired on television.

"I think there were good moments in *Requiem* and some near-great ones," Serling said.

In 1958, Serling won his third consecutive writing Emmy, this one for *The Comedian,* his *Playhouse 90* adaptation of Ernest Lehman's novella about a bullying, egomaniacal television comedian (played by Rooney). Edmond O'Brien, Kim Hunter, and Mel Tormé also were in the cast. Other Serling scripts produced by *Playhouse 90* in the late 1950s included: *The Velvet Alley,* with Art Carney as a suddenly successful television writer who loses sight of what is truly important; *The Rank and File,* starring Van Heflin as a factory worker whose ambition lands him at several moral crossroads; *A Town Has Turned to Dust,* a study of racial prejudice that lost some of its punch due to changes demanded by nervous CBS censors; and *Bomber's Moon,* with Robert Cummings, Martin Balsam, and Rip Torn as World War II flyers stationed in England.

Looking for themes that will recur in *The Twilight Zone* and will frame its lessons, you'll be able to identify many of what he might have called preoccupations: the fundamentally decent person tossed into the middle of a morally ambiguous situation; the worn-out professional coping with dissatisfaction, obsolescence, or just being forgotten; the aging warrior striving to keep on his feet as the ground is being cut out from under him; the worth of the individual; the yearning for simpler times; the enduring spirit battling to survive under the merciless assault of forces beyond one beleaguered person's control.

Again and again, Serling was drawn to the individual faced with a moral crisis, a midlife crisis, a crisis of quiet desperation. We've all been there, or will be there, and it's this recognition that makes Serling's writing so incredibly timely and timeless.

Playhouse 90 was the most ambitious and prestigious of television's golden-age dramas, but it was a script Serling had written for another anthology series, *Westinghouse Desilu Playhouse,* that truly opened the door to *The Twilight Zone.* Starring William Bendix and Balsam, Serling's *The Time Element* was about a bookie and bartender convinced that he's time traveling in his dreams to December 6, 1941, the day before the attack on Pearl Harbor. It aired November 24, 1958, and was pretty much a *Twilight Zone* episode before there was a *Twilight Zone.*

Serling was wearying of the battles with network censors, and *The Time Element* convinced him that it was possible to be a moralist in disguise. While many, like Mike Wallace, were convinced

Rod Serling about the time he opened *The Twilight Zone* for business. *Courtesy CBS Photo Archive*

that Serling was through with serious work, the writer would soon prove that he was just getting warmed up. Everything that Rod Serling had experienced and everything that he had written going into this new phase of his career shaped the lessons presented so engagingly and imaginatively on *The Twilight Zone,* which began its five-season CBS run on October 2, 1959. Serling wrote twenty-eight of the first-season's thirty-six episodes, and these scripts included such enduring gems as "Walking Distance," "The Purple Testament," "The Monsters Are Due on Maple Street," "A Stop at Willougby," and "A Passage for Trumpet." Through with serious work? On June 20, 1960, *The Twilight Zone* earned Serling his fourth Emmy.

Two major *Twilight Zone* contributors were recruited during that first season, Richard Matheson and his close friend and fellow fantasy writer Charles Beaumont. George Clayton Johnson saw his first teleplay produced during the second season. When Serling won a fifth Emmy in 1961, he recognized the importance of these writers by hefting the golden statuette and telling them, "Come on over, fellas, and we'll carve it up like a turkey."

Another *Twilight Zone* contributor, Earl Hamner Jr., penned the first of his eight scripts for the third season. The series jumped from a half hour to an hour with its eighteen-episode fourth season, returning to a half hour for its fifth and final season. The last original *Twilight Zone* aired in 1964, and the series immediately began a robust afterlife in syndication. By then, the show had transformed Rod Serling into the most recognized writer on the planet. During the 1960s and 1970s, people who couldn't pick Norman Mailer or Saul Bellow out of a police lineup knew Rod Serling. They knew the voice, the face, the mannerisms. *The Twilight Zone* had turned a well-known and acclaimed writer into that awful and bewilderingly amorphous American creation—a celebrity. It's a status that few writers attain, and it invites yet another comparison with Mark Twain. There aren't many in their league—two beloved American writers who enjoyed spending summers with their families at beloved upstate New York retreats (Twain at his sister-in-law's Quarry Farm in Elmira, Serling at the Lake Cayuga cottage near Ithaca). Both were invariably caricatured or photographed smoking (Twain with his cherished cigar, Serling with the ever-present cigarette). Both wrote scathing indictments of the human race's capacity for cruelty and ignorance.

Each idealized his hometown, drawing on cherished boyhood memories to fashion some of his best writing. Each was survived by a daughter who wrote an insightful memoir about him: Clara Clemens published *My Father: Mark Twain* in 1931; Anne Serling published *As I Knew Him: My Dad, Rod Serling* in 2013. Each was a bit of a ham, enjoying the spotlight and reveling in the affection of admirers. You rather think that Serling would have agreed with a conclusion Twain reached near the end of his life: "Praise is well, compliment is well, but affection— that is the last and final and most precious reward that any man can win, whether by character or achievement. . . ." Twain and Serling won it by character *and* achievement.

Many are fond of quoting F. Scott Fitzgerald's line about there being no second acts in American lives. They're probably misusing the line, since there's evidence that Fitzgerald didn't believe it. Anyone with doubts about the line can happily point to Serling's career, which more than refutes this oft-cited sentiment. It obliterates the whole notion of no second acts. That's because, as you already know, *The Twilight Zone was* the second act. The illustrious first act, of course, was Serling's mighty contributions to television's golden age of the drama anthology. Serling lived such a crowded life, he even managed a post–*Twilight Zone* third act before his death at fifty. It featured honored TV movies, screenplays, and his contributions to the NBC horror anthology *Night Gallery.* Fueling each phase was Serling's strong sense of morality.

"Now just what is morality?" Serling said during a March 1971 speech in Akron, Ohio. "I'm not able to begin to give you a definition of it . . . I do know, however, that if a churchgoing Calvinist reads three books of the Old Testament each morning and lives a life of perpetual abstinence, all he has to do is say the word 'nigger' once, and, in my book, he is not a moral man.

On the other hand, if a college student swings, tosses around four-letter Anglo-Saxon profanities, and does not know a catechism from a cartoon, if he holds out his hand to a ghetto child or takes a train ride down to Alabama to help register black voters or rises to his feet to publicly speak out for what might well be an unpopular cause, then I say this morality is a pure and remarkable thing."

So when you go back to that radio report on that hot June day in 1975, and you consider the totality of this whirlwind career, you are left with one of the most compelling lessons of all: keep fighting, keep swinging. No matter how many times life knocks you down, no matter how many emotional body blows you must absorb, no matter how many devastating punches crash through your guard, keep fighting. Like the hero of *Requiem for a Heavyweight,* Rod Serling refused to give up. He refused to give up on himself. He refused to give up on the causes and beliefs he held dear. He refused to give up on his fellow human beings.

He had the boxer's mentality. You don't stop swinging. You keep throwing leather until the man rings the bell, ending the fight . . . or the man counts ten. There is something deeply heroic about how he kept fighting. "For us the heartening thing is that there are still things to strive for," he said. So those that follow the lessons of *The Twilight Zone* are challenged by Serling to fight "for something a little bit better."

One writer-producer who innately understood this was Gene Roddenberry, the *Star Trek* creator who followed the "moralist in disguise" path blazed by Serling on *The Twilight Zone.* "The fact that Rod Serling was a uniquely talented writer with extraordinary imagination is not our real loss," Rodenberry said at a July 7, 1975, memorial service held for Serling. "These merely describe his tools and the level of his skill. Our loss is the man, the intelligence and the conscience that used these things for us.

Rod Serling gets the portrait treatment for an NBC newspaper advertisement promoting the horror anthology *Night Gallery*. *Mark Dawidziak collection*

"No one could know Serling, or view or read his work, without recognizing his deep affection for humanity, his sympathetically enthusiastic curiosity about us, and his determination to enlarge our horizons by giving us a better understanding of ourselves."

ONE GIANT SPOILER ALERT

The stories presented on *The Twilight Zone,* including the twist endings laced with irony, have become pop-culture coin of the realm. They are shared reference points, instantly recognizable among contemporaries, joyously handed down generation after generation. Still, there might be some who have not yet discovered the land that "lies between the pit of man's fears and the summit of his knowledge." This page is for them.

The plots of these episodes will be discussed. Resolutions will be revealed. Many a *Twilight Zone* tale stressed the importance of playing fair, and that's what this spoiler alert is all about.

For the already initiated and for the record, not every episode gets covered. This book touches on about one hundred of the 156 episodes that aired during the 1959 to 1964 run of *The Twilight Zone.* This in no way suggests that these are the one hundred best episodes. Some classic episodes and some of my all-time favorites are not included, merely because they don't fit the fifty chosen life lessons. That's a primary author's lesson. Leave something for the sequel.

Nor does this book cover the 1985 to 1989 revival series,

which began on CBS, then jumped to syndication. Nor does it cover the twenty episodes in the 2002 to 2003 incarnation that aired on UPN. For this book, at least, we're sticking with the classics. Some lessons are illustrated by single episodes, others by two or more. And some episodes are used to illustrate more than one lesson.

Nor should the reader in any way assume that this book covers every lesson or everything I learned in *The Twilight Zone*. This is a representative sampling, not a comprehensive list. And others may look at the same episodes and see different but equally valid lessons. The point is, there's always room for more, but how could there not be in a dimension that's as vast as space and as timeless as infinity?

ALWAYS KEEP YOUR HEART OPEN TO THE MAGIC THAT COMES YOUR WAY

"THE BIG TALL WISH"

(ORIGINAL AIRDATE: APRIL 8, 1960)

Some people don't believe in magic, yet it exists. Ignore that at your own peril. Now, I'm not talking about Las Vegas stage illusions or spells cast by wizards with Hogwarts degrees. I'm not talking about Disneyesque fairy godmothers or time-honored superstitions covering everything from the number between twelve and fourteen to black cats, cracked mirrors, and strolls under ladders. I'm talking about the kind of magic that touches all of us—or can touch all of us—in one form or another. There are three requirements, however. First, you must believe in the magic. Second, you must be able to recognize the magic. Finally, you must be able to accept it. And that's not as easy as it sounds, as the first-season episode "The Big Tall Wish" drives home with the devastating power of a perfectly timed left hook.

Rod Serling stepped back into the boxing ring for this story. It was familiar territory for him. He'd laced up the gloves for several bouts after joining the army. He returned to "the square circle" for the 1953 *Kraft Television Theatre* production *The Twilight Rounds* (yes, *Zone* wasn't the first time he'd used *Twilight* in a title) and, of course, for the towering *Playhouse 90* production *Requiem for a Heavyweight*. "The Big Tall Wish" introduces us to boxer Bolie Jackson (Ivan Dixon), "an aging, over-the-hill relic of what was, and who now sees a reflection of a man who has left too many pieces of his youth in too many stadiums for too many years before too many screaming people." The aging athlete, businessman, teacher, salesman, you name it—there's that familiar theme that so fascinated Serling. As Bolie contemplates his battle-scarred face in the mirror, the keeper of the Twilight Zone tells us that this past-his-prime prizefighter "might do well to look for some gentle magic in the hard-surfaced glass that stares back at him."

It's good advice, because, just before his big comeback fight at Saint Nicholas Arena, Bolie breaks his hand. Henry (Steven Perry), the little boy who loves him, makes "a big tall wish" because Bolie is his friend and he has been hurt enough already. Bolie is about to be counted out by the referee, but Henry's wish reverses the outcome, and it is Bolie who finds himself standing over an unconscious opponent, hand raised in victory. Later that night, Henry confesses that Bolie won because of the big tall wish. "It was magic, Bolie," Henry tells him. "We had to have magic then." He begs Bolie to believe in the magic, because, "If you don't believe, Bolie, it won't be true. That's the way magic works." Bolie can't accept the miracle. He has been too beaten up and beaten down by life. "I can't believe," he says. "I'm too old. And I'm too hurt to believe." This refusal reverses the reversal of fortune, and Bolie is back in the ring, being counted out.

On the most surface level, and not a very sublime one, "The Big Tall Wish" can be viewed as a *Twilight Zone* variation on the adage that cautions us against looking a gift horse in the mouth. That works, yet this beautifully written, filmed, and acted episode has a far more moving payoff punch. If we stop with the moment that Bolie loses the fight, then, as poignant as it is, this is merely the story of a self-described "tired old man" who has run out of wishes and dreams and hope. "When do they suddenly find out that there ain't any magic?" Bolie asks Henry's mother, Frances (Kim Hamilton), before the fight.

But the fantasy aspect of Henry's wish is not the real magic at work in this episode. The real magic is what's behind the wish. A child's love makes the big tall wish come true, and Bolie's refusal to believe in the magic does nothing to diminish that love. After the beaten fighter returns home, Henry still believes in him and still is proud of him. The big tall wish is just an expression of the love, which is the real magic. Do we have any doubt that Bolie will continue to be the beneficiary of that magic? They're heading for a hockey game the next day, to a place where they can laugh and yell and eat hot dogs. Do we have any doubt that, as clearly as Bolie sees life's hardships and injustices, Henry has given him something worth wishing for—something worth fighting for?

"Got to believe," Henry says again and again. And in those three words is the reminder that magic takes all kinds of forms, including the restorative and transformative powers of love, faith, hope, and belief. George Clayton Johnson returned to this idea with his equally moving third-season episode "Kick the Can," in which Sunnyvale Rest Home resident Charles Whitley tries to convince others in the home for the aged that there's magic in acting young and playing a favorite childhood game. His lifelong friend, Ben Conroy, has grown too cynical to believe. And the magic passes him by. He can't believe in it, recognize it, or accept it.

"Maybe there is magic," Bolie says at the end of "The Big Tall Wish." "And maybe there's wishes, too. I guess the trouble is, there's not enough people around to believe."

Still, you don't need to believe in literal magic to believe in the magic powering this episode. It's all around you. It can be the faith of a child. It can be faith in yourself. It can be the devotion of a parent or the enduring loyalty of a best friend. You find this magic in all those things placed in the category of "those lovely intangibles" by *Miracle on 34th Street,* a film that's deeply magical but one that can be viewed as literally or metaphorically so. Whichever camp you are in, there's magic in this film that should work for you. The same thing applies to the best of the *Twilight Zone* episodes. The magic is what gets us through, allowing us to crawl off the canvas and continue. At the end of the episode, Bolie hasn't really lost. He hasn't lost Henry's love or belief in him. We don't feel sorry for Bolie because he could have been a champion. We smile for him because there is a little boy who loves him deeply enough to have made the big tall wish.

The end of *It's a Wonderful Life* assures us that no man is a failure who has friends. "The Big Tall Wish" amends that: no person is a failure who has someone making those big tall wishes for him or her. Love and belief . . . magic, indeed. And it's a one-two combination that can deliver the knockout blow to at least some of life's woes. Life will continue to be a fight for Bolie Jackson. It probably will be tough for little Henry, too. We can't expect anything else for them. But these will not be lives bereft of hopes and dreams. The earlier moralist in disguise, Mark Twain, advised: "Do not part with your illusions. When they are gone, you may still exist, but you have ceased to live." May you never run short of that kind of magic in your lives. It's our big tall wish for you . . . from the Twilight Zone.

GUEST LESSON: MEL BROOKS
I've asked a wide variety of Twilight Zone *fans and people associated with the series to submit their favorite lesson or lessons from the land of shadow and substance. You'll find these scattered throughout the book. Some kept their responses to one line. Some sent several paragraphs. Some zeroed in on a specific episode. Some addressed the entire show. Some made it personal.*

Some made it humorous. Some made it profound. I put no limits on length or approach.

First up, some thoughts from Mel Brooks, one of those rare show business legends to have won an Oscar, Emmy, Grammy, and Tony. The director of The Producers, Blazing Saddles, *and* Young Frankenstein *is a longtime* Twilight Zone *devotee. It's good to be a* Twilight Zone *fan. This was his response.*

The greatest lesson I learned is that you need to reserve judgment and seriously buy into the creation and design of the filmmaker. You've got to give it all up and go along with the magic. Every time I watched *The Twilight Zone,* I was completely ready to surrender to it. That's what the mystery of creation is all about. Give yourself over to that wonderful, wonderful mystery.

FOLLOW YOUR PASSION
"A PASSAGE FOR TRUMPET"
(ORIGINAL AIRDATE: MAY 20, 1960)

Sooner or later, most fledgling writers are hit with that dusty piece of advice: "Write about what you know." I first stumbled over it during a ninth-grade English class at a Long Island junior high school. The problem was, I was in the ninth grade. What did I know? The words, which seemed so wise in tone and directness, were meaningless to me. They seemed to open a mysterious door that led . . . nowhere. I can remember trying to apply those words to my thirteen-year-old life and thinking "What do I know?" For that age, except in the rare cases of true prodigies (a category for which nobody was nominating me), the advice is badly phrased. Amend it slightly. Instead of "write about what you know," make it write about what you love, what you're passionate about, what you're interested in, what fires you up, what rocks your socks and pings your pong. *That* I would have understood. And while others my age might have said sports or cars, I would have said show business in all of its forms—movies, the theater, television.

Following that passion, I've been writing about movies, the theater, and television for more than thirty-five years, and getting a weekly paycheck for it, year after year. Years later, I would hear this advice phrased as "follow your bliss," "follow your heart," "follow your dream," and "follow your passion." Journalists who use this as a road map have a fighting chance to grow old in the business. Think of sportswriters who never get over the thrill of going to the game. Think of movie and TV critics. The happiest of the breed got to where they are by following their passion.

Joey Crown (Jack Klugman) remembers the music and the things that make life worth living in "A Passage for Trumpet," written by Rod Serling. *Courtesy CBS Photo Archive*

Writing is just our way in here, because the follow-your-passion lesson can be applied to just about anything. You'll find a poignant illustration of this lesson in the Serling-penned first-season episode that hits one of the show's highest notes, "A Passage for Trumpet." Jack Klugman and Burgess Meredith both starred in four episodes of *The Twilight Zone*. You could say that "A Passage for Trumpet" contains one of Klugman's best performances, but you could say that about any one of the four. He plays Joey Crown, a musician ready to give up on himself, ready to give up on everything. He has lost his direction. He has lost his sense of purpose. He has lost his bliss, which is the drive to produce glorious music from his beloved trumpet. Without this heavenly expression of his inner soul, he's trapped in a Hell of his own making.

Such a loss must cause great pain, and Joey is numbing the pain with alcohol. "For old times, when you had it," says a musician friend, slipping money into Joey's pocket. Had what? Ah, we know what he has lost—what he has thrown away. Without his music, Joey feels like "just plain ordinary nothing." He's down, but is he out? That's the main question posed by Serling in this episode.

It sure seems as if Joey is heading for a dead end. He's about to blow it, and I don't mean his trumpet. He pawns the instrument, using the money to get drunk. He emerges from the bar lower than ever. He decides to commit suicide by stepping in front of a truck. He wakes in a shadow world where no one can see him or hear him. Convinced he is dead, Joey is lured by the sound of a trumpet, and the angelic fellow (played by John Anderson) with the horn can see him and hear him. The stranger's name is Gabe, "short for Gabriel," and he's sort of an expert on trumpets. Joey isn't a ghost, Gabe tells him. He's not dead. And he can choose life, if he wishes. He can go back.

Joey concedes that he may have forgotten how terrific certain things can be. Primary among these: "Maybe I forgot about the music I could make on this horn and how nice it sounded. . . . Somewhere along the line, I forgot all the good things." Unlike Clarence, the angel who shows George Bailey that it's a wonderful life, Gabe uses sweet music to awaken the part of Joey gone dead. Joey is called back to life, if you will, by the very thing he has tried to throw away. It is one sweet wake-up call, to be sure. Joey very much wants to go back and reclaim first his trumpet, then his life. "The bugle and me, till death do us part," he says.

Cut to Joey playing that trumpet on the roof of his apartment building. Just as Gabe's music lured him toward the light, Joey's music has cut through the night and lured a lonely newcomer to the city. Nan (Mary Webster) wonders if Joey might show her the city. Can there be any doubt that they'll make beautiful music together?

Like so many episodes of *The Twilight Zone*, "A Passage for Trumpet" has more than one lesson to teach us. Certainly Gabe is telling Joey (and us) to recognize, appreciate, and embrace second chances. Another lesson? Joey himself tells us that it really is a wonderful life, if you can recognize, appreciate, and embrace the things that make you happy. Still another? Serling's cautionary tale also is a call to arms, reminding us to make the most of the talents and opportunities we have been given. "That's an exceptional talent, Joey," Gabe tells him. "Don't waste it."

Important lessons all, yet we can't forget that Joey ultimately finds his way by again following his passion. He's once again in tune with the soulful jazz music he loves, and it hasn't only saved his soul, it has found him a soul mate. He is recalled to life, as Dickens puts it in *A Tale of Two Cities*. He is released from his personal Bastille of pain and disillusionment. He is alive, not just because he's breathing in air but because he's filling the air around him with divine music and with life-affirming possibilities.

GUEST LESSON: JACK KLUGMAN

I had the distinct honor of twice interviewing Jack Klugman, star of four Twilight Zone *episodes, two written by Rod Serling ("A Passage for Trumpet" and "In Praise of Pip"), one by George Clayton Johnson ("A Game of Pool"), and one by Richard Matheson ("Death Ship"). He also was featured in Serling's* Playhouse 90 *drama* The Velvet Alley. *We talked at great length about* The Odd Couple *and* The Twilight Zone, *two of my all-time favorite series, and he offered up a lesson of sorts, although not one specifically solicited for this book (since I hadn't yet thought of it). But I can't resist including this.*

I learned that there are certain playwrights, like Rod Serling, who just suit me. It was a joy to play his characters and to roll his words around in my mouth. What characters he gave you to play! What words he gave you to say! Lovely words. They just seemed to resonate with me. There have been three writers that seemed to most suit me: Rod Serling, Clifford Odets, and Neil Simon. With Neil Simon, it was the humor and the rhythms. With Odets, it was the staccato style and muckraking attitude. But with Rod Serling it was the anger, the defiance, and the fire. He brought such fire to everything he wrote.

READ EVERY CONTRACT . . . CAREFULLY

"ESCAPE CLAUSE"

(ORIGINAL AIRDATE: NOVEMBER 6, 1959)

I have not signed a contract at any point in my life without Rod Serling standing behind me. I've never actually turned around to make certain that he was there. I didn't have to. I knew he was there. I could picture him, lit cigarette perched between two fingers of an upraised hand. I could sense him, ready to launch into one of those "submitted for your approval" narrations if . . . if I carelessly agreed to something foolish. My job, therefore, is not to give Rod any excuse to start talking. I have not always succeeded. I would have stupidly agreed to any terms when I signed my first book contract at the age of twenty-five. And that's precisely what I did. I wanted a book published in the worst way, and to paraphrase Abraham Lincoln, that's what I got. Rod went on for about two hours that time: "Picture of an idiot about to the cut the rope that will drop the two-ton safe dangling over him."

I've learned with each contract, getting a little sharper and shrewder, book by book. It's all in the wording, what's in there and what isn't. It's all in the details, how something is phrased and what terms are lurking in the fine print. And as the familiar old maxim warns us, the Devil is in the details.

That's literally true in the *Twilight Zone* episode that sparked the idea for this book, Serling's "Escape Clause." That's the one with David Wayne as the thoroughly unpleasant hypochondriac Walter Bedeker. What makes the bilious Bedeker easy pickings for the Devil, here called Mr. Cadwallader (Thomas Gomez), is not simply an obsessive preoccupation with his health. It is his obsessive preoccupation with himself. Or as Serling puts it, "He has one interest in life, and that's Walter Bedeker." He has only one concern about society, and that is, "If Walter Bedeker should die, how will it survive without him?"

You see, Walter is worried about every germ and disease, but not about his vision. He's so blind to the hopes and cares of his fellow human beings, he can't see the foolishness of making this deal with the Devil. He is given immortality and indestructibility in exchange for his soul. There is an escape clause, which Bedeker haughtily dismisses, even as we're thinking, "Oh, oh, pay attention." If he ever tires of the agreement, he can summon Cadwallader and head for Hades.

Bedeker has not only signed a bad deal, he has constructed his own Hell on Earth. He soon becomes bored. And he has only himself to blame. He has been granted immortality, and what does he do with it? What's his plan? There is none, except to pursue things that make Walter Bedeker happy, and he soon runs out of those. He has no desire to help others or improve the world or make some kind of contribution. There is nothing to live for, so he thinks about getting a charge out of dying (or at least experiencing it with the assurance of survival). He hopes that drinking poison or stepping in front of a train will provide a momentary thrill. But when his wife tries to stop him from jumping from the roof of their apartment building, she falls to her death, instead, and Bedeker confesses to murdering her. He wants to experience the electric chair. To his horror, he is sentenced to life in prison, no possibility of parole. Forever in the same cell? Time to call Mr. Cadwallader. Time to give the Devil his due. Time to exercise the escape clause. Time for Rod to start talking: "Walter Bedeker, lately deceased, a little man with such a yen to live. Beaten by the Devil, by his own boredom—and by the scheme of things in this, the Twilight Zone."

The lesson here? It could be as simple as, if you deal with the Devil, you're going to get burned. But one more applicable to everyday life would be: don't just read the contract, consider the consequences of every clause from every conceivable angle. Think of how much grief many Americans would have been spared by following this advice during the subprime lending crisis that hit at the same time as the 2007 to 2009 recession. Consider all those who signed adjustable-rate or balloon-payment mortgage contracts, certain there was nothing there that could come back and bite them in the assets.

A healthy familiarity with *The Twilight Zone* and Rod Serling's writing inspires a healthy respect for complete and precise wording in any kind of contract, whether it be a bargain with the Devil or a wish granted by a genie. In "Make Me Laugh," a 1971 episode of *Night Gallery*, Serling has a swami caution an eager would-be wisher. He tells of a Civil War buff who wished to be in Lincoln's shoes and found himself in an insane asylum claiming to be a woolen sock (had to be restrained from sticking darning needles into his head). The contract was fulfilled, but not on the expected terms. That's because they were not specified. The Civil War buff might as well have been signing an adjustable-rate loan without considering the consequences. His next stop? It's far worse than what would be in store for him in the Twilight Zone. He's headed into Serling's Night Gallery. Pay particular attention to those nasty loopholes and possible ramifications. As anyone who has watched enough of *The Twilight Zone* knows, you don't leave that much open to chance, fate, irony, the universe, or whatever deity or demon may be holding your belief cards.

Read the contract. Don't sign too quickly, and don't settle for too little, even when drawing up life's metaphoric contract for yourself. Here's an example I typically share with my students at Kent State University. When I was staring at my senior year at George Washington University, a familiar question was hanging over me: Will I find work after graduation? I still can summon the anxiety of that moment. More than thirty-five years later, I imagine a *Twilight Zone* scenario with Rod Serling appearing before my desk at the school newspaper. I'm in a particularly vulnerable emotional place and he's holding a contract. "Here, sign this," he says, "and you'll always be guaranteed a weekly paycheck for writing. You'll always be what you most want to be—a working writer."

Picture, if you will, how quickly I would have leaped over the desk to snatch the paper out of his hands and sign. But this is Rod, not Mr. Cadwallader. He is not playing a game of gotcha. He's out to teach a different kind of lesson. "Hold on," he says with a smile. "Don't sign yet. I didn't say you'd make enough to support yourself, let alone a family. Let's change the contract to say you'll be guaranteed a weekly paycheck for writing, and that paycheck will be sufficient to feed and house yourself and a family."

How could I have missed that? All right, now let me sign. But Rod again holds up his hand.

"Not so fast," he says. "I didn't say what kind of writing you'd be doing. You could be spending your life writing safety warnings or manuals on how to put together blenders. I'm willing to offer you the same contract, but you're guaranteed a living writing about things you love—movies, theater, television."

At this point, I'm begging. "Please! Please let me sign." But Rod goes on. "It gets better. You also can have books published, plays produced, magazine work, fiction, nonfiction. . . ." Now

I'm wrestling to get the contract out of his hands. But there's more. And there has been in my life . . . much more. The point is, I probably would have signed the first contract, without thinking, without hesitation, without considering the possible ramifications. So, when there's a contract in front of you, remember, Rod is right behind you. Don't give him a handy excuse to start talking about you.

GUEST LESSON: DICK VAN DYKE

Although he never appeared in an episode of The Twilight Zone, *Dick Van Dyke was (and is) a big fan of the show and Rod Serling. His acclaimed series,* The Dick Van Dyke Show, *ran on CBS at the same time as* The Twilight Zone, *and one of its most memorable episodes, "It May Look Like a Walnut," was a playful nod to Serling's wondrous land.*

The lesson is to always appreciate and cherish the kind of creative, imaginative, and original writing found on *The Twilight Zone*, because that kind of writing hasn't been seen since.

NOBODY SAID LIFE WAS FAIR

"TIME ENOUGH AT LAST"

(ORIGINAL AIRDATE: NOVEMBER 20, 1959)

True story. There were six of us, sitting around a table at the Du-par's Restaurant on Ventura Boulevard in Studio City. We had strolled over there after dinner, searching, we said, for coffee and pie, but really just looking for an excuse to keep the lively conversation going for a while. The group included two writers who know a thing or two or three about writing fantasy stories: Harlan Ellison, the author of landmark science fiction and horror tales, and Charles Edward Pogue, whose screenwriting credits include *Dragonheart* and the 1986 remake of *The Fly*. You could say that I met Harlan through *The Twilight Zone*. Having written celebrated episodes of everything from *The Outer Limits* to *Star Trek*, Harlan was a creative consultant for the 1985 CBS revival of *The Twilight Zone*. I was the TV critic at the *Akron Beacon Journal*, and I'd read acres of Ellison, dazzled by the intoxicating terrors of his *Strange Wine* and the searing insights of his television criticism in *The Glass Teat*. So, naturally, I asked my best network contact to arrange for an interview. By then, Harlan's dissatisfaction with commercial television was firmly on the record. Why, then, I

Henry Bemis (Burgess Meredith) wanders through the rubble of a world destroyed by war in Rod Serling's "Time Enough at Last." *Courtesy CBS Photo Archive*

asked in 1985, was he heading back into the killing fields? "I don't consider myself working for television," he told me. "I consider myself working for *The Twilight Zone,* which is very much like being part of a myth—a great legend. I can't think of anybody, no matter how adamant they are about not working in television, who would risk going to the grave not being able to say 'I once worked on *The Twilight Zone.*'"

The relationship with CBS, predictably enough, did not survive. Our friendship did. Thirty years later, the conversation continues. But back to Du-par's and that warm January night. The talk drifted toward *The Twilight Zone* and our all-time favorite episodes. Someone mentioned "Time Enough at Last," Serling's adaptation of the short story by Lynn Venable. It contains perhaps the most memorable twist ending payoffs of any episode. It features one of the most heart-stopping images ever served up by Serling and his team. You know what I'm talking about. Yes, those darn broken glasses. And if it's not the most iconic of all *Twilight Zone* episodes, it's on most everyone's top-ten list.

It was no surprise, therefore, that everyone at the table fell into the kind of beaming exaltation that's hardly uncommon when two or more *Twilight Zone* fans are gathered . . . everyone, that is, except me. Not showering sufficient praise on "Time Enough at Last" could be viewed as a fifth-dimension form of blasphemy. Such reluctance to join the benediction required an explanation, and this is the one I offered that night.

I've never been crazy about "Time Enough at Last," even though John Brahm's direction is sensational and Burgess Meredith's performance is heartrending. I will readily concede the episode's considerable artistic merits. The power of Meredith's performance is undeniable. But there is something about this story that always has left me feeling mighty uneasy. You know the story. Meredith plays bank teller Henry Bemis, "a bookish little man" devoted to literature and the joy of reading. The world lines up to deride him for this, and, at the head of the line are his grumpy boss and snappish wife. He happily sneaks off to the bank vault and uses his lunch hour to pursue his love of books—a love that the world around him doesn't seem to understand. Well, the world around him is about to go bye-bye. A nuclear war erupts when Henry has his nose buried in a book, and the bank vault protects him from the worldwide devastation. He may just be the last man on Earth. He is about to commit suicide when he spies the ruins of a library. He stacks books on the stone library steps, planning years and years of reading. But his glasses fall to one of those stone steps, smashing the lenses and leaving him incapable of seeing the words on the pages of his beloved books.

Now, here's my problem. I can't help but view this as a violation of basic laws governing *The Twilight Zone*. The people singled out for this kind of terrible and ironic smackdown generally are the recipients of well-earned just deserts. Through greed, spite, prejudice, or bullying, they've turned themselves into one giant target for a cosmic comeuppance. Let the punishment fit the crime. But what is meek Henry's crime? He loves books. He prizes the printed word. He wants to read. He wants to share his great passion for Dickens and the story of *David Copperfield*. His boss tells him plainly what is wrong with him: "You, Mr. Bemis, are a reader." How dare he? And for this he is singled out for one of the bleakest fates ever visited on a denizen of the Twilight Zone. Seems more than a bit extreme, don't you think?

It has been argued by some of my *Twilight Zone* friends that Henry's crime is a study in isolation—that his single-minded pursuit of books has shut him off from the people in his life. And the punishment for this is the ultimate isolation. All right, if you must, but I'm not buying. Henry is the one bullied and picked on in the early part of this episode. He is surrounded by mean, grumpy, unpleasant, impatient people. His response to this? He harbors no hatred for his fellow inhabitants on the planet. He does not give into bitterness or anger.

Serling describes Henry as a fellow "whose passion is the printed page but who is conspired against by a bank president and a wife and a world of tongue cluckers." Those are

Rod's words, not mine. Clearly, our sympathies are meant to be with Henry. His wife, a first cousin of the hellish housekeeper Mrs. Danvers in *Rebecca*, cruelly taunts Henry by asking him to read her some poetry in the book he has secreted. He is momentarily giddy over the notion that she might share his love of literature, but that notion is dashed on the cold realization that she has defaced the book, making it unreadable. She declares poetry "a waste of time." Henry's uncomprehending answer is a plaintiff and sorrowful "Why?" Why, indeed.

Henry's plight seems all the more harrowing as we move through the decades since "Time Enough at Last" aired, watching books and the written word rise higher and higher on society's endangered species list. For those of us who side with Henry, the better Meredith episode is "The Obsolete Man," Serling's second-season cautionary tale about a librarian standing up to a book-banning society. The world can't make room for a reader like Henry in "Time Enough at Last." "The Obsolete Man" argues that maybe we should—a message that has grown in resonance as reading and reading skills have diminished.

But what lesson are we to derive from the story of Henry Bemis? Serling hints at one in his closing narration, referring to the "best-laid plans of mice and men—and Henry Bemis." Any horror fan can tell you how to translate that: "Never (ever) ask, What could possibly go wrong?"

Still, maybe the bigger lesson is in the bitter pill we must swallow in the shattering conclusion. "That's not fair," Henry says, examining the broken glasses. "That's not fair at all." No, it isn't fair. And in its very unfairness is the echo of one of my mother's favorite sayings. When one of us would wail that something wasn't fair, she would invariably pull out "Nobody said life was fair." I didn't like it when she said it then. I didn't like it when that truth hit Henry Bemis in the glasses. But, with something like clarity, I did recognize the truth of it. Nobody said life was fair. A subset of this lesson is the title of Harold Kushner's 1981 book, *When Bad Things Happen to Good People*. Henry is a good person, so I always hope for the ending where he finds the ruined remains of an optometrist's store and locates a pair of glasses that work for him. That works for me.

GUEST LESSON: TOM FONTANA

In the interests of balance, it must be conceded that "Time Enough at Last" has inspired something more than the "life isn't fair" response from many a Twilight Zone *devotee. We offer, then, two widely different interpretations, both wonderfully personal, from keen observers of television's storytelling legacy. The first is from Tom Fontana, the writer-producer whose long list of distinguished credits includes* Oz *(which he created for HBO),* St. Elsewhere, Homicide: Life on the Street, *and* Copper.

I love books. No Kindle for Mama Fontana's little boy. I want paper, to fondle and sniff, to underline astonishing passages and sometimes even to shed a tear upon. So there's no surprise in saying that "Time Enough at Last"—starring the extraordinary Burgess Meredith as Henry Bemis and adapted by the awe-inspiring Rod Serling from a story by Lynn Venable—taught me all that I needed to know about surviving in a harsh and unforgiving world. The lesson is simple: always own a backup pair of glasses. . . .

GUEST LESSON: ROBERT J. THOMPSON

This response to "Time Enough at Last" is from Robert J. Thompson, author, TV historian, and communications professor at Syracuse University.

I get some street cred on this because I teach at a university that is in the birthplace of Rod Serling, and not far from where he grew up in Binghamton and where he spent his summers on Cayuga

Lake. And at fifty-six, I really think that "Time Enough at Last" is the one a professor should be most concentrating on. The fellow in that episode tries to share his love of reading with everybody, and they just don't care. That's what I've done all my life. I've constantly tried to tell eighteen-to-twenty-two-year-olds how much this stuff matters, and they won't listen. And I'm someone who has spent forty-five years of my life so proud of the incredible library I have acquired, walking around stack after stack of books. And now . . . I'm realizing that this stuff is going to ultimately completely bury me. So that ending speaks to academic hubris. Let's face it, professors do tend to put that kind of pursuit of learning over everything else. And there is hubris to that. The idea at the end of the episode is that all that wisdom still is there. It has not gone away, but instead of Bemis's being able to tap into it, it mocks him. All the minds of centuries are available to him, and just a little thing like an inadequate optic nerve completely takes it away. We spend our lives acquiring the world's wisdom, and, in the end, it's a simple thing like a ninety-nine-cent pair of reading glasses that can dislodge you. It's a sobering moment when you realize what a fine line it is between the secrets of the universe and simply sitting in a stack of paper. For a person slouching toward his sixties with countless volumes weighing down his house, that's a very profound lesson. You've got to add a little Camus to this whole thing. That realization was a lesson of *The Twilight Zone,* too.

KEEP YOUR INNER CHILD ALIVE
"NIGHTMARE AS A CHILD"
(ORIGINAL AIRDATE: APRIL 29, 1960)

Fantasy writers are world-class experts at keeping their inner child alive. Spend some quality time with them, either in conversation or through their published works, and you quickly realize that the inner child is not some distant voice or faint echo to these spinners of wondrous tales. It is loud and intense, sometimes shouting with joy at the universe's many gifts, sometimes screaming in fright at the terrors lurking in dark closets, something laughing with a giddiness that is its own magical kingdom. "The child is in me still and sometimes not so still," said Fred Rogers, the proprietor of *Mr. Rogers' Neighborhood,* whimsically expressing a sentiment that would be instantly understood and appreciated by most authors of fantasy, horror, and science-fiction stories.

It is not an easy trick to pull off, by the way, but it is an emotionally rewarding one. What makes this so challenging is that, even before childhood is over, there are persistent voices trying to badger the child into submission—other voices, other glooms. You are probably well acquainted with the chorus, because it follows you into adulthood. "Act your age." "Oh, grow up." "Don't be so childish." "You're too old be behaving that way."

If anything, the insidious process has been accelerated by technology, exposing too many precious childhoods to the deadly rays of a commercial-driven pop culture. From the moment a child leaves the safety of the playpen, he or she is under attack, as creativity and imagination battle for supremacy against the forces of conformity and societal stereotypes. And the attack even can come from other children. Ray Bradbury, whose writing so influenced *The Twilight Zone,* remembered how, at the age of nine, he almost had thrown away those things that were most precious to him. He had already become a major fan of Buck Rogers, carefully cutting out the comic strips from the local newspaper and keeping them as a special, ever-expanding tome. The kids at his school learned about this and teased him unmercifully. Embarrassed and a little ashamed, he tore up the collection and threw it away. For a month, he walked through his fourth-grade classes, stunned and empty. And after a month, he dissolved into tears and couldn't understand why. "Who had died?" he wondered. Then the answer hit him like a rocket, "Me, that's who!" Buck Rogers was gone and life simply wasn't worth living. Then he thought, those kids who teased him weren't his friends. The people who got him to tear up those strips and tear his life down the middle were his enemies. "I went back to collecting *Buck Rogers,*" he said. "My life has been happy ever since. . . . Since then, I have never listened to anyone who criticized my taste in space travel, sideshows, or gorillas. When such occurs, I simply pack up my dinosaurs and leave the room."

That's why fantasy writers, as well as actors and many a genius, have a tough time relating to Saint Paul's much-quoted line: "When I became a man, I did away with the things of the child." They hold on to *Buck Rogers* and such things. Those inclined toward the New Testament probably prefer the moment

Jesus tells the apostles that the way to paradise is to "become like little children." The much-stressed distinction here is to remain childlike, not childish. And if you can manage that, certainly your inner child will lead you to some heavenly destinations.

I sat next to Harlan Ellison during a screening of the documentary about him, *Dreams with Sharp Teeth*. Another acclaimed fantasy writer (and *Twilight Zone* fan), Neil Gaiman, was on the screen, remarking how Harlan was, at the same time, one of the greatest writers of the twentieth century and "an alternately impish and furious" eleven-year-old. I became aware of Harlan impishly and furiously pounding the arm of his chair, repeating, "I'm seven. I'm seven." When I turned and asked him what was wrong, Harlan replied, "I'm seven. He's got it wrong. I'm seven years old."

All right, that's settled. As you can see, Ray Bradbury celebrated his inner child. Harlan Ellison could tell you the age of his inner child. And Rod Serling . . . well, Rod Serling wasn't just that fellow in the dark suit, dispensing lessons through clipped phrasings and clenched teeth. There was the practical joker Rod and the life-of-the-party Rod. There was the alternately impish and playful Rod who put lampshades on his head, imitated a gorilla, and loved the Pirates of the Caribbean ride at Disneyland. There was the Rod who could always summon the carousel and cotton candy memories of summer nights in the Binghamton of his childhood. His daughter Anne describes him as "nostalgic and childlike."

"The most sophisticated people I know—inside they are all children," Jim Henson observed.

But being in touch with your inner child means being alive to the fears as well as the joys of childhood. The nightmares go along with the dreams, and how deliciously terrifying they can be. Schoolteacher Helen Foley, the lead character played by Janice

Rule in Serling's "Nightmare as a Child," is suppressing those fears—and one nightmare in particular. "A little girl will lead her by the hand and walk with her into a nightmare," Serling says in his opening narration.

The little girl is Markie (Terry Burnham), who keeps pushing Helen to remember something buried deep from when her mother was murdered. Markie, it turns out, is Helen as a little girl. Markie is the part of herself she needs to remember in order to save herself. A man named Peter Selden (Shepperd Strudwick) has turned up at Helen's door, and, yes, he killed her mother. Now he wants to eliminate the only witness . . . Helen. The traumatic experience has been blocked from Helen's mind all these years, but Markie is there to remind her what she saw—what *they* saw. Talk about being in touch with your inner child.

Still, Helen has done everything in her power to lose touch with that place and time (not without reason). She has pushed it all away to the point of forgetting that her childhood nickname was Markie. She even forgot what she looked like as a girl. She's incapable of recognizing the little girl she once was.

Although Helen has forgotten this inner child, Markie demands to be recognized. "I'm here," she seems to be saying. "I've always been here. Now you're going to hear me." Helen does hear her, and just in time. The moral of this story might well be, keep your inner child alive and she might just save your life.

Writing decades before "Nightmare as a Child" first aired, G. K. Chesterton sagely observed: "Happy are they who still love something they loved in the nursery. They have not been broken in two by time; they are not two persons, but one, and they have saved not only their souls but their lives."

Helen heals the break and no longer is two. She has saved not only her soul but her life. We can take this literally in "Nightmare as a Child," or we can take it spiritually. Either way, we can be thankful that Rod Serling had no trouble keeping his inner child alive. Without that gift, *The Twilight Zone* would not have been possible. Symbolically, he gave the central character in this episode the name and profession of a favorite high school teacher in Binghamton. Something here demanded an echo of the old hometown.

GUEST LESSON: HARLAN ELLISON

The fiercely outspoken Harlan Ellison is also one of the most fiercely talented writers to have set his sights on the science-fiction, fantasy, horror, and speculative-fiction fields. His mountain of awards attests to that. But Harlan's writing spans many more genres, and his published works include mystery, television and film criticism, essays, columns, and scripts. Ellison's teleplays were produced for The Outer Limits *and* Star Trek, *as well as the 1985 CBS revival of* The Twilight Zone. *Among his many books are* Ellison Wonderland, Spider Kiss, I Have No Mouth and I Must Scream, The Glass Teat, Strange Wine, Shatterday, Stalking the Nightmare, *and* An Edge in My Voice.

I didn't write for the original *Twilight Zone,* as you know, but I had the privilege of knowing two of the writers whose magnificent talents helped shape it: Charles Beaumont and Richard Matheson. I remember almost every episode intimately, and my favorite is "Two," the one with Charles Bronson and Elizabeth Montgomery. It speaks to the aftermath of war. Why is it the favorite? Because it is. And the lesson? I have no idea what the lesson is, kid. I'm eighty-one years old. Things don't have lessons for me anymore. There are great memories and there are small memories, and that's a great memory of the original *Twilight Zone.*

DIVIDED WE FALL
"THE MONSTERS ARE DUE ON MAPLE STREET"
(ORIGINAL AIRDATE: MARCH 4, 1960)

"THE SHELTER"
(ORIGINAL AIRDATE: SEPTEMBER 29, 1961)

The phrase appears on the great seal of the United States: *E pluribus unum*. It is Latin for "Out of many, one." Or, if you will, "One out of many." Originally, it referred to the notion of many states forming one sovereign nation. Later, as the Statue of Liberty welcomed "huddled masses yearning to breathe free," the country's unofficial motto took on a melting pot interpretation, celebrating that out of many races, religions, nationalities, heritages, beliefs, ancestries, and ethnicities towered one nation made stronger and more vital by their inclusion. In our differences, there was strength. It has often been remarked in the twenty-first century, however, that Americans are more divided and polarized than at any time since the Civil War. Watching these divisions with growing alarm, historian Arthur Schlesinger observed, "We've got too much *pluribus* and not enough *unum*." Lurking in those words is the echo of Abraham Lincoln's warning that a house divided against itself cannot stand.

That warning rumbled across the decades, and a little more than a century after Lincoln reminded us that we were supposed

Steve Brand (Claude Akins) and Charlie Farnsworth (Jack Weston) don't quite realize that "The Monsters Are Due on Maple Street." *Courtesy CBS Photo Archive*

to be living in a *United* States, it found powerful metaphoric expression in one of Rod Serling's most significant and insightful scripts, "The Monsters Are Due on Maple Street." Having observed in horror how the insidious forces of fear, suspicion, paranoia, mistrust, ignorance, hysteria, and prejudice could divide us during the Red Scare reign of Joseph McCarthy, Serling served up a suburban parable that demonstrated how swiftly and monstrously friend could be turned against friend, neighbor against neighbor, American against American. He shows us how quickly *unum* gets trampled underfoot when *pluribus* gives way to a mob mentality.

To emphasize that this could happen anywhere at any time, Serling sets his story on Maple Street, U.S.A. It is a late-summer Saturday, precisely 6:43 p.m. Time for barbecues, ice-cream cones, and chats with friends on the gliders of front porches. The idyllic picture is shaken by a meteor blazing overhead. Or is it a meteor? When a total power failure mysteriously shuts down even cars, portable radios, and the telephone service, young Tommy (Jan Handzlik) says it is just like every science-fiction story he has ever read. That's how the aliens infiltrate society. The aliens look just like us. His suggestion is greeted with laughter . . . until a neighbor's car suddenly starts, all by itself. Why does his car start when no one else's will? And how did it start when Les Goodman (Barry Atwater) wasn't even standing near it? And, hey, another neighbor has spotted Les looking up at the sky at night, as if he were waiting for something or somebody. It's sure looking like they found their communist . . . uh, alien.

"Let's not be a mob," says levelheaded Steve Brand (Claude Akins), pleading for everyone to remain calm. But whipped up by loudmouth Charlie Farnsworth (Jack Weston), the increasingly fearful neighbors let suspicion run wild. "You're letting something begin here that's a nightmare," Les tells them. How right he is. Panic takes over as the once-friendly neighbors go on a witch hunt for "fifth columnists from the vast beyond."

"Well, believe me, friends, the only thing that's gonna happen is that we're going to eat each other up alive," Steve says. It's a prophetic statement. Hopelessly divided, Maple Street falls. At the conclusion, two aliens discuss how easy it is to destroy the fabric of society. All you need is to do is shut off the power and introduce the shadow of doubt. It is an age-old tactic, divide and conquer.

"The Monsters Are Due on Maple Street" is an American tragedy that Serling delivers with a word of caution: "The tools of conquest do not necessarily come with bombs and explosions and fallout. There are weapons that are simply thoughts, attitudes, prejudices—to be found only in the minds of men. For the record, prejudices can kill and suspicion can destroy, and a thoughtless, frightened search for a scapegoat has a fallout all its own—for the children, and the children not yet born. And the pity is that these things cannot be confined to the Twilight Zone."

So deep does this caution run, it can be viewed as an indictment of those who search for scapegoats or those who see enemies where none exist. When you go searching for monsters, be careful that you don't turn into one.

The episode also can be viewed as a warning against fearing people just because they're different. And it can be taken as a chilling alarm bell, reminding us to be on guard against all those nasty little things that threaten to divide us. That way lies not only tragedy, Serling is telling us, but madness. Charlie Farnsworth is looking for an enemy, and, instead, he runs headlong into the realization made famous by the *Pogo* comic strip: "We have met the enemy and he is us."

Serling revisited these themes for the third-season episode "The Shelter," also set in a suburban America everytown. Larry Gates stars as a beloved doctor who has built a basement shelter big enough for himself, his wife, Grace (Peggy Stewart), and their twelve-year-old son, Michael. The government announces a UFO threat on the radio, telling everyone to head for their shelters. The problem is, ol' Doc Stockton is the only one who has taken this precaution. As in "The Monsters Are Due on Maple Street," friends and neighbors give in to fear and panic. They give voice to feelings of mistrust and prejudice. It is, as Serling tells us in the opening narration, a nightmare—another nightmare, another descent into madness. Once again, the monsters prove to be us. While not as powerfully written as its *Twilight Zone* predecessor, it does hit home, purposely set in a typical home in a typical American town.

"No moral, no message, no prophetic tract, just a simple statement of fact," Serling says after the tale is told. "For civilization to survive, the human race has to remain civilized."

Of course, there is a moral and a message and a lesson here. For the human race to remain civilized, the humanity we share ultimately must prove stronger than those very human frailties that constantly are working to divide us. Serling believed we could find that strength. He gave us these nightmares as a way of pushing us toward that dream.

For me, "The Shelter" also hit home in a personal way. It aired a few weeks after my fifth birthday, and, a short time later, my father decided we needed a bomb shelter. He was an extremely capable fellow, so he dug out a sort of subbasement and, following one of those government pamphlets, added a bomb shelter to our house on Long Island. It was stocked with water and provisions, but, after a couple of years, the panic over a nuclear exchange receded just a bit. By that time, I'd fallen under the spell of those old Universal horror films, and the bomb shelter became my special place of refuge. It became my dungeon, and, indeed, it was a cool and damp environment. I collected bottles and jars of any odd shape I could find, and with the addition of a child's chemistry set, I had my very own mad scientist's laboratory. It was the corner I called my own and a place for the imagination to run wild. My den of imagination these days is an office at the top of our Ohio house. We call it the Bell Tower. Story of my life—from the Dungeon to the Bell Tower. The Dungeon still exists in my boyhood home, now owned by my nephew. He inspects building and construction sites, and he tells me it is so solidly built, it has to stay. But imagine what the residents of Maple Street would have thought of me. "He spends all of his time down in that dungeon." Think of those wonderful quirks that have defined you, and then imagine what the Maple Street mob might have thought of you.

GUEST LESSON: MARC SCOTT ZICREE

Everybody who cherishes The Twilight Zone *owes a great debt to Marc Scott Zicree, who wrote the first history of the series,* The Twilight Zone Companion. *The book put dozens of people associated with the show on the record, setting the standard for histories of television series. Zicree also has contributed scripts to several shows, including* Beauty and the Beast, Forever Knight, Babylon 5, *and* Star Trek: The Next Generation.

Here's what I learned from *The Twilight Zone,* and Rod Serling in particular: we can either live in a universe of love and compassion, or chaos and destruction. The choice is ours, made every day, every moment, by the actions we consciously or unconsciously take . . . and you can file that under *L* for Life Lessons.

DON'T LIVE IN THE PAST

"WALKING DISTANCE"
(ORIGINAL AIRDATE: OCTOBER 30, 1959)

"THE TROUBLE WITH TEMPLETON"
(ORIGINAL AIRDATE: DECEMBER 9, 1960)

"ONCE UPON A TIME"
(ORIGINAL AIRDATE: DECEMBER 15, 1961)

"NO TIME LIKE THE PAST"
(ORIGINAL AIRDATE: MARCH 7, 1963)

"THE INCREDIBLE WORLD OF HORACE FORD"
(APRIL 18, 1963)

A h, the good old days. For Martin Sloan (Gig Young), the stressed-out businessman in Rod Serling's moving first-season episode "Walking Distance," that phrase means the idyllic summers of his youth. It brings to mind band concerts in the park, merry-go-round rides, games of hide-and-seek, and chocolate sodas with three scoops. For Booth Templeton (Brian Aherne), the aging actor at the center of writer E. Jack Neuman's second-season episode, "The Trouble with Templeton," the good old days were the Roaring Twenties, when he and his late wife, the vivacious Laura (Pippa Scott), starred in one Broadway hit after another. It brings to mind a giddy panorama of opening nights; adoring audiences; and, most of all, Laura, "the freshest and most radiant creature God ever created." Both men are discontented with the world around them. Both feel run-down, tired, out of time, and out of place. Both yearn for

Martin Sloan (Gig Young) walks into the past and encounters his younger self (Michael Montgomery), carving his name on the park's bandstand in Rod Serling's "Walking Distance." *Courtesy CBS Photo Archive*

what they remember as an idyllic past. Both will follow that yearning, literally walking into the past, by way of the Twilight Zone.

Both Martin and Booth must learn to live in their own time. Both must realize, with a resolve tinged with melancholy, that they can't live in the past. It's a difficult lesson for each of them. It's a difficult lesson for many of us. Neuman told Marc Scott Zicree, author of *The Twilight Zone Companion*, that the idea behind "The Trouble with Templeton" was not only "you can't go home again" but "you shouldn't go home again, ever." That thought runs through both these beautifully crafted excursions into the middle ground between light and substance.

"Walking Distance," like "The Monsters Are Due on Maple Street," ranks among Serling's strongest *Twilight Zone* scripts, and that's saying something. Young is mesmerizing as Martin, a man living "at a dead run." He is the vice president in charge of media at a New York City advertising agency. Fed up with the rat race, he bolts from the Big Apple, finding himself within walking distance of the aptly named Homewood. It is his hometown. It is where he grew up, and it has come to symbolize serenity and happiness. We'll call this place Homewood, but you could call it Binghamton. You could call it any place or time held wistfully dear in your memory.

Martin wonders, would Homewood still feel like home? He decides to find out, strolling a mile and a half while a garage mechanic works on his car. That's the geographic distance. By fifth-dimension measurements, he is walking twenty-five years into the past . . . his past. Once there, he learns that he can't stay. It's one summer to a customer, says his father (Frank Overton), who finally comes to believe the adult Martin's time travel claims. This summer belongs to the young Martin Sloan. "Don't make him share it," sympathetic father says to weary son. Yet he says good-bye with a bit of advice.

"Maybe when you go back, Martin, you'll find that there are merry-go-rounds and band concerts where you are," Pop tells him. "Maybe you haven't been looking in the right place. You've been looking behind you, Martin. Try looking ahead."

Martin Sloan is successful in most things, the understanding Serling says, "but not in the one effort that all men try at some time in their lives—trying to go home again." How in touch was Serling with this realization? Remember, this is the writer, successful in most things, who, each summer, made a pilgrimage to Binghamton, walking its streets and wishing and remembering.

The same lesson is aimed at Booth in "The Trouble with Templeton." Arriving late on the first day of rehearsal for a new play, he is taken to task by an obnoxious boy wonder director. Like Martin escaping from New York, Booth bolts from the theater, desperate to get away. Like Martin, he wishes for a time of contentment. He wants to once again be with Laura, eighteen when they were married, twenty-five when she died. "Yesterday and its memories is what he wants, and yesterday is what he'll get," Serling tells us. So Booth Templeton leaves the theater and promptly steps into 1927. There he finds Laura and another ghost from his past, writer-director Barney Flueger (Charles Carlson). But they seem so different—cold and frivolous and hedonistic. Booth stumbles back to his own time, but he's brought with him a script titled "What to Do When Booth Comes Back." Laura, Barney, and the rest were putting on a play for his benefit, and the message is, don't live in the past. You have a part to play, and it's in the present—in your own time.

"They wanted me to go back to my own life, and live it," Booth says.

It's precisely what Martin's father wants him to do in "Walking Distance." Other *Twilight Zone* episodes also offer the same lesson, in a variety of ways. Richard Matheson's third-season contribution "Once Upon a Time" goes the comedic route, with Buster Keaton as Woodrow Mulligan, a janitor stumbling on a time machine and transporting himself from 1890 to 1962. There he meets Rollo, a scientist who wishes to travel to the past. Woodrow feels hopelessly out of place in 1962. Rollo soon is discontented with 1890. Each must live in his own time. So, again, don't live in the past . . . unless, of course, as with Woodrow, you're from the past, and then it's okay.

In "No Time Like the Past," a Serling hour-long episode from the fourth season, Dana Andrews plays Paul Driscoll, a time traveler who, after several failed attempts to change the past, opts for escaping to a small Indiana town in 1881. Like Martin,

Booth, and Rollo, he eventually learns you just can't live in the past.

One other *Twilight Zone* twist on this theme was the only episode written by Reginald Rose (*12 Angry Men*), "The Incredible World of Horace Ford." Another of the fourth-season hour-long episodes, it stars Pat Hingle as a man obsessed with memories of his childhood. He, too, learns that it is dangerous to live in the past, but with a brutal difference. Martin and Booth view the past in a nostalgic haze; and, for the most part, those views are justified. Achingly, the good old days were every bit as good as they remember. There is nothing wrong with their memories, just the wish to escape into them. "The Incredible World of Horace Ford" is more of an exercise in "nostalgia ain't what it used to be." In Horace's case, his memory is faulty. The past was not the wonderful place he recalled. There was poverty and brutality. Maybe, if he makes an effort in the present, Horace will find that *these* are the good old days . . . or could be. Either way, the message is the one framed by Martin's father. Look for merry-go-rounds and band concerts in your own time. Either way, the lesson is the same.

GUEST LESSON: MARTIN GRAMS

A remarkably prolific show business historian, Martin Grams has authored books on several radio and television shows. His topics range from TV's The Time Tunnel *and* Alfred Hitchcock Presents *to radio's* The Shadow *and* Suspense. *He added mightily to fifth-dimension scholarship with his incredibly detailed study,* The Twilight Zone: Unlocking the Door to a Television Classic.

In "Walking Distance," an advertising executive named Martin Sloan built a wall against future pain rather than let his troubles flow through him. Focusing too much on the misconceptions, defenses,

and preformulated reactions, he let the stress of his daily routine get the better of him. He ran away like a little child, only this time he did not run way from home . . . he ran to it . . . hoping to relive a time when he was ignorant of the news, never had to answer to anyone, and responsibilities meant deciding what flavor ice cream to eat. Now is where we are and will always be; and this is where we can create ourselves anew, reinvent ourselves, improve ourselves, change the world through our own inner transformation. I found it fitting that on *The Twilight Zone,* Martin Sloan received this lesson through his father, who had been dead many years hence. When we seek guidance beyond the good Lord above, we consult our parents. It is only natural. Disapproval needs only pass through—stop focusing on the worst of the day. And in today's society of smart phones, tablets, and fast-paced work assignments, we can all learn to unplug from time to time and stop focusing on the past. The future is bright if we embrace it. And a walk in the woods to take in the fresh air and sound of relaxation is not a bad thing.

DOGS REALLY CAN BE YOUR BEST FRIEND

"THE HUNT"

(ORIGINAL AIRDATE: JANUARY 26, 1962)

"LITTLE GIRL LOST"

(ORIGINAL AIRDATE: MARCH 16, 1962)

Another *Twilight Zone* moment. It is a sunny August day as I sit down to write this entry about the two third-season *Twilight Zone* episodes with dog heroes: "The Hunt," in which a hound named Rip guides seventy-year-old mountaineer Hyder Simpson all the way home (to the pearly gates), and "Little Girl Lost," in which a family pet named Mack rescues a six-year-old girl who has slipped into another dimension. I'm getting a later start than I intended. That's because, just as I was firing up the computer, there was a knock at the side door of the house. The next-door neighbor was standing there with a panting medium-size dog—the type you immediately know is friendly. And he was . . . just a real charmer. He reminded me quite a bit of our first dog, Dakota, who greeted every person, dog, cat, squirrel, or rabbit he encountered as an old lodge brother. Brian, our neighbor, wanted to know if I recognized the dog. I didn't, but this clearly was someone's beloved pet. He responded to commands. He was well groomed and well fed. He was a gentle soul, and he was wearing a collar. Someone was missing this dog. I snapped his picture with my phone and texted it to my wife. Did she

Hyder Simpson (Arthur Hunnicutt) will be glad his hound dog, Rip, is along for the trip he needs to take in "The Hunt," by Earl Hamner Jr. *Courtesy CBS Photo Archive*

recognize this little dog lost? She didn't. So we gave him some water and food, and Brian agreed to keep him for a while in his fenced-in backyard. I decided to get back to work. I knew before I sat down again that it was a lost cause, as lost as the big-eyed pooch in my neighbor's backyard. You see, to the left of my desk is a splendid portrait of Rod Serling, a gift from an artist friend in Tennessee. Well, Rod loved dogs. All animals had a friend in Rod Serling, but he was particularly fond of dogs. And if I looked up from the computer screen, Rod's eyes were boring into me. It I concentrated just on the screen, I kept seeing the face of the lost dog, which seemed to morph into the animated face of Max, the Grinch's dog in *How the Grinch Stole Christmas!* How could I extol the heroic nature of dogs and desert one in need?

Lesson learned. I headed back down, picked up one of our spare leashes, and told our dog, Dombey, to guard the house. Dombey is a corgi/basset mix, which I contend makes her a corset. I gathered the lost dog and we started to patrol the neighborhood. He walked along at a brisk pace on the red leash. Not five minutes later, I spotted a car slowly cruising down the next street. I pointed to the frisky dog at the end of the leash. The car headed for us and pulled over. Little dog lost was on his way home, and I was on my way back to *The Twilight Zone,* in the proper frame of mind. What put me in that frame of mind were the expressions of great relief and indescribable joy on the faces of the two people in that car. You'd think they were being reunited with their best friend.

Which brings us to "The Hunt" and "Little Girl Lost," episodes that aired within two months of each other in 1962. No need to overstate the lesson here. When the dog surrendered his wild nature and entered the dwelling places of humans, a bond was forged that was as enduring as it was profound. Rudyard Kipling described this moment: "When the Man waked up he said, 'What is Wild Dog doing here?' And the Woman said, 'His name is not Wild Dog any more, but the First Friend, because he will be our friend for always and always and always.'" If you are one of those people who can look into the eyes of a dog and not feel that, then these episodes will have little impact on you. But Rod Serling was one of those people who felt that bond and celebrated it. You can sense that in the delightful pictures of Rod with his dogs. His daughter Anne recalls him playing with dogs on the ground "like a littermate."

And yet, as fond as he was of our canine companions, Rod didn't write either of these episodes. There's no question, however, that he endorsed the payoffs in both. The first of the two tales about tail-wagging heroes, "The Hunt" was written by Earl Hamner Jr., later to find greater success on CBS with his semiautobiographical series, *The Waltons*. Veteran character actor Arthur Hunnicutt plays the recently deceased Hyder Simpson, whose dog, also recently deceased, keeps him from making a devil of a wrong turn in the afterlife. Simpson doesn't realize he is dead. When he and Rip reach a gate, a friendly fellow says it's the entry to Heaven. Simpson can go right in, the fellow says, but Rip isn't allowed.

"Any place that's too highfalutin for Rip is too fancy for me," an incensed Simpson says. "What kind of outfit you runnin', don't allow no dogs?"

He decides to mosey on. Down the road a piece, he meets an angel who explains that gate was the entry point to Hell. The gatekeeper wouldn't let Rip in because, catching a hint of brimstone, he would have warned Simpson of the danger.

"A man, well, he'll walk right into Hell with both eyes open," the angel says. "But even the Devil can't fool a dog."

It's a lovely tribute to the fidelity and nobility we ascribe to man's best friend. And Simpson's loyalty to Rip also saves him from making a disastrous mistake. Having left behind what he believes to be Heaven, he declares, "It would be a Hell of place without Rip." Why, yes, that's precisely what it would be. Hyder Simpson and Earl Hamner are not the only ones who think so. Robert Louis Stevenson, author of *Treasure Island* and *The Strange Case of Dr. Jekyll and Mr. Hyde,* said, "You think dogs will not be in Heaven? I tell you, they will be there long before us." That quote is a close cousin to James Thurber's "If I have any beliefs about immortality, it is that certain dogs I have known will go to Heaven, and very, very few persons."

A dog also saves the day in "Little Girl Lost," written by frequent *Twilight Zone* contributor Richard Matheson. It's based on his short story of the same title, and that story was inspired by a real moment of fright. Matheson's daughter had cried out in the night, and he went to check on her. She wasn't in the bed. She wasn't on the floor. He felt under the bed. Nothing. Finally, he realized she had fallen out of the bed, rolling all the way underneath it to the back wall. When he first felt under the bed, she was so far back, he couldn't reach her. It became one of those classic "what-if?" moments for the writer. What if there was a portal to another dimension near the bed and a little girl fallen through it? You could hear her crying, but you couldn't see or touch her.

This is the nightmare facing Chris and Ruth Miller (Robert Sampson and Sarah Marshall). Their physicist friend Bill (Charles Aidman) figures out what happened to little Tina (Tracy Stratford). Adding yet another personal touch, Matheson chose names from his own family. He married Ruth Ann Woodson in 1952. They had four children, including Tina and Chris.

Mack, the family dog, charges through the hole and finds the little girl. At her father's urging, Mack brings Tina closer and closer to the portal.

"Man, what a mutt!" says Bill, and we're nodding in agreement.

Just as the hole is about to close, Chris, halfway through the portal, gets a grip on Tina and Mack. Bill pulls them to safety, and another near disaster is averted thanks to the faithful dog.

The moral? "Travelers to unknown regions would be well-advised to take along the family dog," Rod Serling tells us in the closing narration to "The Hunt." "He could just save you from entering the wrong gate." Or save you after you've slipped into a bad place. Hey, that's what friends are for.

BEWARE THE PERSON WHO SAYS, "I DARE YOU"

"THE SILENCE

(ORIGINAL AIRDATE: APRIL 28, 1961)

"THE GRAVE"

(ORIGINAL AIRDATE: OCTOBER 27, 1961)

You know the schoolyard scene in humorist Jean Shepherd's semiautobiographical *A Christmas Story* where Schwartz dares Flick to place his tongue on a metal flagpole. It's a blustery winter day, and Schwartz claims said tongue will be quick frozen to said flagpole. Flick says, "Are you kidding? Stick my tongue to that stupid pole? That's dumb."

"That's 'cause you know it'll stick," taunts Schwartz.

"You're full of it."

"Oh, yeah?"

"Yeah!"

"Well, I double-dog-dare ya!"

"Now it was serious," Shepherd tells us in narration. Next would come the "triple dare you," and then "the coup de grace of all dares," the "sinister triple-dog-dare."

"I triple-dog-dare ya!" yells Schwartz.

It was, as Shepherd says, a slight breach of playground etiquette, skipping the triple dare and "going right for the throat." But it is effective, as the smug look on Schwartz's face assures

Gunman Conny Miller (Lee Marvin) encounters Ione (Ellen Willard) on his way to the ominous location indicated by the title of Montgomery Pittman's "The Grave." *Courtesy CBS Photo Archive*

us. Flick takes the dare with predictable results. Call the fire department and pry that trapped kid from the flagpole.

Here's the thing. Flick had it right when he said, "That's dumb." Sticking your tongue to a metal flagpole on a winter day is dumb. Being goaded into it is dumb. Taking the dare is dumb, dumb, dumb. Yet how many of us are susceptible to the manipulative ritual, even before it reaches triple-dog-dare phase? Come on, own up to it. You've been there. We all have. And what was the result? Metaphorically speaking, we're left screaming for help, arms windmilling, looking like a perfect fool (well, nobody's perfect). It's bad enough on the playground, where you at least expect such childish rites of passage. But the bigger the child, the bigger the consequences, so beware the person who says "I dare you." There might just be forces at play of which you are ignorant. Those forces might be of the scientific and natural order, dictating that, due to the thermal conductivity of metal, a wet tongue will indeed stick to a flagpole once the temperature drops to near freezing. Those forces also might be cosmic, making the individual who accepts the dare a thermal conductor attracting the lightning bolts of irony. People who accept wild challenges for the thrill of it all are called daredevils. If you are not one of these adrenaline junkies (or a glutton for punishment), you might want to be leery of the devilish type tricking you with dares. Nothing good can come of it, particularly if you are within daring distance of the Twilight Zone.

Two episodes underscore this point, and you know when someone takes a dare in *The Twilight Zone*, the payoff is going to have an ironic force that would make O. Henry wince. "The Silence" is Rod Serling's fifth-dimension reworking of an Anton Chekhov short story, "The Bet." As Chekhov's title suggests, the dare in this tale takes the form of a bet. Franchot Tone stars as Archie Taylor, a retired colonel who deeply resents that the peace of his exclusive men's club is constantly shattered by ever-chattering Jamie Tennyson (Liam Sullivan). Most members of the club find Tennyson something of a windy bore, but the effect of his self-important blather on Taylor is positively Poe-like. Multiplying the aggravation factor to telltale dimensions, Tennyson represents everything Taylor resents: lack of refinement, lack of manners, lack of breeding, lack of taste. He is, in Taylor's estimation, "a shallow, talkative, empty-headed ne'er-do-well." Now, don't hold back, Archie. Tell us what you really think. Tennyson is also suffering from a lack of funds. He is deeply in debt, and Taylor knows it. So Taylor proposes a wager. It's pretty much an I dare you. He dares Tennyson to remain completely silent for a year. If he can manage this seemingly impossible feat, Taylor will give him half a million dollars. Money talks, as they say, so talkative Tennyson agrees to fall silent, confined to a glass structure built in the club's unused game room. Here he can be under constant observation.

Chekhov's story ends on a note of salvation for the fellow who makes the dare and the fellow who takes it. Serling's version has a tragic twist. Tennyson wins the bet, and Taylor is forced to admit that he doesn't have the money. Tennyson has gone through this terrible ordeal for nothing. Even worse, he now reveals how he won the bet. Knowing he couldn't remain silent for a year, he had the nerves to his vocal cords severed. He rips off the scarf around his neck, revealing the scar, and the look on his face speaks volumes.

If the fate of poor Jamie Tennyson isn't enough to convince you of the foolishness of taking a dare, consider what happens to gunman Conny Miller (Lee Marvin) in writer-director Montgomery Pittman's splendidly spooky Western episode, "The Grave." A word about Montgomery Pittman. He wrote only three *Twilight Zone* episodes, so he is not placed in the same pantheon of lead contributors with Serling, Matheson, Beaumont, and Johnson. But his batting average was extremely high. Those three episodes, all airing in the third season, are "Two," "The Grave," and "The Last Rites of Jeff Myrtlebank." He not only wrote these three gems, he directed them (also directing two episodes written by others). Each is very different in tone. Born in Louisiana, Pittman first tried his hand at acting, then turned to writing. His credits included episodes of such Westerns as *Maverick, Sugarfoot, Cheyenne, Colt .45*, and *The Deputy*. Adding director to his résumé, the cigar-chomping Pittman made his *Twilight Zone* debut with Serling's second-season episode "Will the Real Martian Please Stand Up." He died of cancer in June 1962, just four months after "The Last Rites of Jeff Myrtlebank" aired. He was forty-five. Oh, he had the gift. What *Twilight Zone* tales might he have told?

One that he did tell, "The Grave," starts with townspeople ambushing and gunning down notorious outlaw Pinto Sykes (Richard Geary). The town leaders had hired Conny to track down Pinto. Dying, Pinto says that Conny didn't try to catch up with him. He even waited for him in Albuquerque and sent word where he was. So Pinto died with a warning for Conny. If Conny dares to get anywhere near Pinto's grave, the dead outlaw will reach up and grab him. You can feel the wind and the cold in this wonderfully atmospheric episode. And you know things aren't going to end well for Conny. Indeed, Tennyson's fate seems mild in comparison. Then again, Pittman adds more fatal character flaws to Conny's makeup. He is a bit of a bully and a coward. One of the people he bullies, young Johnny Rob (James Best), dares him to visit Pinto's grave. Johnny Rob and gambler Steinhart (Lee Van Cleef) bet Conny that he doesn't have the courage to get within grabbing reach of Pinto's grave. They give him a bowie knife, which Conny is to plant near the tombstone to prove he was there. The next morning, they find Conny's lifeless body sprawled across Pinto's grave. Something pulled him down. A knife mistakenly plunged through his own coat? Pinto's spirit? Conny's own inner fears?

What truly brings him down, though, is that he can't back down when someone says, "I dare you." Like Tennyson, he takes the bet. And it's a sucker's bet. Or as Serling tells us in the closing narration to "The Silence," "If you don't believe it, ask the croupier, the very special one who handles roulette—in the Twilight Zone." Go on and ask. I dare ya.

GUEST LESSON: JONATHAN HARRIS

Best known for his delightfully over-the-top portrayal of Dr. Smith on Lost in Space, *Jonathan Harris appeared in two second-season* Twilight Zone *episodes: as a creepy doctor in the splendidly eerie "Twenty Two" ("Room for one more, honey.") and a lawyer in "The Silence." A few years before his death at eighty-seven in 2002, he talked at length with TV critic David Bianculli and me about everything from his work on golden-age anthology shows and* The Bill Dana Show *(with Don Adams playing an early version of the character he soon would play on* Get Smart*) to* Lost in Space *and* The Twilight Zone. *It was a marathon of great stories. He talked about working with Lou Costello ("a very nice man") on an episode of* General Electric Theater. *He talked about working for producers Irwin Allen and Sheldon Leonard, wonderfully impersonating them when necessary. And when Rod Serling's name came up, he made an observation that might have been directly solicited for this book (although, as with Jack Klugman, it wasn't). This is what he had to say (in grand theatrical style).*

When you worked with writers like Rod Serling, you learned that you didn't need fancy sets, big special effects, and lavish budgets. It was the writing. We had words! We had words! We had substance. You start with the words or you ain't got nothin'!

IT'S NEVER TOO LATE TO REINVENT YOURSELF

"MR. DENTON ON DOOMSDAY"

(ORIGINAL AIRDATE: OCTOBER 16, 1959)

"THE LAST FLIGHT"

(ORIGINAL AIRDATE: FEBRUARY 5, 1960)

"NERVOUS MAN IN A FOUR DOLLAR ROOM"

(ORIGINAL AIRDATE: OCTOBER 14, 1960)

"THE NIGHT OF THE MEEK"

(ORIGINAL AIRDATE: DECEMBER 23, 1960)

"STATIC"

(ORIGINAL AIRDATE: MARCH 10, 1961)

Rod Serling wrote a third-season *Twilight Zone* episode called "Five Characters in Search of an Exit." Never mind the story for now. All we need from that episode is the title, which could serve as the theme for this particular chapter. I'd like to introduce you to our five characters, each the principal player in another *Twilight Zone* episode: Al Denton, Terry Decker, Jackie Rhoades, Henry Corwin, and Ed Lindsay. Know what they have in common, besides a travel ticket stamped by Rod Serling? Each is, indeed, a character searching for an exit—an exit from the dead end where their life choices have deposited them. Each is in need of that chance for renewal, that shot at redemption, that opportunity to reinvent himself. And for each of them, an exit will present itself. A door will swing open, and we'll be rooting for them to grab that ticket and go through it.

Henry Corwin (Art Carney), a fired department store Santa Claus, is the recipient of a Christmas miracle in Rod Serling's "The Night of the Meek." *Courtesy CBS Photo Archive*

Necessity is the mother of reinvention, at least in *The Twilight Zone,* which often returned to the theme of redemption. The irony pendulum could often swing with tragic consequences in these morality tales. When someone stubbornly refused to get out of the way, holding fast to ignorance or prejudice, the pendulum had no choice but to strike that person right in the vices.

Those incapable of change might as well hang a giant bull's-eye around their necks. Their hatreds become a kind of supercharged electromagnet attracting that pendulum with frightening speed and deadly accuracy.

Still, when change was possible, the pendulum could swing the other way, in the general direction of, yes, redemption. Here is a lesson for individuals, societies, nations, and, if it comes to that, planets. It's never too late. Often enough, the twist ending on a *Twilight Zone* story bestowed the benefits of redemption and renewal on someone who has taken a depressingly wrong turn. If they embraced the change, they were rewarded with an exit leading toward—call it what you will—rebirth, reformation, transformation, reclamation, revival, rejuvenation, salvation. Take your pick. Plenty more where those came from. So the coward turns into the hero. The nervous, frightened man becomes strong and self-assured. The hopeless drunk finds hope and a calling. The cantankerous old man becomes the romantic young suitor. The gunfighter gets to hang up his guns and become a man of peace.

As evidence, consider the cases of Al, Terry, Jackie, Henry, and Ed. I know this sounds like the members of a 1950s doo-wop group or a Rotary Club bowling team. But each of them is facing a desperate battle not to be one of life's gutter balls.

One of the earliest episodes, Serling's "Mr. Denton on Doomsday" gives Al Denton (Dan Duryea) two chances to reinvent himself. When we first meet Al, the once-feared gunfighter is a pathetic sight. The town drunk, he is relentlessly humiliated by the small western town's rowdies and bullies. As Serling tells us, he "would probably give an arm or part of his soul to have another chance, to be able to rise up and shake the dirt from his body and the bad dreams that infest his consciousness." He has sunk about as deep into the pit of self-hatred as it is possible to go. But Fate is about to play a hand, in the magical form of a little man named Henry J. Fate (Malcolm Atterbury). And Fate, Serling reminds us, "can help a man climbing out of a pit." For a brief couple of seconds, Fate gives Al the ability to get off two unbelievable shots that turn the chief bully (Martin Landau) into an ex-bully. He has won back his self-respect, finding the strength to give up the bottle, but now he fears a return of the nightmare that drove him to drink—the challenges of every young gun thinking he can outdraw him. Yet Fate steps in a second time, arranging it that Al and his young challenger (Doug McLure) are equally fast, injuring each other's shooting hands. Now Al is free to truly reinvent himself, never again identified by the gun strapped to his side or the bottle in his shaking hand.

Another first-season episode, Richard Matheson's "The Last Flight," finds World War I British flyer Terry Decker (Kenneth Haigh) fleeing a 1917 aerial battle, deserting his best friend. He has left his comrade to a certain death. But after flying through a mysterious white cloud, he touches down at an American air base in France . . . in 1960. He learns that his friend became a decorated hero in World War II. There was only one way his friend could have survived. Terry must have saved him. There it is—the second chance . . . the shot at redemption. Terry again flies through the mysterious cloud, returning to 1917, where he heroically rescues his friend.

Jackie Rhoades (Joe Mantell) is the title character in Serling's second-season episode "Nervous Man in a Four Dollar Room." He has been given a job by a gangster. He is to murder a bar owner who won't play ball. He's trapped. Jackie doesn't have the courage to stand up to the gangster, who is demanding that he cross the ultimate line. Looking in the mirror, this nervous little man sees a stronger, better Jackie aching to get out. This is the man he could be. This is the man he *will* be if he embraces the change. Jackie can be a thing of the past, replaced by John

Rhoades, who has found his exit, "with one foot through the door and one foot out of the Twilight Zone."

Henry Corwin (Art Carney) is the drunken department store Santa in another of Serling's second-season episodes, "The Night of the Meek." Henry finds his salvation in a magical bag that grants wishes and allows him to reclaim his shattered life. Gift by gift, he reinvents himself into the person he wants to be: a real Santa. A story told with heartwarming Dickensian flourishes, "The Night of the Meek" takes a broken man and gives him a purpose. Being open to the magic and ready for the miracle, he is granted not only his ultimate wish but the greatest gift of the season: salvation. The funny and touching episode is a lovely Christmas gift from a writer born on Christmas day.

And finally there is Ed Lindsay (Dean Jagger), a cranky bachelor who gets his second chance through an old radio that's every bit as magical as the cloud Terry flies through or the ratty old bag Henry finds. The centerpiece of the second-season episode "Static," written by Charles Beaumont and based on a story by Oceo Ritch, this radio has incredible reception. It pulls in a signal all the way from the fifth dimension, delighting Ed with beloved shows from the past. The programs remind him of a time when he was happy and had hopes. They lure him back to 1940, giving him a new lease on what was a wasted life. "All Ed Lindsay knows is that he desperately wanted a second chance and he finally got it," Serling says.

Yes, he does. When we first meet Al, Terry, Jackie, Henry, and Ed, each seems beyond the reach of that second chance. But, whether he fully realizes it or not, each wants to change, and that's what makes this rejuvenating brand of *Twilight Zone* magic work. It is magic made up of equal parts hope, optimism, and renewal. All those elements are very much a part of *The Twilight Zone.*

GUEST LESSON: MARK OLSHAKER

Mark Olshaker was a fourteen-year-old ninth grader when he met his hero, Rod Serling, in Washington, D.C. They remained friends until Serling's death ten years later. Olshaker is an Emmy-winning filmmaker, New York Times *bestselling nonfiction author, and critically acclaimed novelist. The books he has written with John Douglas, beginning with* Mindhunter, *have sold millions of copies, been translated into many languages, and, along with his Emmy-nominated film,* Mind of a Serial Killer, *for the PBS series* NOVA, *made Olshaker a sought-after speaker and consultant on criminal justice and victims' rights issues. He is the author of the highly praised novels* Einstein's Brain, Unnatural Causes, Blood Race, The Edge, *and, with Douglas,* Broken Wings. *He is president of the Norman Mailer Society, past chairman of the Cosmos Club Foundation, a member of the board of directors of the Rod Serling Memorial Foundation, and a member of the editorial board of Rod Serling Books.*

Sitting with Rod one time, I asked my hero and friend if he wished that the things he wrote about in *The Twilight Zone* would actually happen. He quickly replied, "Yes, but not to me!" For once in his extraordinary, passionate, and all too brief life, I think he was being disingenuous. Because they *did happen* to all of us—his viewers and disciples—in that fifth dimension he created, beyond that which is known to man. I am of that vast boomer cohort nurtured on the *Zone;* and, at least in part, it is why we became the generation idealistic enough to believe that anything was possible and skeptical enough to question whether anything was true. The title of my friend Mark's book, therefore, is literally accurate, and those of that generation who have not grown too cynical or complacent still exist in that wondrous land whose boundaries are that of imagination, and always will. So Rod is the spiritual father of us all.

GETTING TO THE TOP COMES WITH A PRICE—STAYING THERE

"MR. DENTON ON DOOMSDAY"

(ORIGINAL AIRDATE: OCTOBER 16, 1959)

"A GAME OF POOL"

(ORIGINAL AIRDATE: OCTOBER 13, 1961)

We're not quite through with Mr. Denton, the gunfighter-turned-drunk-turned-gunfighter who put in such a useful appearance in the previous chapter. He has yet another lesson to teach us. This one is about the price you pay for single-mindedly clawing your way to the top of any much-coveted mountain. The price is steep, and it takes many forms, but let's start with just one. There is this little revelation: getting to the top is only half the trick. The other half is staying there.

Al Denton learned this by going through the soul-crushing crucible of constantly proving he was the fastest gun in the West. The weight of it pounded him, shattered him, nearly destroyed him. It drove him into a bottle, almost pushing him beyond the point of no return. Granted, his is an extreme case, since proving you're the best in Al's particular profession literally means kill or be killed. Metaphorically, though, any champion in any field can relate to Mr. Denton's dilemma. Being a champion means defending the crown. It goes with the territory. And "uneasy lies the head that wears the crown" doesn't begin to describe it. There will always be a challenger out there who is a little younger, a little hungrier, a little more gifted, or, maybe, a little faster.

One of the simplest and giddiest games of our youth was the one we called king of the hill (but also known as king of the mountain or king of the castle). The rules were downright primal. First, you'd find a decent size hill or pile of dirt (new housing developments were good for this). Then the players would make a mad scramble to reach the top. The first at the peak proclaimed himself the king of the hill. And so he was . . . for

Legendary champion "Fats" Brown (Jonathan Winters) watches Jesse Cardiff (Jack Klugman) line up a shot in "A Game of Pool," by George Clayton Johnson. *Courtesy CBS Photo Archive*

as long as he could hold that lofty summit. The other players, of course, were trying to knock him off. If one succeeded, the new monarch shouted, "I'm king of the hill." And so he was, until someone knocked him off. The chaotic fun continued this way until the would-be emperors and deposed dirt sovereigns headed home, gloriously muddy or dusty, depending on recent weather conditions. Some never stop playing king of the hill, and that's not necessarily a bad thing. From this mind-set are born champions and heroes, musical virtuosos and heads of state.

Some are just born with that inner drive to be the best in a highly competitive field, from high finance and high-powered politics to entertainment and sports. They push themselves to be the top gun. They make whatever sacrifice is necessary to get that edge. They practice and train until body and spirit are exhausted, then they practice and train some more. They will reach the top of the mountain, at all costs. They will proclaim themselves the king of the hill.

For some, it's about power. For others, it's about ego or excellence. Whatever is fueling the ambitions and obsessions, it is not condemned out of hand by the basic tenants of *The Twilight Zone*. There is, however, a gigantic caution flag waving over that road to the top: be aware of the sacrifices you'll need to make to be the best and to keep proving you're the best. Or, as Rod Serling put it in his introduction to writer George Clayton Johnson's third-season episode "Game of Pool," "trying to be the best at anything carries its own special risks in or out of the Twilight Zone." Indeed, it does. Al Denton found out about the special risks when he became the fastest gun in the West.

"I was good," Al says. "I was real good. I was so good that once a day someone would ride into town to make me prove it. And every morning I'd start my drinking a few minutes earlier. Until one morning, the guy who asked me to prove it turned out to be sixteen years old."

Jesse Cardiff, played by Jack Klugman (making the second of

his four outstanding *Twilight Zone* appearances), finds out about them in "A Game of Pool." Jesse is a pool shark weary of hearing about the legendary skills of the late "Fats" Brown (Jonathan Winters). He mouths off about how he could beat Fats, but falls into stunned silence when Fats appears in Clancy's pool hall. They are alone, and Fats proposes a game with the highest stakes of all. If Jesse loses, it will cost him his life. Jesse naturally balks, but Fats goads him into accepting the terms.

"For my money, you don't want to be the best bad enough," Fats tells Jesse. "It's a proud thing to be the best at anything, but then you wouldn't know about that."

Jesse wins. "I beat the king of the hill . . . and now I'm the best," he crows. Fats has warned him that he might win more than he can imagine. After his death, Jesse finds out what those ominous words mean. As Serling explains, "being the best of anything carries with it a special obligation to keep on proving it." So now it is Jesse who must continually answer the challenges of players certain they can beat him. Jesse has been handed the bill, and he now sees the steep price he has paid (and must continue paying). Fats, relieved of a champion's pressures, has gone fishing. Like Al Denton, Fats finds a measure of happiness, peace, and contentment only when he no longer needs to defend his crown.

Fats tells Jesse that the stakes for this game are life and death. He's not overstating the case. When Jesse is dead, he might just realize that he hasn't had much of a life. He tells us as much when listing the joys he has sacrificed in order to endlessly practice breaks and bank shots in deserted pool halls. He hasn't seen a movie in years. He hasn't been on a date. Indeed, at the top of their professions, both Al and Jesse are tragically lonely fellows. They are, we surmise, cut off from relationships, from family, from friendships, from everyday pleasures. They are kings of their respective hills, but those are desolate, isolated spots.

Is this the price every champion must ultimately pay? No, but these cautionary tales more than suggest that it is the risk that every champion and every would-be champion runs. They also more than suggest that the risk is greatly multiplied when the wrong reasons are behind the need to be king of the hill. Al's path to the top was littered with the bodies of gunned-down men. And Jesse wants to wield his pool cue as a weapon against all those who made him feel small. Victory might be assured, but it most assuredly is going to be hollow.

So the message here isn't that it's best to avoid being the best. The message is to look deep inside yourself and be sure. Be sure that you want to take this road. Be sure that you understand the sacrifices involved. And be sure you're undertaking this climb to the top for the right reasons. Sounds downright tricky and more than a little dangerous, doesn't it? That's because it is. It's not supposed to be the least bit easy. That's why we fly a caution flag over this steep and rocky road.

> **GUEST LESSON: GEORGE CLAYTON JOHNSON**
> *Four outstanding* Twilight Zone *scripts were written by George Clayton Johnson: "A Game of Pool," "Nothing in the Dark," "Kick the Can," and "A Penny for Your Thoughts." Four other episodes were based on his stories: "The Four of Us Are Dying," "Execution," "The Prime Mover," and "Ninety Years Without Slumbering." He also wrote the first-season* Star Trek *episode "The Man Trap" and, with William F. Nolan, the novel* Logan's Run. *He sent this five word-lesson in early March 2015.* Twilight Zone *fans celebrated his life and mourned his passing, on December 25, 2015 (which would have been Rod Serling's ninety-first birthday):*
>
> **To look beneath the surface.**

TAKE CARE OF YOUR OWN INNER DEMONS BEFORE YOU GO MEDDLING WITH OTHERS'

"THE HOWLING MAN"

(ORIGINAL AIRDATE: NOVEMBER 4, 1960)

Charles Beaumont's splendidly atmospheric second-season episode "The Howling Man" is based on his short story of the same title. H. M. Wynant plays David Ellington, a weary traveler on a walking tour through central Europe after the horrors of World War I. He is lost and far off course. Indeed, he has gone much further astray than he can possibly imagine. He is stumbling his way into . . . the Twilight Zone. And, having made his way there, he will be going even further astray.

Caught in the middle of a violent storm, Ellington, on the verge of collapse, reaches the door of a remote abbey. At first told he may not enter, the sick, exhausted, and far-from-happy wanderer is eventually taken in by the eccentric order of monks. Most eccentric of all is their leader, the booming-voiced Brother Jerome (John Carradine). As he recovers, Ellington keeps hearing a strange howling sound that echoes throughout the abbey. Seeking the source of this unearthly howl, he finds a ragged but seemingly gentle man locked in a cell. The prisoner tells Ellington that Brother Jerome is insane, and he begs to be released. "They're mad, Mr. Ellington," he says. "All of them. Raving mad."

Brother Jerome declares that the howling man is none other than the Devil himself. What really holds him prisoner is a simple piece of wood, the staff of truth, which has been placed across his cell door. Ellington is now certain that Brother Jerome is madder than a March monk. He releases the prisoner, who immediately reveals himself to be—you guessed it—the Devil,

The Devil (Robin Hughes) is on the loose in "The Howling Man," by Charles Beaumont.

Courtesy CBS Photo Archive

and an appalled Ellington watches as he escapes. Hell is on the loose, and it leads to World War II.

Ellington was not the first jaded soul to be duped by the Devil on *The Twilight Zone*. But typically, as in the case of Walter Bedeker in "Escape Clause," the only person who gets burned is the deluded individual who believes he can outsmart the Devil. Ellington's actions have tragic consequences that extend well beyond his own personal fate. His realization of this terrible responsibility turns him into a haunted man, obsessed with re-capturing the Devil.

"We are each our own Devil, and we make this world our hell," Oscar Wilde observed about seventy years before Ellington let the Devil out of his cell. Ellington, at the very least, has made this world his own purgatory. Why is he such easy pickings for the Devil locked inside? Why does he fall into the trap? It's not because of what's inside the cell. It's because of what's inside himself: hubris. Convinced that he knows better than Brother Jerome, he is unable to look beyond surface appearances. Brother Jerome seems fanatical and insane, so he must be fanatical and insane. The prisoner seems innocent and rational, so he must be innocent and rational. We might see this as a warning against easy assumptions or judging on appearance, but the bigger lesson is found in examining why Ellington makes the easy assumption.

He is an educated man of learning and sophistication, and the Devil plays on this. To Ellington, these robed monks are no better than cleaned-up peasants groveling in ignorance and isolation. Ellington knows better. Jerome, after all, must be an ignorant, superstitious zealot, at best; a lunatic, at worst. Ellington is absolutely certain that he's right. He *must* be right.

"I suppose you fancy yourself a sophisticated man," Brother Jerome says to him. "You consider us to be primitive because we live here in solitude, away from the so-called real world."

If Ellington could suspend judgment for a while, he might see the truth. Wisdom can be standing before you in all sorts of shapes and forms, and so can evil. And how many times have we been warned that the Devil can take a pleasing shape (or, at least this time, a sympathetic shape)? Perhaps a man of Ellington's erudition would also be aware of Baudelaire's words of caution: "The Devil's finest trick is to persuade you that he does not exist." Some might take that literally, but it's equally valid in a metaphoric sense. How many devilish people in pleasant shapes have you encountered? Think of how sparsely populated the halls of Congress would be without them.

Hubris blinds Ellington to the truth, and yet another well-worn proverb (this one actually from Proverbs) warns us that, "Pride goes before destruction, and an haughty spirit before a fall." None of this time-honored advice gets past David Ellington's wall of hubris. It makes him the perfect patsy in "The Howling Man." His inner demons prove to be his undoing. And we all have inner demons.

A parable recorded in Matthew speaks to this. The translations differ slightly in wording, but the meaning always comes through loud and clear: "Why do you see the speck in your brother's eye but fail to notice the log that is in your own? First take the plank out of your own eye, and then you will see clearly to remove the speck from your brother's eye." While Brother Jerome may have his failings, they are nothing compared to the hubris and hypocrisy blinding Ellington. That plank in his eye even blinds him to the obvious reality of a frail piece of wood keeping the Howling Man a prisoner. He removes the staff of truth and casts it aside (as terrifying a bit of symbolism as you could ask for at that awful moment). And as the nightmarish storm builds around Ellington, we hear the echo of words from a story Beaumont undoubtedly knew well, Robert Louis Stevenson's *The Strange Case of Dr. Jekyll and Mr. Hyde*: "My Devil had long been caged, he came out roaring."

Brother Jerome pleads with Ellington to see things from a "different point of view," to listen "with an open mind." He doesn't. He can't. His fatal flaw isn't doubt. If he entertained doubt, he would seek the truth and put the staff of truth to the test. He makes no room for doubt. He can't be wrong, and that is precisely where he does go wrong.

Perhaps nobody can subdue the Devil in an individual or in mankind for long. Yet, if we recognize it for what it is, we at least can be on guard against the evil lurking within. This is the bitter lesson learned by David Ellington, who stares at us with imploring eyes and pleads, "You must believe."

GUEST LESSON: JAMES GRADY

Investigative journalist and novelist James Grady's best-known book is the espionage thriller Six Days of the Condor *(made into a 1975 film as* Three Days of the Condor, *starring two* Twilight Zone *veterans Robert Redford and Cliff Robertson and directed by Sydney Pollack, who played a director in "The Trouble with Templeton"). Grady says he "grew up in awe of* The Twilight Zone *in a small, rural* Twilight Zone–*like town in the 1950s and 1960s, sixty miles west of the Rockies, thirty miles south of Canada, and a zillion miles from any other reality (Shelby, Montana). The show rocked my world." His lesson, the briefest in the book, is just one word, but it's a powerful one:*

Believe.

BEAUTY TRULY IS IN . . .

"EYE OF THE BEHOLDER"
(ORIGINAL AIRDATE: NOVEMBER 11, 1960)

Yet another *Twilight Zone* moment while writing this book (and, folks, I'm not making these up). This entry is being written on September 26, and late on September 26, at that, because I have been completely stuck on how to start a discussion of one of Rod Serling's most poignant and beautifully crafted scripts, "Eye of the Beholder." So I'm doing what any dutiful, dedicated, responsible writer would do under such trying circumstances . . . procrastinating. And there's nothing like good ol' Facebook for work avoidance. But I no sooner start scrolling through the news feed when I see that several friends have posted pictures of Donna Douglas. Today, I learn, would have been her eighty-third birthday (she died January 1, 2015). I had no idea, of course, but the realization sends me scurrying back to *The Twilight Zone*. That's not just because Donna Douglas, best known as Elly May Clampett on *The Beverly Hillbillies*, is the "face" of this rightly acclaimed episode. It's also because Donna Douglas was the very first *Twilight Zone* star I met and interviewed. That was in August 1980, during my stint as the arts and entertainment writer at the *Kingsport*

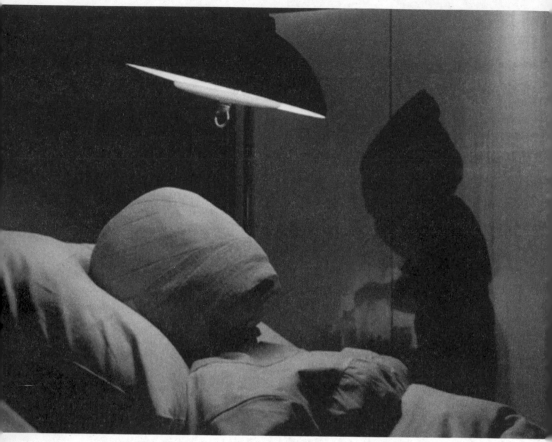

Janet Tyler anxiously waits to see if surgery has made her look normal in Rod Serling's
"Eye of the Beholder." *Courtesy CBS Photo Archive*

Times-News, a fifty-thousand-circulation newspaper in upper-
east Tennessee. Dressed in the familiar Elly May costume, she
was in Kingsport to film a commercial spot for mobile homes.
I was dispatched to do a story about her visit. We had a long
talk, mostly about *The Beverly Hillbillies,* but I wasn't going to
miss the opportunity to ask her about *The Twilight Zone,* "Eye
of the Beholder," and Rod Serling.

She remembered being tested and accepted for the role. She
remembered how thrilling it was to work on an episode that
became a classic. She remembered Rod Serling as "both a genius
and a nice man."

"They're always rerunning that episode," she said with a laugh. "It's one of the most famous *Twilight Zone* shows, and I get asked about it all the time. After Elly May, that's what people most know me for."

And with good reason. "Eye of the Beholder" is as innovative as it is imaginative, as powerful as it is profound. As Marc Scott Zicree points out in his history of the series, everything works on a remarkably high artistic level in this episode: the direction by Douglas Heyes, the performances, Serling's writing, the camera work of George Clemens, Bernard Herrmann's atmospheric score, and William Tuttle's makeup designs. And its message has only grown in relevance and resonance.

The episode's payoff scene is so iconic, it has become one of those *Twilight Zone* moments that has seeped into the pop-culture consciousness. Indeed, we are so familiar with the big reveal that we tend to forget just how innovative this episode seemed when it first aired

Her head wrapped in bandages, Janet Tyler is undergoing a last-chance procedure to make herself beautiful. "Ever since I was a little girl, people have turned away when they looked at me," she tells her doctor. Her deformed features have condemned her to a life of loneliness in a society where the motto is "conform to the norm." Janet longs to be normal, to be accepted, to be loved. Her hideous face cuts her off from all these hopes and dreams. This is the eleventh operation to correct her unfortunate condition, and that's the maximum number of attempts allowed by the state. If this operation fails, she will be sent to a segregated community where other such hopeless cases are confined. Waiting for the bandages to be removed, Janet (voiced by Maxine Stuart) makes a heartbreaking plea to her doctor. She wants to leave her hospital room for a few minutes. She wants to sit outside in the garden for a little while, "just to feel the air, just to smell the flowers, just to make believe I am normal. If . . . if I sit out there in the darkness, then the whole world is dark and I'm more a part of it like that, not just one grotesque, ugly woman with a bandage on her face, with a special darkness all around her. I want to belong. I want to be like everybody."

Throughout the cleverly shot episode, the faces of the doctors, nurses, and orderlies are kept in shadows. When the bandages are removed, we see the astonishingly beautiful face of Donna Douglas. At the same time, we hear the doctors yelling that the operation has been a total failure. No change! No change at all! She still is a grotesque sight to them. Then we see the faces of the doctors and nurses. Tuttle's makeup concept is piglike—what would be grotesque by our standards of beauty.

At the end, Janet goes off with Walter Smith, a representative of the segregated village where she will be sent. Also by our society's standards, he is as handsome as she is beautiful. He assures Janet that she will be accepted and she will be loved. Then Serling adds the postscript: "Where is this place and when is it, what kind of world where ugliness is the norm and beauty the deviation from that norm? The answer is, it doesn't make any difference, because the old saying happens to be true. Beauty is in the eye of the beholder, in this year or a hundred years hence, on this planet or wherever there is human life, perhaps out among the stars. Beauty is in the eye of the beholder. Lesson to be learned in the Twilight Zone."

This would not be the last time *The Twilight Zone* would speak to the dangers of conformity mandated by a totalitarian state. Serling returned to the theme in another inventively filmed second-season episode, "The Obsolete Man." And a fifth-season episode, "Number 12 Looks Just Like You," written by John Tomerlin and based on a Charles Beaumont story, also explores the notion of a society where unattractive people are not tolerated.

Each of these wonderfully crafted episodes attacks conformity from a different angle. Each celebrates the individual in a different way. Each has a lesson that has taken on greater implications as we have moved deeper into the twenty-first century.

In this era of cyberbullying, anonymous online comments, and relentlessly packaged (and unrealistic) ideas of beauty, "Eye of the Beholder" spits in the eye of anyone devaluing an individual because of his or her looks. It's an insidious process, and, thanks to everything from action movies to commercials, it can put ugly ideas into even very young children. Consider the *20/20* experiment, in which the TV newsmagazine had two women—one extremely pretty, the other just attractive—teach to the same level of efficiency to an elementary school class. The students overwhelmingly thought that the prettier woman was the better teacher. This was one of several instances where the more attractive man or woman was invariably preferred, in everything from job interviews to sales. But the elementary school experiment was particularly disturbing because the responders were children.

Janet Tyler tells her doctor that the state doesn't have the right to make ugliness a crime. No, the state doesn't, but society does have that power, and technology has made it easier to use that awful power in all sorts of corrosive ways. Among the many lovely interludes in "Eye of the Beholder" is the one where Janet's doctor talks, looking deeper into her face and seeing the truly beautiful human being there. Why shouldn't we be allowed to be different? It's a dangerous question that the doctor asks, prompted by his ability to look beyond the surface. Beauty is skin deep? We proclaim it, but we don't act as if we believe it. Why shouldn't Janet be part of normal society? Her doctor can do no more than ask, because his way is blocked by the two words prized by the state: glorious conformity. That's the ugly reality he is facing.

GUEST LESSON: JAMES L. BROOKS

Acclaimed as a director, producer, and writer, Jim Brooks created or cocreated such shows as Room 222, The Mary Tyler Moore Show, Rhoda, Phyllis, Lou Grant, *and* Taxi. *As a producer, his name has appeared on* The Tracey Ullman Show *and* The Simpsons. *He also has written and directed many award-winning films, including* Terms of Endearment, Broadcast News, *and* As Good as It Gets. *His lesson is drawn from "Eye of the Beholder."*

I guess, wasn't everybody's favorite the one where you got the operation on the person to create beauty? And the lesson? Some son of a bitch has figured out how to have a great ending!

(That son of bitch, of course, was Rod Serling, but, to paraphrase the famous line from Owen Wister's The Virginian, *when Brooks called him that, he smiled . . . with admiration.)*

BE YOUR OWN PERSON
"MR. BEVIS"
(ORIGINAL AIRDATE: JUNE 3, 1960)
"NUMBER 12 LOOKS JUST LIKE YOU"
(ORIGINAL AIRDATE: JANUARY 24, 1964)

Like the second season's "Eye of the Beholder," the fifth season's "Number 12 Looks Just Like You" tackles issues of beauty, appearance, and conformity. They are parallel parables in many ways, but, in the later episode, those themes are explored on a futuristic landscape where standards of beauty are used as an all-out attack on individualism. In "Eye of the Beholder," everyone considered ugly is sent to an isolated village. In "Number 12 Looks Just Like You," everyone at the age of nineteen undergoes a transformation surgery that makes him or her beautiful. There are only so many perfect models of beauty, however, so you end up looking like millions of other transformed people. Why wouldn't you choose to be one of the beautiful people, just like everybody else?

Eighteen-year-old Marilyn Cuberle (Collin Wilcox) has her doubts. Her father committed suicide after his transformation. Why? Marilyn views the operation as a state-mandated guarantee of conformity, and it is a dangerous view to hold. Her mother (Suzy Parker), her uncle Rick (Richard Long), and her friend Valerie (Pam Austin) all try to convince her that transformation

Pam Austin and Richard Long are two top models for the futuristic society in "Number 12 Looks Just Like You." *Courtesy CBS Photo Archive*

is her path to happiness and contentment. She will, after all, be beautiful, just like everybody else. "The transformation is the most marvelous thing that could happen to a person," her mother says.

Marilyn is a nonconformist, like her father. She believes in "the dignity of the individual human spirit." She resists the transformation. She reads the works of Shakespeare and Dostoyevsky, even though books have been banned. She sometimes wants to feel sad and cry, rather than gulp down the ever-handy glass of Instant Smile. Uncle Rick tells her, "You're different," and he sure doesn't mean it as a "you'll show the world" compliment.

Everyone assures Marilyn that she'll feel great when she looks and thinks like everybody else.

"Yes, but is that good, being like everybody?" she asks Uncle Rick, who looks like all the other men in the episode. "I mean, isn't that the same as being nobody?"

It's the resounding question at the heart of the episode first credited completely to Charles Beaumont (it is based on his story, but John Tomerlin wrote the script). Unlike Janet Tyler in "Eye of the Beholder," Marilyn is not considered ugly or deformed. Marilyn may not be pretty, as she herself tells us, but she also isn't homely. Janet's crime is deviating so much from the standard of beauty that she must be sent away. Marilyn's crime is not wanting to be as beautiful as everyone else.

It goes well beyond that, of course. Marilyn wants to think for herself, to retain her own identity, to be her own person. "When everyone is beautiful, no one will be," her beloved father told her. "They don't care if you're beautiful or not, they just want everyone to be the same." While she puts up a determined and noble fight, the state ultimately must win. Marilyn is forced through the transformation, and, with it, is a psychological adjustment. She comes through the procedure with a new attitude, pleased that now she looks exactly like Valerie.

The surrendering of her individuality is heartbreaking to the viewer. The final image of the vapid and transformed Marilyn is tragic, disturbing, and a thousand times more chilling than anything in "Eye of the Beholder." "Portrait of a young lady in love—with herself," Serling tells us. "Improbable? Perhaps. But in an age of plastic surgery, bodybuilding, and an infinity of cosmetics, let us hesitate to say impossible."

Janet leaves the hospital with some hope of happiness. Marilyn is a shell of a young woman, steamrolled by a society that will not tolerate a questioning mind. The lesson is a stern one. Marilyn is forbidden to stray from the only path deemed acceptable for her. If you have the ability to wander off in your own direction, grab that opportunity and find your own road to happiness and personal fulfillment. The roadblocks probably won't be as formidable as the ones Marilyn faces, yet they could take the form of peer pressure, platform politics, societal expectations, familial demands, pop-culture trends, or any kind of group thinking that demands an individual join the herd and walk in lockstep.

This lesson gets a somewhat more whimsical and lighthearted workout in Serling's first-season episode "Mr. Bevis." Orson Bean plays accident-prone, happy-go-lucky, ever-optimistic James B. W. Bevis, an amiable oddball with a fondness for loud clothes, zither music, model ships, and the works of Charles Dickens. Children and dogs love him. His employers, and they change frequently, are exasperated by him. Bevis is a square peg not making much effort to fit into a round world. He likes to smile, and he likes to make others smile. His existence has "all the security of a floating crap game," Serling explains. "But this can be said of our Mr. Bevis; without him, without his warmth, without his kindness, the world would be a considerably poorer place, albeit perhaps a little saner." At the end of a day when everything goes wrong, Bevis gets a visit from his guardian angel, J. Hardy Hempstead (Henry Jones). He arranges for everything that went wrong to go right. Fortune shines on Bevis, but, in doing so, robs him of the inner glow that so warms the world. Success means responsibility. And responsibility means surrendering everything he loves—loud clothes, zither music, and all. Bevis has been taken off the eccentric road that made him happy. He wants to go back to being his own person. Hempstead understands and grants his wish.

There is magic here, too, which Bevis understands so well. So does Rod Serling, who believed that conformity is the enemy of this brand of magic: "The magic of a child's smile, the magic of liking and being liked, the strange and wondrous mysticism that is the simple act of living." And, yes, living as your own person. The lesson comes by way of tragedy in "Number 12 Looks Just Like You" and comedy in "Mr. Bevis," both routed through the Twilight Zone.

GUEST LESSON: MICK GARRIS

Mick Garris is a director specializing in horror tales. He was at the helm of the miniseries versions of Stephen King's The Stand, The Shining, *and* Bag of Bones, *as well as the film versions of King's* Sleepwalkers *and* Riding the Bullet. *He is the creator of two horror anthology series, Showtime's* Masters of Horror *and NBC's* Fear Itself. *Also a writer, he won a 1986 Edgar award for an episode of Steven Spielberg's NBC anthology series,* Amazing Stories.

The Twilight Zone surely was the most influential of all the TV shows in the genre. It blazed trails and burned its outré offerings into the minds of kids who would take the lessons they learned from Professor Serling and build upon them to create the horror and fantasy of the following generations. Show me an author, a screenwriter, or a filmmaker who works in dark or speculative fiction, and I'll show you a *Twilight Zone* addict. And by all means, count me among them. I know it bent my sensibilities for good when I stumbled across it after my proper bedtime, and it rests like a wooden stake in my heart.

COUNT YOUR BLESSINGS
"THE MAN IN THE BOTTLE"
(ORIGINAL AIRDATE: OCTOBER 7, 1960)

A publicist recently asked me how long I've been a TV critic. I told her, "Well, let me put it this way: they use carbon14 to date my earliest reviews." There's not much sense denying that I'm pretty much in the Jurassic category when it comes to longevity on the beat. When I began getting paid by a newspaper for reviewing television, Jimmy Carter was president, *Laverne & Shirley* was the top-rated show in the country, and there were only three networks. As the number of channels started to multiply, so did the complaints I heard from other TV critics. On a fairly regular basis, a colleague would make a point of commenting on how tough the job is—how debilitating, how onerous, how demanding, how challenging, how awful, how miserable. Where two or more are gathered, the whining will commence. Yet, no matter how beaten down I've been by chasing deadlines and dealing with breaking stories, in my mind, I go to a blue-collar neighborhood bar, somewhere on the west side of Cleveland. I'm sitting between two unemployed steelworkers. We're all drowning our sorrows, and one of them glances down at me and asks, "What's your problem?"

And without blinking, staring straight ahead, I say with complete disgust, "Well, I'm a TV critic, you see. I watch television for a living."

They exchange quizzical glances, then look back down at me. "Do they pay you for that?" one of them asks.

"Yeah, the bastards give me a check every week," I grunt back, sounding like Humphrey Bogart after Ingrid Bergman broke his heart in *Casablanca*. "And it clears, if you can believe it. Tough break, huh?" Now, in my mind, this is a one-way ticket to the parking lot for a well-deserved round of asswhuppin'. And this scenario never fails to bring clarity.

Change the perspective. Alter the point of view ever so slightly, and what seems like a curse is, in actuality, a great blessing. What seems like a burden is an incredible privilege. How many less fortunate souls on this planet would look at the kind of life we lead and think, with considerable envy, "What a lucky stiff! What lottery did he win?"

It's like that marvelously giddy scene at the end of director Frank Capra's *It's a Wonderful Life*, a film with moments that foreshadow the eerie spirit of Serling's *Twilight Zone*. George Bailey (Jimmy Stewart), so relieved to have escaped a hellish world in which he'd never been born, returns home to find the kids, as well as the authorities with a warrant for his arrest. The warrant soon will be torn up as the town rallies around George, but, at this point, he is still facing the shadow of scandal, bankruptcy, and jail. That shadow drove him to despair and the brink of suicide. He returns from his encounter with a guardian angel and exclaims, "Isn't it wonderful? I'm going to jail!" Nothing has changed, except George's point of view. The shadow has been utterly destroyed by an appreciation of his many blessings. He was fixated on the problems and could see nothing else. Now he sees the bigger picture and can say with a genuine sense of joy, "I'm going to jail!" He isn't, of course, but now he realizes that the real jail to fear is the prison of gloom we build for ourselves. We all occasionally need to be reminded of a piece of advice from a writer who would have enjoyed spending time in the Twilight Zone, Charles Dickens: "Reflect upon your present blessings—of which every man has many—not on your past misfortunes, of which all men have some."

This is precisely the lesson that Arthur and Edna Castle (Luther Adler and Vivi Janiss) learn in "The Man in the Bottle," a second-season *Twilight Zone* episode penned by Rod Serling. They are, as the master of the fifth dimension tells us, "gentle and infinitely patient people, whose lives have been a hope chest with a rusty lock and a lost set of keys." In other words, they get by, barely, by paying the bills that most need paying. They run a neighborhood shop specializing in antiques, knickknacks, and curios. And every dollar counts. A soft touch, Arthur gives one of those precious dollars to an old woman far worse off than he is. She gives him a bottle, telling him that it's a family heirloom. He doesn't believe her for a second, but he's touched by her desperation. Knowing what a kind man Arthur is, she confesses that the bottle is something she fished from the trash.

When Arthur knocks over the bottle, a genie emerges and grants them four wishes. Edna wants nothing to do with it at first. She thinks nothing good can come from such magic. But she's wrong. Something good *will* come of it. A dubious Arthur first points to a broken pane of glass in a display case. It's a sign of their hand-to-mouth existence. As a test, he challenges the genie to fix it. The glass is magically repaired, and the Castles suddenly realize that they can have anything for the asking. So they ask for a million dollars. Staying true to their generous nature, they find happiness in giving much of it away to badly off friends and neighbors. Then the Internal Revenue Service comes calling, demanding they pay taxes on the money. They're left with five dollars. Thinking he can outsmart the genie and the Twilight Zone (and we know where this usually leads), Arthur wishes to be the ruler of a country. He specifies that it must be in the twentieth century and that he can't be voted out of office. The genie complies, and Arthur realizes he is Adolf Hitler near the end of World War II. These dark, unforeseen consequences force Arthur to use his final wish as an escape hatch. He just wants to return to his old life: "I wish I were back where it all started."

But like George Bailey, he has returned from the nightmare with a new perspective on life. "Funny thing, though," he tells Edna. "This place . . . this place doesn't look half bad. . . . And since we obviously can't afford a brand-new life, suppose we give the old one a paint job or something." Smiling with a similar appreciation, Edna tells him, "I think that's a very good idea."

So something good has come of this brand of magic. Each wish brought them closer to the realization that life wasn't so bad, after all. And maybe they came out a little bit ahead in another way. They got a fixed pane of glass out of the deal. Just as they're enjoying a good laugh about this, Arthur accidentally hits the glass with a broom handle, returning it to the cracked condition. They look at the glass and each other, then laugh even more heartily and lovingly over being fortunate enough to have a shop with a display case with a broken pane of glass.

It is a lovely bit of symbolism, reminiscent of another element in *It's a Wonderful Life*. Throughout the film, George returns home, beaten down by his battles to make a living and keep the building and loan going. Going up the stairs, he grabs the newel-post, only to have the top come off in his hand. It is a daily reminder to him of the things they don't have and can't afford. It begins to symbolize his frustrations and resentments. Yet when George returns from the nightmarish vision created by the wish that he had never been born, he bounds up the stairs of his home only to have that wooden dome again come off in his hand. This time, though, he grabs that wooden dome with elation and kisses it. Oh, to be so rich as to have a newel post in need of repairing . . . or a broken pane of glass. And George deserves to be that rich, as do the Castles, who, remember, delight in helping others. When Arthur and Edna have money, they give it away. Despite their encounters with magic, life isn't going to get magically easier for George, Arthur, or Edna. What has changed is not their condition but their attitude. They've learned to count their blessings, and they've learned there are many to count. Their message to us is that we should try to learn this without a visit from an angel named Clarence, a genie dispatched from the Twilight Zone, or a one-way ticket to a parking lot on the west side of Cleveland.

DON'T LET SUPERSTITIONS RULE YOUR LIFE
"NICK OF TIME"
(ORIGINAL AIRDATE: NOVEMBER 18, 1960)

Like his dear friend Richard Matheson, Robert Bloch was a master of the horror tale, a prolific writer, and a sneakily funny guy. Both wrote landmark horror novels in the 1950s (*I Am Legend* by Matheson, *Psycho* by Bloch). Both were huge influences on Stephen King. Indeed, there is a wicked Bloch witticism King is fond of quoting (and has been widely and wrongly attributed to him): "Despite my ghoulish reputation, I have the heart of a small boy. I keep it in a jar on my desk." Unlike his dear friend Richard Matheson, however, Bloch never wrote for *The Twilight Zone*. He did get near the land of shadow and substance with his novel version of the screenplay for *Twilight Zone: The Movie* (1983). But Bloch contributed some of the most memorable scripts to another anthology series, NBC's *Thriller,* the 1960 to 1962 horror-and-mystery parade overseen by host Boris Karloff. Why this trip around the Bloch, as the pun-addicted writer might have put it? Well, the fellow who first opened the Bates Motel for bloody business had a keen appreciation of the writing done by dear friend Richard

Newlywed Don Carter (William Shatner) falls under the spell of a fortune-telling machine, much to the alarm of his wife (Patricia Breslin), in Richard Matheson's "Nick of Time." *Courtesy CBS Photo Archive*

Matheson. As we get set to discuss a sensational *Twilight Zone* episode by Matheson, "Nick of Time," I can't resist passing along something Bloch told me during a lengthy chat in 1992. We got around to discussing advice for young writers. "There is little that can be said about the mechanics of the business (writing)," he said. "But I'd say that Richard Matheson is a wonderful role model. . . . I'd tell anyone wanting to be a writer to read Richard Matheson."

Good advice. And note, if you will, that Bloch didn't say "anyone wanting to be a horror writer." Nor did he say "anyone wanting to be a fantasy writer," or "science-fiction writer," or "television writer," or "short-story writer," or "screenwriter," or "Western writer." All those terms could have been used to describe Richard Matheson. But there's no genre specified here. You want to be a writer? Read Matheson. Consider that an extra lesson, courtesy of Robert Bloch.

How fortunate for *The Twilight Zone* (and us) that Matheson and another of his close friends, Charles Beaumont, became, after Serling, the show's leading writers. Among Matheson's many memorable contributions to the series was the second-season episode "Nick of Time," which stars William Shatner as a newlywed who almost surrenders his free will to the powers of superstition. One of Serling's openings for the show reminded us that the Twilight Zone was the middle ground between science and superstition. This story demonstrates just how dangerous the footing can be in the superstition part of that territory.

Handsome and successful Don Carter (Shatner) is on his way to New York City, wondering if he'll get that promotion to office manager. He and his wife, Pat (Patricia Breslin), experience car trouble in the little town of Ridgeview, Ohio. They visit the local diner, where they find a Mystic Seer tabletop fortune-telling machine decorated with a winking, grinning Devil. "Ask Me a YES or NO Question," the sign on the metallic box says. "Does He/She Love Me? Will I Become Rich? Is My Future Bright?" Ask your question, put a penny in the machine, and a printed card gives you your answer. Prone to be superstitious, an intrigued Don starts pitching pennies into the devilish contraption. He is soon convinced that the machine can accurately predict the future. For instance, he asks the machine if he'll get that promotion. The answer is, "It has been decided in your favor." He calls the home office, only to find out that, sure enough, the promotion is his. An increasingly horrified Pat tries to convince Don that it was his talent and ability, not the machine, that secured the job. But Don is hooked. The honeymoon looks to be over, until Pat convinces him that they must not become slaves to fear and superstition and the hellish fate this machine represents. Pat's love and faith restores his confidence in himself. Don asserts his independence from superstition, telling the machine he'll make his own decisions: "We'll drive out of this town and go where we want to go—anytime we please." There is a snapper, however, and after the Carters leave, another couple enters. Looking worried and a bit disheveled, they head nervously for the machine. "Do you think we might leave Ridgeview today?" they ask. "Is there any way out? Any way at all?"

There is a way out, and the Carters have found it. Matheson always liked the title of this episode because it has two meanings. Don and Pat are saved in the nick of time from the insidious trap that snares the other couple. And superstition can become the nick that cuts into your life. But there is a third possible meaning. Old Nick is a colloquial name for the Devil.

One of the many reasons "Nick of Time" works so well as a *Twilight Zone* lesson is Matheson's marvelous understanding of human nature. Matheson isn't suggesting that it's wrong to have superstitions. He is saying it is dangerous to be ruled by them. Don't be obsessed with them. Don't become an addict. The writer knows that even the most skeptical, scientific, doubting, or cynical among us might harbor a superstition or two. There is in this the echo of something the great agnostic and magnificent debunker H. L. Mencken once told an interviewer. The Sage of Baltimore said that he found the person following a superstition "an amiably comic character," like "the man who believes that Friday is an unlucky day. I should add at once that

I am one of those who do believe that Friday is an unlucky day. Like nearly all agnostics, I'm very superstitious. And I would no more undertake any work of importance on Friday the thirteenth than I'd jump off a house."

Dostoyevsky voices a similar observation in *The Brothers Karamazov:* "Since man cannot live without miracle, he will provide himself with miracles of his own making. He will believe in witchcraft and sorcery, even though he may otherwise be a heretic, an atheist, and a rebel." And William Faulkner warned against the hubris of thinking that, on all levels, education and experience necessarily places an individual "beyond superstition and impervious to mindless fear."

While the rational mind might reject superstition, Matheson knows that we're not always rational creatures. Part of us sides with Groucho Marx when he observed, "If a black cat crosses your path, it signifies that the animal is going somewhere." Another part of us, as Mencken and Faulkner realized, is unwilling to go so far as to tempt fate.

Matheson doesn't even rule out the possibility that the machine does have magical powers. The episode is so slyly designed, you can interpret it either way. It could be all coincidence. Or it could be a little supernatural corner in a little diner in the little town of Ridgeview. There is a bigger lesson at play here, and it isn't hinged on whether or not the machine has the ability to predict the future. This is underscored when Pat says they must get away from the diner.

"Even if it's true?" Don asks.

"Especially if it's true," she replies, then splendidly giving voice to Matheson's real lesson: "It doesn't matter whether it can foretell the future. What matters is whether you believe more in luck and in fortune than you do in yourself. Well, you can decide your own life."

Beautiful moment. Beautiful lesson.

GUEST LESSON: BRANNON BRAGA

Starting his Hollywood career as an intern on Star Trek: The
Next Generation, *writer-producer-director Brannon Braga
penned numerous episodes of that series, as well as* Star Trek:
Voyager, *and* Star Trek: Enterprise. *He also coauthored the fea-
ture films* Star Trek: Generations *and* Star Trek: First Contact.
He has been an executive producer on several shows, including
Star Trek: Voyager, Star Trek: Enterprise, Threshold *(which he
cocreated),* 24, FlashForward, Terra Nova, *and cable channel*
WGN America's *first scripted series,* Salem *(the horror drama
he cocreated with Adam Simon). In 2014, he was an executive
producer and director on* Cosmos: A Spacetime Odyssey, *Fox's
new version of Carl Sagan's series.*

"Long Distance Call" had a tremendous impact on me. That's the
one where the dead grandmother tries to lure her grandson to join
her in death. I saw the episode when I was twelve years old and
my own beloved grandmother had just passed away. The episode,
unsettling even by today's standards, helped me to confront my
own issues of loss and grief. *The Twilight Zone* at its best!

LET IT GO
"*KING NINE* WILL NOT RETURN"
(ORIGINAL AIRDATE: SEPTEMBER 30, 1960)
"ONE MORE PALLBEARER"
(ORIGINAL AIRDATE: JANUARY 12, 1962)

Maybe one of the most difficult life lessons to learn and put into practice is let it go . . . whether we're talking about resentment, guilt, jealousy, fear, anger, regret, disappointment, prejudice, indiscretion, betrayal, hurt, failure, or whatever negative experience from your past that you carry around day after day, year after year. It only grows heavier the longer you carry it; still you hold fast and tight to it, as if this awful burden were something precious beyond measure. It begins to weigh you down, slow you down, and ultimately break you down. You may look fine to friends and family members, but psychologically your shoulders are beginning to sag and stoop. You're beginning to stumble and stagger under the weight of this terrible load. In extreme cases, it will bring you to a complete halt.

Such extreme cases are at the center of two episodes written by Rod Serling, the second season's "*King Nine* Will Not Return" and the third season's "One More Pallbearer." In both these stories we find men overwhelmed by past experiences. Each is left an emotional wreck because he's been unable to let go of negative feelings. One is almost crushed by what he's carrying around. The other is crushed.

In the case of James Embry, brilliantly portrayed by Robert Cummings, the burden is one of guilt. When we first encounter Embry, he is lying unconscious near the wreck of the *King Nine,* a B-25 bomber that crashed in the North African desert during World War II. We learn that Embry, a captain in the Army Air Corps, is the commander of the *King Nine.* Struggling to his feet and inspecting the wreckage, he searches for his crew. They're nowhere to be found. He glimpses visions of his men— visions that fade and disappear like mirages. He finds the grave of one. Then, overhead, he sees four jet aircraft streaking across the sky, flying in formation. At first, he wonders what kind of aircraft they are. Then he realizes they're jets. "Jets? Jet aircraft? How did I know about jet aircraft?" he wonders. "This is 1943. There's no such thing as jet aircraft. But I know about it." Driven to hysterics, he collapses. The scene shifts to 1960, where Embry is in a hospital bed. He was brought in that morning, after seeing a headline about the wreckage of the *King Nine* being found intact in the African desert. Checking with the Pentagon, the doctors learn that Embry missed that fatal flight because of illness. He was discharged from the army a short time later due to recurrent fevers. The implication is that he was discharged because of psychological reasons. He has been carrying around this load of guilt for seventeen years. "I should have been on the plane," he tells the doctor and the psychiatrist in his room. "I should have gone on that mission. I chickened out."

"You didn't chicken out," the psychiatrist tells him. "You had no way of knowing that plane wasn't going to come back. Now you'll realize it more as time goes by and you'll feel better for it. It's out in the open now. You don't have to hide it in a pit deep inside of you. That's what's been hurting you all these years."

The psychiatrist assures him his trip back to the *King Nine* was a hallucination triggered by that newspaper headline. We get the feeling that James Embry, who did nothing wrong, is ready to let it go. We get the idea that he'll be all right. And we're glad for him. Negative feelings, after all, particularly those built up in our minds over the years, don't always play fair. They're not always rational. So, as with superstitions, we're all prone to them. They can sneak up and grab you at vulnerable moments, even when you're on guard against them. Again, we see an example of how the profound understanding of human nature is what made the storytelling on *The Twilight Zone* so insightful and timeless.

Still, this being *The Twilight Zone*, a mind-bending ending is in order. When a nurse brings by Embry's clothes, one of his shoes falls over. The doctor and the psychiatrist see that it is full of sand.

Paul Radin (Joseph Wiseman), the lead character in Serling's "One More Pallbearer," is an even more extreme case, and his fate is more extreme. Embry is a decent man who can't let go of a guilt that is understandable but undeserved. Radin is a petty man who can't let go of perceived slights from his past. Now he wants to settle three old scores. He wants to make three people pay for what they did to him. He wants to make them grovel. He wants to extract apologies and force them to beg for his forgiveness.

Now, mind you, despite taking some terribly wrong turns in his life, Radin is an incredibly wealthy tycoon. He has prospered. He has millions of reasons to be happy. Yet he apparently doesn't put much stock in that old line: "Living well is the best revenge." He is, indeed, tightly wound proof of an even older adage: "Money can't buy happiness." So he summons three people to the bomb shelter he has installed three hundred feet beneath the Radin Building, a skyscraper in Manhattan. The three people are Colonel Hawthorne (Trevor Bardette), who had Radin court-martialed for refusing a direct order, causing the deaths of a company of men; Mrs. Langsford (Katherine Squire),

the high school teacher who flunked him for cheating and trying to frame another student; and the Reverend Mr. Hughes
(Gage Clarke), who exposed him for driving a young woman
to suicide. Radin has rigged the shelter with a sound system
that will simulate the approach of an all-out nuclear exchange.
He tells his guests that he has advance knowledge of this event.
They may stay in the shelter and survive . . . if they apologize
to him and ask his forgiveness. At this point, you're thinking,
"Paul, baby, let it go."

In fact, his former teacher says as much. "Well, then, may I
make an observation?" Mrs. Langsford asks him. "Just a comment on how incredible this whole thing is, that a man like you,
a millionaire three times over, an important man who walks
with kings and heads of state and industrial tycoons, that such
a man should have a mind so tiny that it could brood over a
high school incident of twenty years ago and let it fester inside
you, as you seem to have done."

It *has* festered. That is precisely what happens when people
hold on to garbage. It begins to stink, and the smell only gets
worse. The garbage should be taken to the curb and left there
for the sanitation department to remove. But people like Paul
Radin proudly display the garbage and tell you how important
it is. He compounds this mistake by wanting to dump this garbage on the heads of others. They simply step out of the way,
much to his amazement. Completely accepting that the world
is about to end, all three turn down his offer and ask to leave.
Radin has piled the garbage so high around himself, he can't
see how highly these three value honor. He can't see it. He can't
understand it. In the Twilight Zone, such a man is bound to
get hopelessly lost. And he does. When his sound effects simulate a nuclear attack, Radin's mind snaps. He believes a bomb
has left the city in ruins and that he is alone in the rubble. He
becomes the victim of his own practical joke, sentenced to a
loneliness of his own making.

"Do you take pride in your hurt?" John Steinbeck has a character ask in *East of Eden*. "Does it make you seem large and tragic? . . . Well, think about it. Maybe you're playing a part on a great stage with only yourself as audience." That's Paul Radin when "One More Pallbearer" begins. In the end, the great theater has collapsed around him. He's sitting amid the rubble that exists only in his mind. We could call it rubble. Or we might call it garbage.

YOU'RE ONLY TRULY OLD WHEN YOU DECIDE YOU'RE OLD

"KICK THE CAN"

(ORIGINAL AIRDATE: FEBRUARY 9, 1962)

L et us return one last time to the eternal wisdom of Mark Twain in order to kick-start our discussion of George Clayton Johnson's sublime third-season episode, "Kick the Can." Much of what the cigar-puffing writer said about old age is reflected in this story about the residents of Sunnyvale Rest Home for the Aged. "I am old," Twain wrote to friends in 1906. "I recognize it but I don't realize it. I wonder if a person ever really ceases to feel young—I mean, for a whole day at a time." Later that same year, Twain observed in an autobiographical dictation, "I am aware that I am very old now; but I am also aware that I have never been so young as I am now, in spirit. . . . I am only able to perceive that I am old by a mental process; I am altogether unable to feel old in spirit. . . . When I am in the company of very young people I always feel that I am one of them." Twain wasn't just blowing smoke here. He made those last remarks when he was about to turn seventy-one (a pretty good run for the early twentieth century, and he had three and a half years more to go). On yet another occasion, Twain said, "The heart is the real fountain of youth."

Charles Whitley (Ernest Truex) thinks the fountain of youth might just be the childhood game of kick the can. *Courtesy CBS Photo Archive*

The life-affirming spirit behind those Twainian thoughts runs through the beautifully acted "Kick the Can" like a joyful ten-year-old boy playing a favorite game on a warm summer evening. Twain's ruminations on age are precisely the kind of thoughts being voiced at Sunnyvale by elderly Charles Whitby (Ernest Truex). He tries to convince the other residents, including his best friend, Ben Conroy (Russell Collins), that age has nothing to do with growing old. They can recapture the spirit of their youth by acting young. Maybe there's magic in a simple

139

game of kick the can. Maybe the heart is the real fountain of youth.

There is a splendidly symbolic scene at the opening of the episode. Charles thinks his son has come to take him home. Charles has misunderstood, and his son gives him the disappointing news. The old man gets out of his son's car, looking very old, indeed. He notices a group of children playing kick the can, and he is drawn to them. He strolls over, picks up the many-times dented can and sits down under a tree. On the porch of the rest home, the elderly residents gather to observe the scene. From the hill behind the tree, the children emerge to wonder who has picked up the can and why. And Charles . . . he sits between, in bittersweet tableau, pulled by two worlds that have a claim on him. Sunnyvale is a dying place, Serling reminds us, but only for those "who have forgotten the fragile magic of youth . . . for those who have forgotten that childhood, maturity, and old age are curiously intertwined and not separate." Sitting beneath that tree, Charles is getting a hold of that idea. Charles is remembering a time when he wasn't Charles but Charlie.

"Don't you remember?" he asks Ben, who has grown sour, sedate, and grouchy in his old age. "Did you ever stop to think of it? All kids play those games, and the minute they stop, they begin to grow old. . . . Maybe there are people who stay young? Maybe they know a secret that they keep from the rest of us. Maybe the fountain of youth isn't a fountain at all. Maybe it's a way of looking at things, a way of thinking."

Ben pushes this idea aside, calling it nonsense. He tells Charles not to go soft. He tells him that this kind of thinking is dangerous. As in "The Big Tall Wish" and other *Twilight Zone* episodes, a lesson here is to be open to the magic in your life.

"You don't believe in magic, do you?" Charles says to his lifelong friend. "There was a time that you did. . . . There is magic in the world, Ben. I know there is. When I fell in love with Mary, kissed her for the first time, that was magic. When my boy was born, that was magic. Friendship is a magic thing."

Yes, it is. Charles is right, and Ben can't see it. This myopic view isn't caused simply by old age. Ben has stopped seeing the possibilities because he has given up on life. He is incapable of taking chances. He has shut down and withdrawn. He has bought into prejudices and stereotypes. You're as old as you feel, the adage assures us, and Charles refuses to feel old. Like Twain, he is "altogether unable to feel old in spirit."

Or, as a proud Twain disciple, George Bernard Shaw, remarked, "You don't stop laughing when you grow old, you grow old when you stop laughing." Shaw's line was a variation on an observation by Oliver Wendell Holmes Sr. and it cuts even closer to the great heart of this episode: "Men do not quit playing because they grow old; they grow old because they quit playing." Charles, the once and future Charlie, innately understands this, and he realizes that Ben doesn't.

"Ben, you're afraid," Charles tells him. "You're afraid of a new idea. You're afraid to look silly. You're afraid to make a mistake. You decided that you were an old man, and that has made you old."

George Clayton Johnson's final script for *The Twilight Zone* frames this lesson in a way that is marvelously touching without becoming maudlin or saccharine. Charles implores the other Sunnyvale residents to give the magic a try. He asks them to sneak out for a game of kick the can. This is the way to recapture the lost spirit of their youth. They are, at first, doubtful and reluctant. "This your last chance," he shouts, adding a plaintive cry: "I can't play kick the can alone!" They agree to join him, and optimistic Charles makes one last bid to win over Ben. Instead of giving the magic a chance, Ben goes to tell the superintendent. When they rush out to the front lawn, however, all they find is a group of children. Ben recognizes one as boyhood chum Charlie. He pleads with Charlie not to leave him behind . . . to take him with them. He pleads with Charlie, just as his friend had pleaded with him to go along with the game. But it's too late for Ben, at least for this night and this summer. Maybe, if the screams of playing children become a lure rather than an annoyance to Ben, there will be another chance to grab the magic . . . another chance to play kick the can.

What "Kick the Can" asks, no matter what age you might be, is whether you have given up. Is it too late for you? If it is, then you've constructed your own Sunnyvale, which, as Serling reminds us at the conclusion, is: "A dying place for those who have grown too stiff in their thinking to visit the Twilight Zone."

If that's not enough, consider the wise words of writer Gabriel García Márquez: "Age has no reality except in the physical world. The essence of a human being is resistant to the passage of time. Our inner lives are eternal, which is to say that our spirits remain as youthful and vigorous as when we were in full bloom. Think of love as a state of grace, not the means to anything, but the alpha and the omega, an end in itself."

GUEST LESSON: JIM BENSON

A TV historian for about thirty years, Jim Benson coauthored Rod Serling's Night Gallery: An After-Hours Tour *(1999), with Scott Skelton. He and Skelton worked with director Guillermo del Toro as historical consultants for Universal Home Video's season-two DVD box set of* Night Gallery. *They teamed up again to produce a "lost episode" of* Night Gallery *for the season-three DVD box set. A member of the editorial board for* Rod Serling Books, *he also provided and produced audio commentary for Image Entertainment's Blu-ray release of* The Twilight Zone. *As the host of the syndicated radio talk show* TV Time Machine, *he has interviewed a multitude of TV celebrities, authors, and experts.*

Two episodes, "The Big Tall Wish" and "Kick the Can," always had a profound impact on me. Both are heartbreaking illustrations of what doubt and cynicism can do to the fragile gifts God or the universe sometimes can bestow upon us—how easily they can slip away when not fully acknowledged and accepted with graciousness and faith. Rod Serling's introduction for "The Jungle" also taught me a lesson—that one can wear an Eagle Clothes suit without a tie and still look damn good.

IF YOU GET UNBELIEVABLY LUCKY, DON'T PUSH YOUR LUCK

"WHAT YOU NEED"

(ORIGINAL AIRDATE: DECEMBER 25, 1959)

"THE PRIME MOVER"

(ORIGINAL AIRDATE: MARCH 24, 1961)

Life's slot machine magically pays off for you. You're suddenly doing far better than you dared hope. So, how many of us foolishly stay on the casino floor, chucking in coins until the house claims everything we have won—and more? When greed overruns gratitude, the pit boss calling you to account is going to bear a strong resemblance to Rod Serling. Two characters run headlong into this lesson in episodes of *The Twilight Zone*. One compounds his avarice with downright meanness, and the pit boss demands a higher price because of his bullying ways. The other simply requires a course correction, and, once back on the proper path, is pushed in the direction of a happy ending. Same lesson—vastly different payoffs.

These aren't stories that condemn the pursuit of wealth or even gambling. In many ways, *The Twilight Zone* encourages gambling—gambling on yourself, on your abilities, on life's possibilities. These episodes are about people seeking to become obscenely rich by exploiting the abilities of others. These tales are about men possessed by an insatiable desire for more, more, and still more. These are studies of two fellows in need of a good lesson. One lives. One dies.

"What You Need," Serling's adaptation of a short story by Henry Kuttner and C. L. Moore (writing under the pseudonym of Lewis Padgett), introduces us to Fred Renard (Steve Cochran), "a sour man, a friendless man, a lonely man, a grasping, compulsive, nervous man." Renard, Serling tells us, "has lived thirty-six undistinguished, meaningless, pointless, failure-laden years," and he is looking for an escape—"any escape, any way, anything, anybody." The anybody he latches on to is Pedott (Ernest Truex, who also starred in "Kick the Can"), an elderly, soft-spoken peddler who shuffles down sidewalks and through shabby bars, telling people what they need. Yes, he has the wonderful ability to look deep into a troubled soul's eyes, then pull from his sales case of wares the one item that can turn his or her life around: a bottle of cleaning fluid, a bus ticket to Scranton, Pennsylvania, a pair of scissors. Renard observes Pedott in action, handing out small miracles, and he wants one. He demands one. Pedott obliges, providing an item that saves his life. Is Renard grateful? What do you think?

Renard is soon back, threatening the kindly old man and insisting he use his abilities to make Renard rich. Pedott, already knowing the answer, asks what will satisfy Renard. The ugly truth is that nothing will or can satisfy this thug. He'll keep coming back for more. So Renard, the fox, thinking he's on the hunt, is actually constructing a trap—for himself. Pedott, the peddler, tells Renard that he can't give him the things he needs most: "serenity, peace of mind, humor, the ability to laugh at oneself." Instead, Renard gets a pair of slippery-soled shoes. It's a rainy night. As Renard goes after Pedott, a car speeds around the corner. In those slick-soled shoes, Renard can't get out of the way and is killed. The shoes weren't what Renard needed. They were what Pedott needed. The old peddler saw that Renard eventually would kill him, so what was needed was a pair of slippery shoes. The fox got tripped up by runaway greed, by his own vices. It put him directly in the hit-and-run path of a vehicle moving at the speed of cosmic justice.

The lesson isn't quite so severe for Ace Larsen (Dane Clark), one of the two lead characters in "The Prime Mover," written by Charles Beaumont and based on a story by George Clayton Johnson. Ambitious Ace and easygoing Jimbo Cobb (Buddy Ebsen) are co-owners of a small café. When Ace learns that Jimbo has telekinetic powers, he takes his partner to Las Vegas and stations him near the roulette, craps, and chuck-a-luck tables. With Jimbo manipulating the roulette ball and the dice, Ace can't lose. He manages to pile up winnings of two hundred thousand dollars in just one evening. It's not enough. Much to Jimbo's disgust, Ace wants more and more. "Ace, you're sick," his girlfriend, Kitty (Christine White), informs him. He certainly is, and she knows what the disease is: good ol' galloping greed.

Jimbo realizes that Ace isn't on a winning streak. He is, in fact, at risk of losing everything that counts: his girlfriend, his best friend, his humanity. Jimbo tries to warn him, but Ace brushes him off by saying, "I can't hear you, Jimbo. I can't hear you at all."

With everything riding on one roll of the dice, Ace loses all the money. Jimbo says his telekinetic powers were so overtaxed, he "blew a fuse." They return to the café, happy with their stations in life. And Kitty accepts Ace's marriage proposal. And when Jimbo drops a broom, he uses telekinesis to retrieve it. He still has the power to move objects with his mind. Jimbo's greater power, it turns out, is his ability to recognize the danger consuming a friend and to move that friend back onto the right path.

Ace is guilty of pushing his luck. Jimbo is there to push him back in the direction of what really counts.

IF LIFE GIVES YOU ANOTHER CHANCE, MAKE THE MOST OF IT

"THIRD FROM THE SUN"
(ORIGINAL AIRDATE: JANUARY 8, 1960)

"THE LAST RITES OF JEFF MYRTLEBANK"
(ORIGINAL AIRDATE: FEBRUARY 3, 1962)

Take a second to ponder the glorious possibilities of second chances. There is a wonderful line (among countless wonderful lines) in the Tom Stoppard play *Rosencrantz and Guildenstern Are Dead:* "Look on every exit as being an entrance somewhere else." So what looks like the end of the trail just might be the beginning of a significantly better path . . . or perhaps, a more hopeful one. It's a way of looking for second chances, and America is a nation built on second chances. That's why Americans adore a good comeback story. We're suckers for accounts of down-and-outers who seize a second chance and make the most of it. We eat up reports about people who fell lower and lower, only to find a road that led to a higher place. The *Twilight Zone* writers not only recognized and encouraged this, they celebrated it. No matter how hopeless something looks, look around. That second chance might be right in front of you.

The *Twilight Zone* plays fair. Characters facing a dead end, either because they chose a wrong path or were forced down that path, typically are given a new direction. This might be related to the lesson about it never being too late to reinvent yourself. Sometimes, after all, second chances are about reinventing yourself. That was true, for instance, in "The Last Flight," in which a World War I flyer gets a second chance to save a friend. That was true in "Nervous Man in a Four Dollar Room," in which a frightened mouse of a man gets a second chance to live life without fear. That was true in "Static," in which an elderly man gets a second chance at romance. And nowhere on *The Twilight Zone* was that more true than in writer-director Montgomery Pittman's delightful third-season episode "The Last Rites of Jeff Myrtlebank."

Talk about second chances. The episode begins with Jeff, played to the humorous hilt by James Best, spoiling his own funeral by sitting up in his coffin. Now that's a comeback for you. Doc Bolton (Edgar Buchanan) swears Jeff was toes-up, stiff-as-a-board, room-temperature, cashed-in, checked-out, crossed-over, kicked-the-bucket, dust-to-dust, dirt-nap, no-longer-counted-in-the-census dead. The dearly departed begs to differ. Jeff insists that the reports of his death were greatly exaggerated. Still, friends and neighbors only grow more suspicious. The old Jeff was amiable and well liked, if a bit lazy and aimless. The new Jeff is a hard worker, handy with his fists, and brimming with confidence. When a group of men decide to run him out of town, Jeff calmly explains that if he's the same person they have always known, they have nothing to fear. But if he has come back with some kind of supernatural powers, they'd better start being really nice to him and his family. Scared yet putting on happy faces, they beat a hasty retreat. Comfort Gatewood (Sherry Jackson), who has agreed to marry him, asks if Jeff really can do all the magical things he described to the townspeople. While denying that he has any special powers, he lights a match without striking it. She notices it. He smiles and tells her not to imagine things.

Jeff and Comfort are still alive today, Serling tells us in the closing narration, and their only son is a United States senator known "as an uncommonly shrewd politician." The talented Pittman's second-chance story, therefore, presents the notion of death as a career move. On second thought, maybe this second chance is another example of a *Twilight Zone* character skirting the dead end and saying yes to life. Whether through magic or grit, or some combination of both, Jeff emerges as a reinvented version of himself. Instead of the last rites, his funeral becomes an opportunity to at last get things right. Some might argue that the fellow who climbs out of that coffin isn't the old Jeff Myrtlebank, and they would be right. That's how reinvention works. The reformed Scrooge isn't the old Scrooge. Charles Dickens gave the old miser a shot at redemption in a most *Twilight Zone* manner, even though, at the beginning of the story, he seems beyond reclamation. Never too late for a second chance, as Scrooge learns after the ghostly visits are done.

Also facing what seems to be a dead end is William Sturka (Fritz Weaver), the scientist in "Third from the Sun," Serling's first-season adaptation of Richard Matheson's short story. Sturka is staring at the inevitability of "a horror without words." It "is the eve of the end," Serling informs us. There will be a nuclear war. "It's coming," Sturka tells his wife. "It will be a holocaust. It will be Hell. It will be the end of everything we know: people, places, ideas, everything. It will all be wiped out." Still, a second chance is hanging out there—many million miles away. Sturka and test pilot Jerry Riden (Joe Maross) plan to use an experimental rocket ship to reach a distant planet. They manage to get away, Sturka with his wife and daughter, Riden with his wife. They escape and hope they are heading for a better place. Monitoring broadcasts from the planet, they know its inhabitants call it Earth. Yes, the second chance is the third planet from our sun.

They have taken almost no personal possessions with them.

What they have packed is hope. Behind the irony of the ending is the hope that our planet can escape the fate of the one they are fleeing. That's the commodity fueling all second chances . . . hope. Even under the most dire of circumstances (the shadow of death hanging over the individual or an entire race), there must be hope. As the character of Andy Dufresne (Tim Robbins) says in *The Shawshank Redemption:* "Remember, Red, hope is a good thing, maybe the best of the things, and no good thing ever dies." Charles Dickens would have endorsed that idea. So would have Rod Serling. You can hear the echo of it wherever second chances live . . . in the Twilight Zone.

GUEST LESSON: JAMES BEST

He was born Jewel Jules Franklin Guy in Powderly, Kentucky. We knew him best as James Best, the prolific performer whose film credits ranged from Shenandoah *with Jimmy Stewart to the low-budget horror flick* The Killer Shrews. *Best guest starred on more than 280 episodes of various television shows, including* Bonanza, Rawhide, Perry Mason, Gunsmoke, Have Gun—Will Travel, The Fugitive, *and* The Alfred Hitchcock Hour *(with Pat Buttram and Collin Wilcox in an adaptation of Ray Bradbury's "The Jar"). Fans of* The Andy Griffith Show *remember him as guitar-playing Jim Lindsey in two episodes. But Best achieved his greatest fame as bumbling Sheriff Roscoe P. Coltrane in the long-running CBS series* The Dukes of Hazzard. *He made three splendid appearances on* The Twilight Zone: *as guitar-playing Johnny Rob in writer-director Montgomery Pittman's "The Grave" (in which he dares Lee Marvin's character to visit the grave of his rival gunman), as the title character in Pittman's "The Last Rites of Jeff Myrtlebank" (playing a man who puts an abrupt end to his funeral by sitting up and leaving his coffin), and as Billy Ben Turner in Earl Hamner Jr.'s "Jess-Belle" (in which a witch's love potion puts him under a spell). He sent this guest lesson just three weeks before his death at eighty-eight from complications of pneumonia in Hickory, the North Caro-lina town he called home since 2006.*

If there is one thing I learned about *The Twilight Zone*, it's this . . . actually, it is more like three things. Don't ever take a dare, or you might end up bewitched or dead for three days.

LESSON 21:

DEATH, WHERE IS THY STING?

"ONE FOR THE ANGELS"

(ORIGINAL AIRDATE: OCTOBER 9, 1959)

"THE HITCH-HIKER"

(ORIGINAL AIRDATE: JANUARY 22, 1960)

"NOTHING IN THE DARK"

(ORIGINAL AIRDATE: JANUARY 5, 1962)

The words you don't want to hear after a knock on the front door are, "It's for you. . . . Tall fellow with a scythe . . . says his name is Reaper . . . G. Reaper." Which of us, upon getting the news, wouldn't be looking for a way out? Which of us wouldn't be looking frantically for a way to postpone, evade, or avoid this close encounter of the grave kind?

This, of course, is not the way the Grim Reaper came calling on *The Twilight Zone*. Mr. Death made several guest appearances on the series, but never in the familiar cartoon visage: robe, hood, scythe, skeletal hand pointing the way. Indeed, death wore many faces, and one of them was the killer good looks of a young Robert Redford. Talk about your basic looks to die for. In three well-loved episodes, very different characters have great difficulty recognizing their guide through death's door. They do their best to keep the appointment with death from occurring. In each instance, however, the main character ends up accepting the inevitability of death, realizing that the face of death is not as frightening as we imagine. "Life is pleasant,"

Going his way? Leonard Strong plays the mysterious title character in Rod Serling's "The Hitch-hiker," based on the radio play by Lucille Fletcher. *Courtesy CBS Photo Archive*

prolific science-fiction author Isaac Asimov observed. "Death is peaceful. It's the transition that's troublesome."

In these three beautifully written episodes, it is, indeed, the transition that proves troublesome. Still, the acceptance of the transition does bring peace. In Rod Serling's "One for the Angels," for instance, sixty-nine-year-old sidewalk salesman Lewis J. "Lew" Bookman (Ed Wynn) manages to convince Mr. Death (Murray Hamilton) to delay his departure until he can make

the big pitch of his dreams: "You know, a pitch for the angels."
It's a trick. Once Lew gets Mr. Death to agree, he resolves never
to make another pitch. Death, however, is not to be denied. A
truck hits Maggie (Dana Dillaway), an eight-year-old neighborhood girl. She has been chosen to take Lew's place, dying at
his appointed time, midnight. Lew is determined that Mr. Death
will not make that appointment. He uses all his salesman's
powers to launch a pitch session that will distract Mr. Death. It
works, and both Lew and Mr. Death agree it was a most per-
suasive pitch—"one for the angels." Lew accepts that life cannot go on forever and that this Death is not such a bad guy
after all. "Well, I guess it's the time for me now," Lew says.
"Well, I'm ready." Yes, he is. Before going, though, he retrieves
his sales case. "You never know who might need something up
there," Lew explains, and then realizes he might be taking too
much for granted. "Up there?" he asks with a smile of hope.

"Up there, Mr. Bookman," confirms Mr. Death. "You made
it." And they walk off contentedly into the soft darkness of a
summer night.

In another first-season episode, "The Hitch-hiker," written by
Serling (and based on the radio play by *Sorry, Wrong Number*
author Lucille Fletcher), twenty-seven-year-old Nan Adams (Inger Stevens) is driving from New York to Los Angeles. A buyer
at a Manhattan department store, she is on vacation. A blow-
out in Pennsylvania slows her down. She has no idea how much.
After resuming her journey, Nan keeps seeing the same hitch-
hiker (Leonard Strong) along the side of the road, beckoning
her to stop for him. She is frightened by the creepy figure. Each
sighting unnerves her more, even though he's "not menacing,
really." If anything, she tells us, he is "drab, a little mousy, just
a shabby silly-looking scarecrow man." Wherever Nan goes, she
sees him. No matter how fast she travels, he is ahead of her. She
admits to a vague sense of disquiet. She sees him at stoplights
and railroad crossings, and the vague feeling turns into fear.

Desperate, she calls home and is told that her mother has suffered a nervous breakdown. It was caused by the death of her daughter, Nan, six days earlier in an automobile accident in Pennsylvania. A tire blew out and her car turned over. "Very odd," she says. "The fear has left me now." She walks back to her car. She knows who the shabby little man is. Mr. Death is sitting in the car. "I believe you're going my way," he says.

Mr. Death, wearing yet another face, returns for the third-season episode "Nothing in the Dark," another gem written by George Clayton Johnson. Gladys Cooper stars as Wanda Dunn, "an old woman living in a nightmare." The nightmare is her extreme terror of Mr. Death. She knows he can take any shape, and she knows he's waiting for her. She lives in the basement apartment of a tenement building that has been condemned. She refuses to move. She refuses to open the door to anyone. That's because "anyone" could be Mr. Death. If Wanda drops her guard for a second, she will be standing at death's door, or so she believes. Her resolve is put to the sternest test when young police officer Harold Beldon (Robert Redford) is shot and collapses right outside her door. She tells him to go away. He tells her he needs help.

"Why can't you leave me alone?" she asks. "I know who you are. I know what you are. . . . Why do you torture me? It isn't fair."

She relents and drags him inside, now convinced he isn't Mr. Death. But she tells him why she can't call a doctor. She doesn't have a telephone. There are no neighbors. They've all moved away. And even if she could summon a doctor, Wanda couldn't take the chance of letting him in. "He might be him . . . Mr. Death," she says. "I know he's out there. He's trying to get in."

Although Wanda once lived in the sunlight, she has condemned herself to living in the dark and the cold, which she hates. When the contractor hired to tear down the building barges his way in,

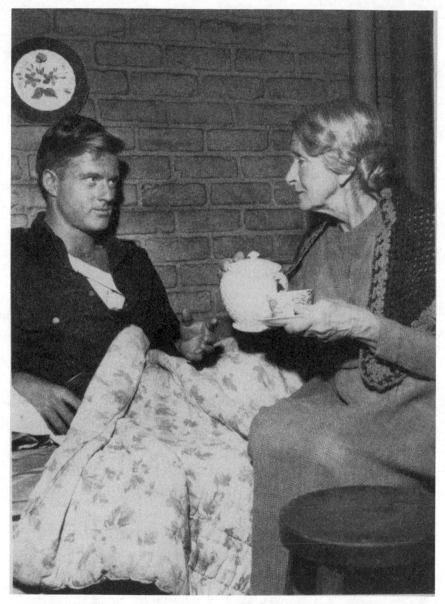

The wounded Harold Beldon (Robert Redford) gains the trust of elderly Wanda Dunn (Gladys Cooper) in "Nothing in the Dark," by George Clayton Johnson. *Courtesy CBS Photo Archive*

he can't see the wounded police officer. That's because Harold really is Mr. Death.

"But you were nice," Wanda says. "You made me trust you."

"But I had to make you understand," the boyish and reassuring Mr. Death tells her. "Am I really so bad? Am I really so frightening?"

Like Lew Bookman and Nan Adams, Wanda must let go of her fear. There is nothing in the dark and the cold except her fear.

"The running is over," he tells Wanda. "It's time to rest." The same words could have been spoken to Lew by the Mr. Death who looks like Murray Hamilton or to Nan by the Mr. Death who looks like Leonard Strong.

"What you feared would come like an explosion is like a whisper," says the Mr. Death who looks like Robert Redford. "What you thought was the end is the beginning." Warmed by this knowledge, they stroll off contentedly into the darkness of a winter night.

Death, where is thy sting? Lew, Nan, and Wanda find it has none. They learn there is some truth to Franklin D. Roosevelt's firm belief that, "The only thing we have to fear is fear itself." Combine that thought with something written by the Roosevelt who preceded Franklin in the White House, cousin Theodore: "Both life and death are parts of the same Great Adventure." Put those two Rooseveltian notions together and you are ready to reap the rewards in these anything-but-grim journeys through the Twilight Zone.

GUEST LESSON: ROBERT REDFORD

Eighteen months before starring with Gladys Cooper in the Twilight Zone *episode "Nothing in the Dark," Robert Redford played a German soldier in the final* Playhouse 90 *production, Rod Serling's* In the Presence of Mine Enemies *(May 18, 1960). Nineteen months after "Nothing in the Dark" aired, he became a Broadway star in the original production of Neil Simon's* Barefoot in the Park *(repeating the role for the 1967 film version). Since then, he has starred in such films as* Butch Cassidy and the

Sundance Kid, Jeremiah Johnson, The Sting, The Way We Were, Three Days of the Condor, All the President's Men, The Natural, Out of Africa, *and* The Horse Whisperer. *He has directed nine films, winning an Oscar for his first,* Ordinary People.

We learned how storytelling could touch us in new and extraordinary ways, and that's because *The Twilight Zone* touched a particular nerve about the surreal and the human in a new and extraordinary way.

EARTH PROVIDES ENOUGH TO SATISFY EVERY MAN'S NEED BUT NOT EVERY MAN'S GREED

"A MOST UNUSUAL CAMERA"

(ORIGINAL AIRDATE: DECEMBER 16, 1960)

"THE RIP VAN WINKLE CAPER"

(ORIGINAL AIRDATE: APRIL 21, 1961)

"THE MASKS"

(ORIGINAL AIRDATE: MARCH 20, 1964)

As we've already discovered, greed is a bad, bad thing to take into the Twilight Zone with you. We're not talking about ambition or the pursuit of prosperity here. We're talking about the kind of extreme avarice that turns the individual into (as Dickens described Scrooge at the beginning of *A Christmas Carol*) "a squeezing, wrenching, grasping, scraping, clutching, covetous old sinner." *Webster's* defines greed as desire for more than one requires or deserves—a lust for wealth far beyond what is necessary for survival, comfort, or basic need. The lesson for this entry was articulated by Mahatma Gandhi: "Earth provides enough to satisfy every man's need, but not every man's greed." It's certainly not a bad thought to keep in mind as the gap between the haves and the have-nots continues to grow at an alarming pace.

Dickens labeled the law-abiding Scrooge a "sinner." Too harsh? Well, there's a reason Dante Alighieri listed greed as one of the seven deadly sins in *The Divine Comedy.* There's a reason Thomas Aquinas assured us that greed "is a sin against God, just as all mortal sins, in as much as man condemns things eternal for the sake of temporal things." Although Gordon Gekko, the corporate raider played by Michael Douglas in *Wall Street* (1987), famously declared that "greed, for lack of a better word, is good," this kind of thinking, if tested in the Twilight Zone, will earn you a swift kick in your runaway aspirations. You might want to be on the side of Dante, Thomas Aquinas, Dickens, and Gandhi.

Simply wanting money won't make you morally bankrupt on *The Twilight Zone.* Arthur and Edna Castle, the couple in Serling's "The Man in the Bottle," wish for money, and they are saved because they are generous and because, deep down, they are in touch with what's truly important. This protects the Castles and guides them to a happy ending. But those who can never have enough will get everything that's coming to them . . . in the Twilight Zone. In Charles Beaumont's "The Prime Mover" (based on a George Clayton Johnson story), Ace Larsen (Dane Clark) is saved when he escapes the grip of greed. There is a line in French playwright Jean Giraudoux's *La Folle de Chaillot* (*The Madwoman of Chaillot*) that cuts to the heart of the matter. The English translation would be, "If they're greedy, they're lost. If they're greedy, they're stupid." *The Twilight Zone* endorses the reality check provided by Giraudoux, not Gekko. So we get a few fifth-dimension indictments of avarice—the kind of avarice that robs the individual of his or her humanity, of all empathetic feelings, of any capacity for kindness.

One of these is a second-season episode penned by Serling, "The Rip Van Winkle Caper." Led by Farwell (Oscar Beregi), thieves make off with a million dollars' worth of gold heading for Fort Knox. The four robbers make for a cave in Death Valley, where, thanks to a gas invented by Farwell, they will sleep for a hundred years in a state of suspended animation. They will awake free and wealthy men, with no fear of being fugitives. At least, that's the plan. A falling rock kills one of the crooks as they sleep through the century. Greed finishes off the rest. De-Cruz (Simon Oakland), eyeing a bigger slice of the golden pie, kills Brooks (Lew Gallo). The stronger, younger DeCruz then starts extorting gold from Farwell. Symbolically, Farwell kills him with one of the gold bars. When a couple finds him stag-gering through the desert, he offers them his gold if they'll give him some water and a ride. Farwell dies, and they assume he was mad. After all, gold has been worthless ever since a method for manufacturing it was perfected. And, in a way, Farwell was mad. All four of the thieves were consumed by the madness of greed, and it destroyed them.

Thieves also fall out in "A Most Unusual Camera," another second-season episode written by Serling. Chester and Paula Diedrich (Fred Clark and Jean Carson) rob a shop and carry away a camera that spits out pictures showing what will hap-pen five minutes in the future. When the camera correctly pre-dicts that Paula's brother, escaped convict Woodard (Adam Williams), will show up, Chester realizes they can make a fortune at the races by using the camera to bet on winning horses. Greed again trips up robbers, this time sending them out the window to their deaths. You can lose your footing, Serling warns, if you become one of "the greedy, the avaricious, the fleet of foot who can run a four-minute mile so long as they're chasing a fast buck."

Serling had already explored the self-destructive nature of greed in the first-season episode "What You Need." Bullying Fred Renard (Steve Cochran) wasn't satisfied with the pile of cash provided through the gifts of an elderly sidewalk salesman (Ernest Truex). He kept coming back for more, until he, too, was tripped up—by slippery-soled shoes greased by greed.

But Serling's strongest indictment of stupidity by way of cupid-ity was his fifth-season gem beautifully directed by Ida Lupino,

"The Masks." Wealthy Jason Foster (Robert Keith) is dying, and he has some loose ends to tie up before he calls it a life. The loose ends are his daughter, Emily (Virginia Gregg); her husband, Wilfred (Milton Selzer); and their two children, Wilfred Jr. (Alan Sues) and Paula (Brooke Hayward). It is Mardi Gras, and Jason has summoned them to his New Orleans mansion. They are there in expectation of inheriting his considerable fortune. Jason is determined to bring these "cruel and miserable people" face-to-face with their ugly natures. He provides each of them with a mask created by an old Cajun. The grotesque masks are reflections of their contorted, selfish souls. They refuse to don the masks, until Jason tells them that this route leads to disinheritance. Not surprisingly, they change their minds and put on the masks. Greed compels them to agree. Jason dies at midnight, and they get to take off their masks. But their faces have taken on the characteristics of the masks. "They now wear the faces of all that was inside them," Serling tells us. Earth provides enough to satisfy every man's need, but the Twilight Zone provides the payoff for those twisted by greed.

WHEN YOU REACH A FORK IN THE ROAD, TAKE IT
"A WORLD OF DIFFERENCE"
(ORIGINAL AIRDATE: MARCH 11, 1960)

The wit and enduring wisdom of Lawrence Peter "Yogi" Berra is to be cherished for its near-surrealistic sagacity. The Hall of Fame baseball legend, who died a few weeks before the writing of this particular entry, once said, "Always go to other people's funerals; otherwise they won't come to yours." There is a wonderful illogical logic there that would befuddle two or more Marx Brothers. This was the guy who once told a group of players to "pair up in threes." This was the man who coined the phrase, "It's déjà vu all over again."

The Marx Brothers are pertinent to this discussion because they were masters of a lunatic brand of illogical logic—madness that is proclaimed with the authority of common sense. There is a classic scene in *A Night at the Opera,* for instance, where Groucho and Chico are negotiating a contract. As Chico expresses disapproval for a clause, it is ripped away from the document. This continues until each brother is holding a slip of paper, whereupon Groucho produces a pen and asks Chico to sign. Chico must finally admit that he can't write. That's all right, Groucho, assures him, there's no ink in the pen, anyway. It all makes perfect sense, to them, maybe. It's entirely fitting that there is one last clause to discuss, and it's the sanity clause. Chico dismisses it with a laugh, saying, "You can't fool me—there ain't no Sanity Clause."

In *Abbott and Costello Meet Frankenstein,* Lou Costello's character tells a huffy customer that his request will cost him overtime because, "I'm a union man, and I only work sixteen hours a day." The huffy customer grumps at him, "A union man only works eight hours a day." Lou responds: "I belong to two unions!" Perfect example of illogical logic, as is the moment in director Frank Capra's *Arsenic and Old Lace* when Teddy Brewster (John Alexander), who thinks he is Teddy Roosevelt, shows Dr. Einstein (Peter Lorre) a picture from "his" autobiography. Referring to the doctor as General Goethals, Teddy tells him the picture shows them at the Culebra Cut portion of the Panama Canal. "My, how I've changed," the doctor observes. Teddy has an explanation: "Well, that picture hasn't been taken yet. We haven't even started work on Culebra Cut." Well, of course. Beautiful example of illogical logic.

You have to think Yogi Berra would have appreciated such observations. And you have to think that Rod Serling must have adored Berra's marvelously quirky Yogi-isms. So many of them could be subtitles for episodes of *The Twilight Zone.* There's one Yogi-ism that could be an illogical logic mantra for the entire series. When, at the end of his playing career, he was moved from the catcher's position to the outfield, he addressed his discomfort by saying, "It gets late early out there." That's *The Twilight Zone.* How many times and for how many characters did it get late early?

Yet another popular Yogi-ism summarizes the lesson you'll find in Richard Matheson's unsettling first-season episode "A World of Difference." "When you reach a fork in the road," Yogi advised, "take it." This is what Howard Duff's character must do, and it's sure not as easy as it sounds. Reality, perception, and the nature of identity often received a Kafkaesque going-over on *The Twilight Zone*, and never more so than in Matheson's nightmare tale.

Businessman Arthur Curtis (Howard Duff) is successful, secure, and happy . . . until he realizes that the phone in his office isn't working. Looking up from his desk, he sees that his office is nothing more than a movie set. Everybody tells him that he is not Arthur Curtis. He is Jerry Raigan, an actor hired to play businessman Arthur Curtis in a film. A Hollywood player whose star power is fading fast, Jerry Raigan is the distorted fun-house mirror image of Arthur Curtis: struggling, insecure, and unhappy. He has an unpleasant ex-wife, a collapsing career, and a drinking problem. Between Jerry and Arthur, there is, indeed, a world of difference.

But which is the reality? Arthur or Jerry? Arthur is convinced that he's trapped in a nightmare world, and, any way you look at it, he is. He tries to convince everybody (and himself) that he is Arthur Curtis. They believe this hallucination is due either to his drinking or a breakdown. Arthur drives to where his home should be. It isn't there. He calls the company where he works. There's no listing for it. When he learns that the movie has been canceled and the sets are about to be torn down, Arthur realizes he has reached the fork in the road and must take it. The Twilight Zone, after all, operates under its own rules and logic. Arthur believes that the office set is the portal back to his reality. It is the fork in the road leading back to his wife and daughter. He takes it, and Arthur Curtis gets back home.

A terrific mindbender of an episode, "A World of Difference" is open to several interpretations. Is Arthur the fictional escape route created in the mind of miserable Jerry Raigan? Or has Arthur slipped into a disturbing dreamscape? Or do they both exist in parallel realities? Or does it matter? Think about it long enough, and you'll hear the mocking laughter of Chico Marx, followed by the humorous-to-haunting words, "There ain't no Sanity Clause!"

The important thing is that Arthur opts for sanity, escaping an insane world. And what are we to make of Matheson's portraying Hollywood as such a soul-destroying, uncaring, cynical place? Arthur reaches a fork in the road that logically shouldn't exist, but sometimes you need to be ruled by illogical logic. In the end, the only thing guiding Arthur's choice of direction is a true-north inner compass pointing toward happiness. Does this fly in the face of logic? In the literal definition of the term, yes, it does. He has tested his belief in Arthur Curtis every way he knows how, and every test confirms that Arthur Curtis doesn't exist. The weight of evidence and common sense should dictate that he concede the point. Yet Arthur refuses to let go of his belief in a better world. And that makes all the difference. As the line from *Miracle on 34th Street* advises us, "Faith is believing when common sense tells you not to."

That faith guides Arthur back home, and the journey recalls yet another Yogi-ism that applies to Matheson's story and to all of us: "If you don't know where you are going, you might wind up someplace else."

WHEN NOBODY ELSE BELIEVES IN YOU, KEEP BELIEVING IN YOURSELF

"NIGHTMARE AT 20,000 FEET"

(ORIGINAL AIRDATE: OCTOBER 11, 1963)

You've probably never heard of Jim Tully. That's not due to any lack of effort on my part. The estimable Paul J. Bauer and I spent nineteen years researching and writing a biography of Jim Tully, a literary superstar of the 1920s and 1930s. He wrote about the American underclass: hobos, Irish ditchdiggers, prostitutes, boxers, railroad workers, circus performers, grifters, drifters, and con men. He died in 1947 and his reputation went into swift decline. By the time *The Twilight Zone* premiered in 1959, he was pretty much forgotten. It was our intention to put him back on the literary map. Despite a biography championed by Ken Burns and four reprints of his works, we failed to bring this dynamic and important American writer back to prominence. This intrusion is neither an abrupt wallow in the self-pity pool nor a shameless plug for that earlier book . . . all right, then again, maybe it is. But it's also a way of smuggling in a bit of Tully advice that sustained us on a road that began twenty-four years ago and also suits one of the greatest of all *Twilight Zone* episodes, Richard Matheson's fifth-season "Nightmare at 20,000 Feet": "Never be so mad as to doubt yourself."

Bob Wilson (William Shatner) definitely spots something on the wing in Richard Matheson's "**Nightmare at 20,000 Feet.**" *Courtesy CBS Photo Archive*

It's good advice, and so necessary at particularly daunting and challenging periods of your life. There were many times during the past twenty-four years when Paul and I have thought about that bit of Tully wisdom. When nobody else believes in you, keep believing in yourself. When most are doubting you, maybe that's when you need to have the most faith in yourself. That's what saves Arthur Curtis, the businessman trying to get back home in Matheson's first-season episode "A World of Difference." It also saves Bob Wilson (William Shatner) and his fellow airplane passengers in "Nightmare at 20,000 Feet." Arthur and Bob could succumb to the "common sense" of everybody around them. They could give up and give in to the diagnosis that they're cracking up. Both find the inner fortitude to stand alone against the overwhelming forces marshaled against them.

It's a familiar theme in Matheson's work. Like Arthur and Bob, so many of Matheson's heroes are loners fighting near impossible odds. You find that in his 1954 novel, *I Am Legend,* about Robert Neville, the ultimate loner battling the undead in a world overrun with vampires. You find that in *The Shrinking Man,* his 1956 novel about Scott Carey, a man gradually cut off from his family and life because, due to exposure to a radioactive spray, he is shrinking one-seventh of an inch every day. You find that in *Duel,* the TV movie based on his short story about a motorist stalked and terrorized by a mysterious truck driver. You find that in *The Night Stalker,* Matheson's adaptation of Jeff Rice's novel about Carl Kolchak, a Las Vegas reporter who discovers that murders are being committed by a real vampire. You find that in his second-season *Twilight Zone* episode "The Invaders," with Agnes Moorehead as "a woman who's been alone for many years" and is now faced with an invasion of tiny aliens. You find that in another of his fifth-season episodes, "Steel," with Lee Marvin as a futuristic boxing manager who must climb into the ring and do battle with a robot. The odds are stacked mightily high against each of them.

"Obviously, that theme reflected my personal feeling about my life in some way, although I lost my sense of that a long time ago," Matheson once told me. "When I was young and single, the sense of isolation was very strong in my work. The individual up against terrible odds."

That definition certainly fits Bob Wilson, the jumpy passenger recovering from a nervous breakdown. He's the only one who sees a gremlin on the wing of the plane. No one, not even his understanding and sympathetic wife, believes him. It's the loneliest feeling in the world, as Carl Kolchak will learn a few years

Agnes Moorehead battles aliens in "The Invaders," another *Twilight Zone* gem penned by Richard Matheson. *Courtesy CBS Photo Archive*

later—to be standing alone, yelling, "Can't you see it? Can't you see the truth?"

No, they can't. Instead, they begin to doubt Bob's sanity. Even he has a few seconds where he doubts his sanity. "It isn't there," he tries to tell himself. "It isn't there!" But he holds on to who he is, what he knows, what he sees.

A friend who's also a veteran television critic suggested that I summarize the lesson with the punch line of an old joke. A man has a flat tire in front of a mental hospital late at night. An inmate at the gate watches him jack up the car, get out the spare, and change the tire. He carefully puts the lug nuts in the hubcap. But, in the darkness, the man trips on the hubcap, sending the lug nuts clattering down a storm drain. He desperately looks into the drain, but the lug nuts are lost. He has no idea what to do until the inmate calmly says, "Why not take one lug nut off each of the other three tires and use those for the spare. It will at least get you home." The man is astonished and grateful for the suggestion. "That's brilliant," he says. "What are you doing in there?" The inmate replies, "Hey, I may be crazy, but I'm not stupid."

Well, as much as I appreciated the suggestion, it doesn't really work, because Bob isn't crazy, despite the alarmed looks and arched eyebrows aimed at him as he rants about the fuzzy being tearing up part of the wing. "Don't look at me like that," Bob says to his wife. "I am not imagining it. He's out there. . . . I realize what this sounds like. Do I look insane?"

No matter what the people around him might be thinking, he is certain that it's real. He is so certain, he puts his life in peril to save the plane. Even when it's all over and his wife is telling him everything is all right, Bob is alone in the realization that everything truly is all right . . . now. He's the only one who knew what danger they were in. He's the only who knows why everything is all right. But as the camera focuses on the damaged wing, Serling tells us that proof soon will be found that supports

Bob's account. While it's nice to know, the nightmare is already over for Bob. He has not only stood up to fear, he has done it alone. And he has conquered it. When nobody else believed in him, Bob opted for believing in himself. When the story begins, he seems to be the most fearful person on the plane. By the end, we realize he is the most courageous. Did I say we were done with quotes by Mark Twain? I lied. Here's another that summarizes another profound lesson to be found in "Nightmare at 20,000 Feet": "Courage is resistance to fear, mastery of fear, not absence of fear."

GUEST LESSON: NEIL DeGRASSE TYSON

Astrophysicist, cosmologist, and author, Neil deGrasse Tyson is also an all-universe Twilight Zone *fan. The host of such TV series as* NOVA Science Now *and* Cosmos: A Spacetime Odyssey, *his many books include* Merlin's Tour of the Universe, Universe Down to Earth, Just Visiting the Planet, One Universe: At Home in the Cosmos, Cosmic Horizons: Astronomy at the Cutting Edge, Death by Black Hole: And Other Cosmic Quandaries, The Pluto Files: The Rise and Fall of America's Favorite Planet, *and* Space Chronicles: Facing the Ultimate Frontier. *His lesson is drawn from a 1961 second-season episode written by Richard Matheson, "The Invaders."*

In "The Invaders," an episode with no dialog, we are treated to the compelling solo performance of a manic, terrified woman with whom we sympathize deeply, as she battles a tiny but formidable alien intruder in her home, only to learn that it is she who is the alien monster and we who are the invaders. An inversion of our worldview—imparting indelible lessons for who and what we are to each other, and to the universe. Dozens of episodes achieved this high bar of storytelling, which represent the *Zone* at its persistent best.

GUEST LESSON: DAVID BIANCULLI

He is the author of the acclaimed 2009 book Dangerously Funny: The Uncensored History of The Smothers Brothers Comedy Hour. *His latest book, published in 2016, is* The Platinum Age of Television: From I Love Lucy to The Walking Dead, How TV Became Great. *His lesson also is derived from "The Invaders."*

For a kid who grew up watching *The Twilight Zone* and ended up becoming a lifelong TV critic, Rod Serling's iconic anthology series provided all sorts of lessons—including the one that you could, indeed, turn your love of television into an actual career. Perhaps the most indelible of all to me, though, came courtesy of Richard Matheson's "The Invaders." Agnes Moorehead is the sole inhabitant of a desolate and tiny farmhouse. She hears a loud sound and soon discovers that a small flying saucer has landed on her roof. A tiny spaceman emerges, and fires at her. The rest of the episode has her fighting the "invaders," finally killing one and taking an ax to the flying saucer, with the other creature trapped inside. That's when we hear the only dialogue other than Serling's narration: the spaceman sending a radio message back home, warning them not to send other ships to this hostile and dangerous planet. That's when the camera pans the flying saucer, settling on the painted words on the exterior: U.S. Air Force, Space Probe No. 1. The valuable lesson there, for me, was all about perspective. Not until the twist ending was revealed did it occur to me that "we" were the invaders—and that, from the other side's point of view, they had every right to fear us and defend themselves. The moral of the story, to me, was to always look at things from perspectives other than your own, and never take anything at face value. And it was a lesson that came in very handy, whether I was playing chess; reading about American history and Manifest Destiny; or, once I entered the real world, covering stories as a reporter.

THAT WHICH DOESN'T KILL YOU MAKES YOU STRONGER

"STEEL"

(ORIGINAL AIRDATE: OCTOBER 4, 1963)

Yet another *Twilight Zone* episode written by Richard Matheson celebrates an individual whose struggle typifies the incredibly indomitable and enduring nature of the human spirit. This time, it's a rugged individual. And this time, unlike in "The Grave," Lee Marvin gets to play a truly courageous fighter named Steel, who tests his mettle by climbing into a boxing ring and facing a robot.

Steel Kelly is another of Matheson's heroes who must fight a lonely and daunting battle—a seemingly unwinnable battle. But Steel's victory doesn't come with his hand raised in triumph. It comes in the form of survival. It comes from enduring terrible punishment so he can earn enough money to keep going. It comes from beating the odds and cheating death, just so he can live to fight another day. Life is going to be like that sometimes. It will dish out sickening body blows and wicked hooks that threaten to take your head off. And when you realize it hasn't killed you, then what? You go on. You go on, a little more battle-tested, a little cagey about when to keep your right up and when to roll with the punches. You're not defeated because you get knocked down. You're only defeated when you don't get back up.

Every fiber in the writer and the fighter who was Rod Serling understood this, and perhaps that's why he again and again returned to the boxing ring as a setting for stories: from the live golden-age dramas *The Twilight Rounds* and *Requiem for a Heavyweight* to the *Twilight Zone* episode "The Big Tall Wish." So, while Serling didn't write "Steel," he certainly must have deeply appreciated its message. After all, he embodied the keep-on-swinging philosophy. As the last line of Paul Simon's "The Boxer" assures us, no matter how many punches have landed, the fighter still remains.

The fighter at the big heart of Matheson's story is Steel Kelly, a one-time heavyweight boxer known for his toughness. Indeed, living up to his nickname, he was never knocked off his feet in the ring.

Set in a future when traditional boxing matches have been abolished, "Steel" presents a time when robots do the fighting for paying customers. Steel has stayed in the fight game by managing Battling Maxo, an outmoded B2 heavyweight model. Due to age and hard use, Maxo is prone to breakdowns. Steel, though, refuses to give up on Maxo. There's still plenty of fight left in the aging android, he insists. Giving up on Maxo would be like, well, giving up. If Steel accepts that Maxo is ready for the scrap heap, then so are whatever dreams he has left. Despite an Everest of problems enumerated by Maxo's mechanic, Pole (Joe Mantell), Steel continues to believe. But Maxo breaks a spring at the worst possible time, right before a scheduled six-round bout. Desperate times call for desperate measures (another hard lesson found lurking in "Steel"), so Steel disguises himself as a robot and goes into the ring against the top-of-the-line B7 model, the Maynard Flash. He doesn't stand a chance. As Serling tells us in his closing narration, "You can't outpunch a machine."

Steel is knocked out in two minutes and twenty seconds of

the first round. The promoter only pays him half of the contracted five hundred dollars, but it will be enough to pay for Maxo's needed repairs. It will be just enough to keep a dream going.

Steel put himself into a fight he couldn't possibly win. He had to lose. The Maynard Flash robot had to win. Yet, although his mechanical arm might be raised in victory, a robot can't really know any kind of victory. Steel has the lost the fight, but he has won a victory. He has won the ability to keep going, to keep fighting, to keep a dream alive. By posing as a robot, Steel demonstrates so grittily what it is to be human—to endure, to survive, to stagger into tomorrow despite the odds. He may not be terribly smart about how he goes about this survival business. There are times when that, too, can be said of all of us. It's one of the things that makes him so wonderfully relatable as a character. He plunges forward armed with obstinacy and animal courage, and gets knocked out. No human opponent could knock down Steel. But a machine can. And life can. Yet he'll get back up. He's down, for the moment. He's not out. As his head begins to clear in the dressing room, he tells Pole how they can get back home, fix up Maxo, and still have a few good fights ahead of them. The sense of hope will not be extinguished. If anything, perhaps it will come back a little stronger, tempered as it has been by the fiery ordeal . . . tempered like steel.

The robot has won the fight because he is made of wires and circuits. Steel has won the victory because he is made of flesh and blood, and, yes, the kind of steel that earned him his nickname.

Matheson's story is proof, as Serling tells us, "that no matter what the future brings, man's capacity to rise to the occasion will remain unaltered." That which doesn't kill Steel makes us feel stronger, as he demonstrates the individual's "potential for tenacity and optimism." In Steel, we see our own determination "to outfight, outpoint, and outlive any and all" obstacles that life throws at us until the last bell really sounds.

"I Sing the Body Electric"—with David White, Charles Herbert, Dana Dillaway, Vaughn Taylor, and Veronica Cartwright—was the only episode of *The Twilight Zone* written by Ray Bradbury.

Courtesy CBS Photo Archive

GUEST LESSON: RAY BRADBURY

Ray Bradbury, a mentor to both Richard Matheson and Charles Beaumont, had a strong indirect influence on the spirit of The Twilight Zone. *Only one of his stories, "I Sing the Body*

Electric," *was turned into a* Twilight Zone *episode, although others were considered. Over a ten-year period starting in 1981, I had the privilege of getting to know Ray Bradbury, interviewing him many times for a proposed book about film, TV, radio, stage, and audio adaptations of his works. We were going to call it* Kaleidoscope: The Many Worlds of Ray Bradbury. *Other projects derailed this idea, but not before many hours of conversation were recorded. We talked about* The Twilight Zone *many times during this period, and he never had an unkind word to say about the series or Rod Serling, although he did think the show should have found ways to do more of his stories. This "lesson" was something he shared in 1989.*

It was a very practical lesson: not to be so involved in working much too hard. That's one of the things I kept in mind when doing my anthology series *The Ray Bradbury Theater*. I used to visit Rod Serling on the set of *The Twilight Zone,* and he looked terribly frazzled because they were doing too many stories in too short a time. I promised myself that I would never put myself under the gun like that. I told myself I'd never work that hard. After we'd done six episodes over two years for HBO, USA [Network] came to me about writing and hosting more. They said, "Well, we want to do eighteen new shows a year." I said, "No, you don't." They said, "Yeah, eighteen new shows." I said, "No, you want to do twelve." And they said, "No, eighteen or there will be no show." I said, "Well, it's sure been nice." They called back two days later and said, "We want to do twelve new shows." I said, "There you go. That's right. You want me to work for you, and I won't do that. I won't work for you, but I'll play for you. And when I can do twelve scripts, I can have a good time. It won't be work. It will be play."

NEVER JUDGE A BOOK BY ITS COVER

"TO SERVE MAN"

(ORIGINAL AIRDATE: MARCH 2, 1962)

IT'S A COOKBOOK!!!!" And it's chockfull of recipes for living . . . or for just staying alive.

One of the most iconic episodes, this third-season entry has more life lessons per square inch than any other patch of *Twilight Zone* real estate. Remember how this disturbing yarn unfolded? Based on a short story by Damon Knight, this Serling-penned script is narrated by Michael Chambers (Lloyd Bochner), a decoding expert telling us about the day the Kanamits arrived on Earth. They promised to end famine and the arms race. And they made good on their promises. When the title of a Kanamit book left at the United Nations is translated, their peaceful intentions seemed certain: *To Serve Man*. But only the title has been translated. As Chambers is boarding a craft for the Kanamit planets, his assistant, Patty (Susan Cummings), rushes up with the news that she has figured out the rest of the book: "Mr. Chambers, don't get on that ship. The rest of the book . . . *To Serve Man* . . . it's . . . it's a cookbook!"

Sure, drop on by the Kanamit home planet. They'd love to

Beware Kanamits bearing gifts. Richard Kiel plays the alien in "To Serve Man," Rod Serling's adaptation of the story by Damon Knight. *Courtesy CBS Photo Archive*

have you for dinner. Gordon Ramsay never cooked up anything this hellish in his kitchen.

Savor that payoff, if you will. Few moments in *Twilight Zone* history are as deliciously chilling as this one. The moral of the story? Well, what exactly is the moral of the story? Take your pick. The tastiest choice on the menu of maxims might be the most obvious: "Never judge a book by its cover—or the title on the cover, for that matter." The familiar expression about never judging a book by its cover is, of course, metaphorical (just like many of the best *Twilight Zone* episodes). It's an admonition against prejudging anything—person, place, political candidate— based on outward appearance. Sound advice, all around, whether used as a guiding principle in preschool or retirement.

Still, you might also be tempted to swallow "To Serve Man" as a science-fiction updating of the Trojan horse tale found in Virgil's *Aeneid* and Homer's *The Odyssey*. That's the one where an elite group of Greek soldiers hid in a giant wooden horse seemingly left as a gift at the gates of Troy. Acceptance of this "gift" led to the sacking of Troy. The cautionary line to emerge from this epic is widely rendered as "Beware of Greeks bearing gifts." Change *Greeks* to *Kanamits,* and you've got one more ingredient that goes into the "To Serve Man" mix. It certainly bears this interpretation, as well. So powerful is the Trojan horse symbolism, the name has been attached to malware—computer programs that promise beneficial results if you install and run them. How relevant a cautionary tale do you want?

"To Serve Man" is such a solid episode, it can support both these constructions . . . and more. Here's another moral more relevant for our times than for the era when this episode first aired: "Conspicuous consumption not only makes for a bad diet, it's a recipe for disaster." What are the Kanamits, after all, if not conspicuous consumers? What is the result of this consumption if not disaster for the human race?

And speaking of consumption, a vegetarian might view "To Serve Man" as a vegan parable heavily spiced with cosmic justice. Love to sink your teeth into a juicy hamburger or a delectable filet? Well, sir, by the end of this episode, the shoe is on the other galactic foot, isn't it?

Or we can use the episode to expand on a phrase that became popular long after it aired: "You are what you eat . . . and, brother, you don't want to become what others eat." Granted, it's not the most relatable life lesson to be found in "To Serve Man," but the practicality of the wisdom is undeniable. If you follow this wisdom trail, you hit a fork in the road where two aspects of human nature collide: suspicion and gullibility. This episode strands you at that fork, asking how you should proceed. Take the wrong road, and you just might end up on a fork being used by a hungry alien at a far-off dinner table.

We're taught that it's good to be cautious but not cynical. Still, if you're not cautious enough, you risk falling into the gullibility trap. This is tricky life lesson footing here, but, hey, nobody said it was supposed to be easy. While you're trying to find your balance, keep in mind that this is a good exercise in critical thinking when dealing with all the Kanamits you might encounter in life. It's not likely you'll be encountering an actual Kanamit anytime soon, so let's substitute some different words. Let's try politicians making election-year promises, telemarketers blitzing you with deals on everything from insurance to credit cards, a particularly pushy breed of used car salesmen, or Nigerian princes sending you e-mails assuring big payoffs in exchange for your financial help. See, there are Kanamits all around you, eager to dine out on your gullibility. Whether they're disguised as politicians or pundits, salesmen or senders of e-mails promising vast sweepstakes winnings, they typically don't resemble a heavily made up Richard Kiel. Everyone is suspicious of the Kanamit at first because he looks so doggone suspicious—like someone crossed Sir Ben Kingsley with a WWF wrestler. The real Kanamits lurking out there are not so easy to spot, and they don't immediately set off the alarm bells. Yet think of the scams, schemes, and sales pitches waiting around every corner every day.

Take the gullibility path and it will lead you to a danger sign that would shake up George Orwell. Could the ultimate message of "To Serve Man" be a cry against a society's willingness to surrender control of our lives to a system or an authority with ulterior motives masked by altruistic promises?

Related to this point and also part of the story is a moral

closely related to the Trojan horse warning. It's an idea that crops up in several *Twilight Zone* episodes: "If something looks too good to be true, it probably is"(see the following entry for more on the episodes that make the maximum use of this maxim). As proverbs go, "Beware of Greeks bearing gifts" runs neck and neck with the one about not looking a gift horse in the mouth. This one had nothing to do with the Greek's horse play in Troy. It's an admonition against being ungrateful. Teeth can determine a horse's age, so this saying, which dates back to at least the 1500s, advises that it would be rude to inspect a gift too closely. It certainly is good advice when you have complete faith and trust in the source of the gift (like the little boy in "The Big Tall Wish," not like soldiers laying siege to your city). While that may be proper etiquette with friends and family, following it blindly in other situations could take you down that unfortunate gullibility path. I mean, let's exercise a little caution here, a little wariness, a little critical thinking. See, if I don't know the source of the e-mail or the horse, of course, I'm really leaning toward the "beware of" interpretation. By all means, look that gift horse in the mouth, in the eye, and, oh, yeah, in that suspicious wooden trapdoor toward the rear. Remember, it's a cookbook! And it's your goose that could get cooked.

So, no matter how you slice it, plenty of food for thought here. As Rod Serling put it in his closing narration to this savory story, "It's tonight's bill of fare on *The Twilight Zone*."

LESSON 27:

IF SOMETHING LOOKS TOO GOOD TO BE TRUE, IT PROBABLY IS

"ONE FOR THE ANGELS"
(ORIGINAL AIRDATE: OCTOBER 9, 1959)

"ESCAPE CLAUSE"
(ORIGINAL AIRDATE: NOVEMBER 6, 1959)

"PEOPLE ARE ALIKE ALL OVER"
(ORIGINAL AIRDATE: MARCH 25, 1960)

"A NICE PLACE TO VISIT"
(ORIGINAL AIRDATE: APRIL 15, 1960)

"THE CHASER"
(ORIGINAL AIRDATE: MAY 13, 1960)

"TO SERVE MAN"
(ORIGINAL AIRDATE: MARCH 2,1962)

Following up on the "To Serve Man" discussion, here's a second course, if you will. There is a familiar old maxim that assures us that "If something is too good to be true, it probably is." We see that in play in "To Serve Man" and several other *Twilight Zone* episodes. Indeed, it was a favorite theme during the show's five-season run. Still, this oft-quoted bit of advice takes us to another one of those forks in the road. If you head down the gloomier path, it can lead to pessimism, preventing you from recognizing the great bargains and splendid opportunities that do occasionally come your way. Really bad direction to go. But the other path, the one that leads into the Twilight Zone, strongly suggests not pessimism but caution. Be open to life's possibilities in matters of personal and business relationships, but always remember to look behind the gleaming smiles and glittering promises. They can be hiding monsters. They can be temporarily blinding to the horrors lurking out there. It's a slippery path, I grant you, and it has been greased with equal amounts of hope and doubt. Staying on your feet can be extremely difficult, and it requires just the proper balance between being open-minded and cautious.

If you find yourself in the Twilight Zone, however, you might want to lean a little on the cautious side. When something looks too good to be true in this realm, you'd best be taking another look . . . a really long look. Don't shut yourself off behind a wall of pessimism, but, for crying out loud, there are Kanamits stomping around, thinking you'd look perfect with an apple wedged in your mouth and a sprig of parsley draped across your brow. The Kanamits in "To Serve Man" come bearing so many wonderful gifts: peace, prosperity, health. How cynical it would be to doubt their good intentions. How ungrateful. How terribly jaundiced. How very smart. Trust me—trusting a Kanamit is not a good idea.

We've also already seen the "if something looks too good to be true" caution flag waved in two first-season episodes written by Serling, "One for the Angels" and "Escape Clause." In the former, sidewalk salesman, Lew Bookman, thinks he has cheated Mr. Death, granted a stay of execution until he can make the pitch of his dreams. He determines not to make any pitches at all. What could possibly go wrong? Then Mr. Death opts for taking a little girl, Lew's friend, instead. In "Escape Clause," Walter Bedeker makes a deal with the Devil, also believing he has indefinitely postponed death. In both cases, the bargains seem too good to be true, and since this is The Twilight Zone, you know they have hard lessons to learn. Different types, though, and that means different destinations. Lew at least learns that he's heading "up there." Walter is heading in the opposite direction.

Three more first-season episodes that drive home this idea in vastly different ways are "The Chaser," "A Nice Place to Visit," and "People Are Alike All Over." Roger Shackleforth (George Grizzard), the central character in "The Chaser," is "madly, passionately, illogically, miserably, all-consumingly in love" with Leila (Patricia Barry), who hardly concedes that he exists. All the affection he sends to her comes back, stamped Return to Sender. Then he buys a love potion from the mysterious Professor A. Daemon (John McIntire). What could possibly go wrong? Roger and Leila get married, but he soon tires of her obsessive love for him. Roger grows so weary of Leila's attentions, he returns to Professor Daemon to purchase some "glove cleaner." The only thing that stops him from murdering Lelia is the news that she is pregnant. Oh, baby, that was close. Based on the short story by John Collier, the script by Robert Presnell Jr. also drives home a lesson we'll get to later: "Be careful what you wish for."

In "People Are Alike All Over," Roddy McDowall plays Sam Conrad, an astronaut heading for Mars with a cargo bay packed with fear and trepidation. His fellow astronaut, Warren Marcusson (Paul Comi), tells him not to worry. He believes, as the title suggests, that people are alike all over. Sam is even more frightened when they crash-land on Mars and Marcusson is killed. The Martians who find him, however, are welcoming, friendly, gentle souls. They treat him as a guest and present him with a house that perfectly duplicates an Earth dwelling. What could possibly go wrong? There are no actual windows. All the doors are locked. And when the living room wall is removed, there are bars. A crowd of Martians gape at him in interest, as if he is an animal in a zoo. That's precisely what he is. Realizing his situation, he gives voice to an ironic thought that echoes throughout the universe: "Marcusson! You were right. People are alike everywhere."

Like Roger and Sam, small-time thief Rocky Valentine (Larry

Blyden) runs into the "if something looks too good to be true" rule. Rocky is shot down by a police officer in the opening of Charles Beaumont's "A Nice Place to Visit," A genial and urbane fellow named Mr. Pip (Sebastian Cabot) explains that he's Rocky's guide and will grant him any wish. He is provided with everything he desires. It truly seems like a slice of Heaven, at first. What could possibly go wrong? Well, everything, in fact, goes right. Then Rocky gets bored. He gets so bored, he asks Mr. Pip if he can be sent to the other place. Laughing with delight, the devilish Mr. Pip tells him he *is* in the other place. That's the Hell of it.

There are more *Twilight Zone* episodes exploring variations on this theme, but this sampling of six stories is sufficient to demonstrate the point. If someone presents an offer too good to be true, and you sense that this person is wearing a mask, rip off the mask. Behind it, you might find a demon, a devil, death, or just a hungry Kanamit.

GUEST LESSON: JOSEPH DOUGHERTY

Joseph Dougherty earned Drama Desk and Outer Critics Circle nominations for his play Digby. *He also wrote the libretto for the musical version of* My Favorite Year. *An Emmy and Humanitas Prize winner for his work on the ABC series* Thirtysomething, *he wrote such HBO movies as the remake of* Attack of the 50 Foot Woman, *directed by Christopher Guest, and the Emmy-winning* Cast a Deadly Spell. *He has contributed as a writer and director to several television series including* Judging Amy, Saving Grace, *and* Pretty Little Liars. *His books include* Comfort and Joi, Trunk Piece, Psychopomp, *and* The Persistence of Phosphors.

There are universal lessons in *The Twilight Zone*: warnings about hubris and the dangers of an ill-considered wish. The reassuring

promise that forces as elemental as death are willing to sit down and talk things over with you. The tantalizing concept that the universe isn't held together by gravity but by irony.

But if you were a kid of a certain age, the most important lesson learned by entering *The Twilight Zone* is that there is such a thing as a "writer."

Rod Serling was the first writer many of us met in the televised flesh. He was a person, a human being, an author, and when he introduced each episode, he also introduced the concept of storyteller as a career choice. There he was, an adult in a grown-up suit, inviting us to sit by the electronic campfire. The subtext was as startling as the tale: "People made these stories. They are handcrafted works. Someone sat down with a thought and a piece of paper and here are the results, submitted for your approval."

Writing was a thing you could do for a living. If you do it well, with generosity, craft, and appropriate pride, what you write might endure.

Maybe that's a lesson, maybe it's a gift. Either way, I found it on *The Twilight Zone*.

THE GRASS IS ALWAYS GREENER . . . OR SO YOU THINK
"ONCE UPON A TIME"
(ORIGINAL AIRDATE: DECEMBER 15, 1961)

Although acclaimed an unquestioned master of the fright game, Richard Matheson had an absolute horror of being typed as a horror writer. For one thing, it troubled him that horror had become a synonym for slasher films, gross-out makeup effects, and torture-porn movies. "I don't like the word *horror*," he said during one of our many talks about his life and career. "I've never liked the word. Horror is something visceral, whereas terror is something mental. I prefer *terror.* . . . *Horror* has become a dirty word. It means blood and guts. It means body parts. Horror had a broader connotation in the old days. Boris Karloff was a horror star. H. P. Lovecraft was a horror writer. Now everybody just thinks of gruesome movie stuff."

Of course, you don't hear people being called terror writers. He also knew that some people thought of him as a science-fiction writer, even though very little of what he wrote actually falls into that genre. But some of it does. So what did he prefer? "Fantasy writer is all right, or storyteller," he said. "That's fine with me."

There was another reason he didn't like being pigeonholed as a horror writer. It was such a limiting label for such a versatile writer. He did write incredibly influential horror, science fiction, and fantasy, but he also wrote Westerns, war stories, mysteries, and comedy. Yes, you read right: comedy. Although few are in danger of identifying him as "comedy writer Richard Matheson," he certainly did scare up his share of laughs. Submitted for your approval, there's "A World of His Own," his delightful first-season *Twilight Zone* episode starring Keenan Wynn as a writer with the power to talk people into existence. Remember, too, that his script for director-producer Roger Corman's *The Raven* (1963) was a spoof that allowed Vincent Price, Boris Karloff, and Peter Lorre to have a giddy good time. That terror trio was joined by Basil Rathbone for Matheson's aptly named *The Comedy of Terrors* (1964). And there was his story "The Funeral," which he adapted for *Night Gallery*. It's about a vampire arranging for the funeral he never had. The man can't write comedy? Don't make me laugh.

Matheson playfully served up the "grass is always greener on the other side of the fence" lesson in a third-season episode, "Once Upon a Time," directed by Norman Z. McLeod. The choice of directors was significant. McLeod had directed the Marx Brothers in *Monkey Business* and *Horse Feathers*, W. C. Fields in *It's a Gift,* Danny Kaye in *The Kid from Brooklyn* and *The Secret Life of Walter Mitty,* and Bob Hope in *The Paleface, My Favorite Spy,* and *Casanova's Big Night.*

Silent screen legend Buster Keaton plays Woodrow Mulligan, a janitor grumbling about the fast pace of life and soaring prices in 1890. We can't actually hear his grumbling, since the 1890 sequences are shot like a silent film, complete with title cards. Tellingly, he is disgruntled in a town called Harmony. His employer, Professor Gilbert (Milton Parsons), is working on a helmet that will transport its wearer through time. Woodrow uses the device to travel to 1962, hoping for a better time. What he finds is more noise, more rush, and much higher prices. He quickly realizes the foolishness of leaving his own time, but the helmet has been damaged. Rollo (Stanley Adams), a scientist specializing in electronics, arranges to have it fixed by a repair shop owner (Jesse White). Rollo, though, only wants it fixed so he can travel to 1890. He yearns for a simpler time. Just as he is about to be transported into the past, Woodrow grabs hold of him, and both are whisked to 1890. While Woodrow couldn't be happier, Rollo soon grows discontented. He is as unhappy and out of place in 1890 as Woodrow was in 1962. He misses transistors, innerspring mattresses, air-foam pillows, frozen TV dinners, electric blankets. What seemed so charming at first now seems dull and barbaric. Understanding Rollo's problem, Woodrow plops the helmet on him and sends him back.

Both Woodrow and Rollo make the mistake of thinking the grass will be greener on the other side of the fence . . . or in another time. "We covet what we see every day," serial killer Hannibal "the Cannibal" Lecter (Anthony Hopkins) tells FBI trainee Clarice Starling (Jodie Foster) in *The Silence of the Lambs*. True, but we also tend to covet what we think we see. How many of us actually see the whole picture and see it clearly? The view isn't really helped by rose-colored glasses, so we see all the positives and none of the negatives on the other side of the proverbial fence. Woodrow gets this almost immediately. Rollo takes a little longer, but he reaches the same conclusion.

You've heard the one about how if we all threw our problems into one big pile and saw everyone else's, we'd take our own back. It's another way of saying live in your own time and your own reality.

A friend who considers himself a true Victorian once remarked that he was born out of his proper time. He believed that his proper time was London in the 1850s. Now, I'm thinking, despite your great expectations, you wouldn't last a half hour in the London that Charles Dickens knew. Imagine the smell. Imagine the summer heat with the Thames a fetid cesspool. Imagine a world without antibiotics, a clean water supply, or doctors who knew to wash their hands. Imagine a world where typhoid and cholera raged for long stretches of the year. I didn't say any of that to my friend. I did point out that he had survived youthful attacks of appendicitis and influenza, both of which might have carried him off in the 1850s. It's natural to yearn for another place and time. It's also natural to see only the picturesque and none of the problems that might stink worse than the Thames in the 1850s.

THE TWILIGHT ZONE

The enduring storytelling power of *The Twilight Zone* was commemorated with a postage stamp issued in 2009. *Courtesy United States Postal Service*

In "Once Upon a Time," Richard Matheson and Buster Keaton drive home the lesson with a slapstick. Woodrow pratfalls his way back home, and the look on his face captures all his euphoria at being back in a place that suddenly looks mighty good to him . . . home, sweet home, to which Rod Serling adds, "To each his own."

GUEST LESSON: LEONARD MALTIN

Film historian (and Twilight Zone *fan) Leonard Maltin regularly updated his indispensable reference book,* Leonard Maltin's Movie Guide (*later* Movie & Video Guide), *from its first edition in 1969 to its last in 2015. The longtime resident movie critic on the syndicated* Entertainment Tonight, *he is the author of many acclaimed books, including* Movie Comedy Teams; The Little Rascals: The Life and Times of Our Gang; *and* Of Mice and Magic: A History of American Animated Cartoons.

Lessons? I don't know. Don't let your eyeglasses break when you finally have time enough to read? Don't actually get off at Willoughby? There aren't really any monsters on Maple Street? I also grew up on *The Twilight Zone* and it was a big part of my younger life, but the big lessons I took away were about storytelling. I still compare many failed (or overlong) movies today to *Twilight Zone* episodes that dealt with the same subject matter much better, and in less than half an hour.

RESPECT YOUR ELDERS
"WHAT YOU NEED"
(ORIGINAL AIRDATE: DECEMBER 25, 1959)
"THE CHANGING OF THE GUARD"
(ORIGINAL AIRDATE: JUNE 1, 1962)

Even as a very young writer, Rod Serling displayed great concern over how society treats the aging and the elderly. It's a concern that runs through each phase of his writing career. Perhaps this stemmed from the loving relationship he had with his devoted parents, Sam and Esther. Perhaps it had more than a little something to do with the values they instilled in him. Whatever the reason, Serling again and again returned to an exploration of aging individuals being marginalized, sidelined, overlooked, pushed aside, abused, or undervalued. Andy Sloane, the burned-out and used-up businessman in *Patterns,* was one such character embodying Serling's belief that getting older shouldn't be viewed as some kind of crime or weakness. Andy is a tragic figure, but Serling had already ventured into this territory from a humorous perspective with *Old MacDonald Had a Curve.* It was aired by *Kraft Television Theatre* before *Patterns*—on August 5, 1953. It tells of an ex–major league pitcher, irascible Maxwell "Firebrand Lefty" MacDonald (Olin Howlin), who frequently exaggerates his record while charging down memory lane at the Carterville Home for the Aged. A freak accident leaves Lefty with an unhittable curve ball. Although sixty-seven, he decides to try out for his old team, the Brooklyn Nationals, who are languishing in last place. The Nationals need a miracle. Lefty needs a new lease on life.

"I think it did show, even at this relatively early date, something of my later preoccupation with the age-youth problem, so obvious in *Patterns,*" Serling wrote in his commentary for *Old MacDonald Had a Curve.* It would continue to be a preoccupation. Behind this preoccupation is an observation made by Willy Loman in Arthur Miller's *Death of a Salesman,* a play that had a profound impact on Serling. Straining for a metaphor, Willy tell his boss that you can't treat a man like a piece of fruit: "You can't eat the orange, and throw the peel away—a man is not a piece of fruit." Wrinkles and gray hairs are well-earned badges of honor, not signs of obsolescence and frailty. The poet, songwriter, cartoonist, author, and performer Shel Silverstein penned a marvelous little poem called "The Little Boy and the Old Man." A little boy confesses there are things he does that embarrass him, from crying to wetting his pants. An old man says he does those things, too. The little boy finally says that grown-ups don't pay attention to him. The old man says it's the same with him.

Serling is constantly reminding us not to forget those who have given so much of themselves to a company, a profession, a school, a family, a movement, or a cause. The timeworn expression is that the parade has passed them by. If they've lost a step, Serling says, then maybe they have earned an honored spot and deserve to be riding along the parade route.

Professor Ellis Fowler (Donald Pleasence) knows this, as well. He's the central character in Serling's lovely third-season episode "The Changing of the Guard." After fifty-one years of teaching at the Rock Spring School for boys, he is being forced into retirement. Feeling as if those fifty-one years mean nothing, Fowler decides to commit suicide. "I gave them nothing," he says of his students. "I gave them nothing at all. . . . I was an abject, dismal failure. I moved nobody. I motivated nobody. I left no imprint on anybody. Now, where do you suppose I ever got the idea that I was accomplishing anything?"

One by one, ghosts of former students step forward to tell him how his teaching inspired them to make courageous choices. Those who will never grow old help an old man to see how much he has accomplished. Their enduring appreciation for him instills the sense of self-respect he is lacking as the system casts him aside. Fowler, wonderfully played by Pleasence, can now retire knowing that his life has meant something. Attention has been paid in "The Changing of the Guard," which plays like a *Twilight Zone* mix of *It's a Wonderful Life* and *Goodbye, Mr. Chips*. The ghosts of these students haunt us, too, making us see Fowler as something considerably more than a tired old man. The one-time students teach us a valuable lesson: here is a man worthy of our respect, our admiration, and our attention.

Throughout his writing life, Serling again and again reminds us to pay attention. Don't just sprint by those who have lost a step or two. Don't drive by those who have been unceremoniously kicked to the curb. Don't refuse to see those who the culture strives to make invisible. Serling had a way of grabbing you on either side of the head and forcing your eyes to look in the desired direction. "See?" you can almost hear him asking in a way that's more a command than a request. "See them. Notice them." Interlaced with this lesson is another favorite Serling theme: the worth and recognition of each individual human life.

Those who don't respect life and respect their elders come to a bad end on *The Twilight Zone*. They have foolishly placed themselves in the category of those asking for it. A leading candidate is Fred Renard in Serling's first-season episode, "What You Need." Renard not only doesn't respect his elders, he bullies a kindly old salesman, Pedott, and he is motivated by greed. Boy, is he asking for it, just like the greedy relatives of "tired ancient" Jason Foster (Robert Keith) in Serling's fifth-season episode "The Masks."

Serling doesn't say respect Andy Sloane, Lefty MacDonald, Ellis Fowler, and Pedott simply because they're elderly. He's telling us to respect them because they've earned it. It's their due. Remember, cold and ruthless Bill Feathersmith (Albert Salmi) is elderly in "Of Late I Think of Cliffordville," Serling's fourth-season adaptation of a Malcolm Jameson short story, and he hardly earns our respect or sympathy. We're more than willing to see Feathersmith get his. Cruel and avaricious, he is everything that Ellis Fowler is not. With all due respect, we applaud both their fates.

JUDGE NOT LEST YE BE JUDGED

"THE FEVER"

(ORIGINAL AIRDATE: JANUARY 29, 1960)

"FOUR O'CLOCK"

(ORIGINAL AIRDATE: APRIL 6, 1962)

I t's easy to misjudge the biblical injunction against judging others. The rule always seems clear enough at first blush: "Judge not lest ye be judged." But every day we need to judge situations, behaviors, motives, actions, reactions. And sometimes there's no getting around it. That means making judgments about people. *To judge* also can mean to evaluate, and that can mean exercising good judgment. To get the full measure of the warning, you need to look at the rest of the caution that goes something like this, depending on your favored translation: "For in the way you judge, you will be judged; and by your standard of measure, it will be measured to you." So when you step back and take a proper perspective look at "Judge not lest ye be judged," you see that we're being told not to be judgmental, hypocritical, vilifying types. Good judgment is, well, good. Bad judgment is being, well, judgmental. That's where the danger lurks, in life and in *The Twilight Zone*.

If you have any doubts, consider what follows this passage in the book of Matthew. It's that indictment of hypocrisy discussed in an earlier chapter—the one about taking care of your own inner demons before you go meddling with others'. How can you tell your brother to remove the speck from his eye when all the time there is a plank of wood in yours? Remove the plank from your own eye. That's good judgment. The echo of this advice can be heard in a line by Molière: "One should examine oneself for a very long time before thinking of condemning others."

How do you keep from sliding down the hypocrisy trail? Try this: "Be curious, not judgmental." There is poetic wisdom in those four words, and, no wonder, since they were said by Walt Whitman. The less deeply curious you are about people, the more judgmental you tend to be. Ol' Walt certainly understood that. Curiosity leads to information, which leads to understanding. Proper evaluation (good judgment), therefore, requires curiosity. You can't shut yourself off. You can't form a sound opinion without information.

The person with the plank in his eye can't see beyond his own prejudices, hatred, and intolerance. That's why judgmental people always tell us so much more about themselves than the people they're judging. That's abundantly the case with Oliver Crangle (Theodore Bikel), the central character in the third-season episode "Four O'Clock" (Serling's adaptation of a short story by Price Day).

A "dealer in petulance and poison," Crangle has made it his life's work to destroy people he judges are evil. Serling tells us he is a twisted fanatic "poisoned by the gangrene of prejudice." He has appointed himself "an avenging angel, upright and omniscient, dedicated and fearsome." In other words, he's asking for it. As judgmental people go, they don't get much more extreme than Oliver Crangle.

His hatred reaches twisted heights, if you will, when, by alchemy, he decides to make every evil person in the world two feet tall. It will happen at precisely four o'clock, as the episode's title suggests. But, at four o'clock, Crangle is the one who shrinks to two feet. His judgmental ways have rebounded on him and brought him up short. A pot called a kettle black, Serling says, rubbing salt into the ironic wounds, "a stone thrower broke the windows of his glass home." Crangle's ranting told us little about the people he viewed as evil. They told us a great deal about himself. He never really wanted to know the people he was judging. He didn't want to really see them. Indeed, he couldn't see them. Blinded by hatred? Yes, in this case blinded and blindsided . . . cut down to size by a metaphoric meteor with his name on it, sent by special delivery from the Twilight Zone

If ol' Oliver had been really curious about people, he might have gotten to know them and avoided that meeting with the meteor. "Try and understand men," another great American writer, John Steinbeck, advised. "If you understand each other you will be kind to each other. Knowing a man well never leads to hate and almost always leads to love."

Another judgmental type who puts himself in the cosmic gun sights is Franklin Gibbs, the miserly and moralizing grump played by Everett Sloane in "The Fever," a first-season episode written by Serling. Gibbs is the type who thinks the Puritans were too fun-loving a group. When his wife, Flora (Vivi Janiss), wins an all-expenses paid trip to Las Vegas, Franklin is anything but pleased. You'd think he would enjoy taking the moral high ground in Sin City, looking down on everything and every person that comes under his shortsighted gaze. Yet the trappings of Vegas only fuel Franklin's defining characteristic: crabbiness.

If Franklin had any curiosity or genuine interest in people, he might have been aware of a basic rule of the con artist's trade. The person who believes he can't be taken is the person most easily took. Franklin looks with contempt at the gambling fools around him. His withering brand of judgment is based on the specks he detects here and there on the gambling floor. He is unaware of that plank blinding him to what is about to happen. What happens is that a drunk gives Franklin a silver dollar and forces him to pull the lever of the one-armed bandit. The machine pays off, and Franklin, so sure of himself and of other people, is infected. He catches the fever. His judgmental ways have set him up to take a fall, both figurative and literal. Before you know it, Franklin is tossing dollar after dollar into the slot machine. When he puts in his last dollar, it jams. He's come up raspberries, and if the machine could make the raspberry noise at him, it would. Utterly destroyed by his own smug self-righteousness, Franklin retires to his room, where he believes he sees the taunting machine coming at him. Hysterical, he falls from the window to his death. We see the one-armed bandit spit out his last dollar. In Franklin's case, what slays in Vegas, stays in Vegas. Being judgmental by nature, he was a good bet for this kind of payoff. Judgmental views are poison, to be sure, and both Franklin and Oliver drink deeply of this dark brew, never realizing that these drinks are on the house in the Twilight Zone.

SHARE WITH OTHERS
"I SHOT AN ARROW INTO THE AIR"
(ORIGINAL AIRDATE: JANUARY 15, 1960)

When we're still wrapped in the self-centeredness of pre-school childhood, we are taught to share with others. Empathy is a far-off concept, yet the virtues of sharing are drummed into us at home, on the playground, and in television shows designed for the kiddie set. The dictate may come from a parent or a purple dinosaur, a loving aunt or a captain named Kangaroo, a kindly neighbor or a mister named Rogers who is in charge of a particularly friendly neighborhood. It must be pretty darn important, this thing called sharing, and it is. Should you find yourself in the Twilight Zone, you'd better believe it is. Your future, our future, just might depend on that. But even as empathy works its way around a maturing consciousness, we find that sharing is easiest during the happiest and most prosperous times. Adversity, though, is the true test of character, and it separates those with genuinely sharing and caring natures from those whose largess is largely a matter of convenience.

"I Shot an Arrow into the Air," a first-season episode written by Rod Serling (working from an idea given to him by Madelon Champion), is a case study in how adversity can bring out the best and worst in us. The spaceship *Arrow One* takes off with eight astronauts on board. There is a malfunction, an explosion, and a crash. Four of the astronauts are killed. Another, the navigator, is badly injured. The commanding officer, Colonel R. G. Donlin (Edward Binns), looks at the desertlike landscape and determines that they're on an uncharted asteroid. They have just five gallons of water, and Donlin realizes their survival hinges on their sharing resources and working together. Flight officer Pierson (Ted Otis) agrees with that, but flight officer Corey (Dewey Martin) doesn't see it that way. He has no intention of sharing the precious water supply. In fact, he gripes about any water being given to the dying navigator. After the navigator dies, Corey and Pierson go out to scout the barren, unforgiving terrain, but only Corey returns . . . with Pierson's water. Corey says he found Pierson dead, and Donlin forces Corey to take him to the body. They find Pierson, not dead but dying. With his last breath, he points to the mountain behind them and draws a symbol in the dirt. It's now down to Corey and Donlin. They are lost in space. The rules don't apply, as far as Corey is concerned. The only thing that matters is his survival, and water is the only thing that will prolong his life. At this point, you're thinking Corey isn't exactly what we call a team player. Taking Donlin's gun, he kills the colonel and is alone with his selfishness. Or is he? Climbing over a mountain, he sees telephone poles. That is what Pierson was trying to draw in the dirt. They didn't crash on an asteroid. They crashed back on Earth, and this is the Nevada desert. It is also the Twilight Zone, so this is where Corey will get his just deserts.

Stepping over Donlin's body, Corey tells the fallen colonel that his problem was that he was "looking for morality in the wrong place." It is a cynical observation that thunders across the decades, as the gap between the haves and the have-nots has grown ever wider. Serling's story has only grown in resonance in this new century, and one compelling reason is because he reduces the sharing question to a matter of the most basic of all human needs—water. As recently as 2014, this fundamental need was underscored by the dangerously high lead contamination in the water in Flint, Michigan. Fifty-five years after "I Shot an Arrow into the Air" premiered, the harrowing statistics tell us that 783 million people do not have access to clean water and almost 2.5 billion do not have access to adequate sanitation. We can broaden the scope of the discussion to include food, wealth, medicine, and education, but, as Serling so keenly understood, water tells the tale.

The Coreys will say you're looking for morality in the wrong place. The Coreys will say why give water to people who are going to die anyway? The Donlins will say you must hold on to what makes us human. The Donlins will say we're all in this together.

Serling, ever on the side of the Donlins, believed passionately in the generous spirit that glows so warmly in the works of Charles Dickens. As we've already seen, this luminous spirit is reflected in many of his *Twilight Zone* episodes. Indeed, if there are parallels to Twain, and there are, then there are just as many to Dickens: a whirlwind of energy who died in his fifties; a sometimes actor celebrated by an adoring public; a great lover of animals, but particularly dogs; a writer on the short side who stood tall on the side of the angels. Dickens, the reformer and the social conscience, used his stature as a writer to blast away at ignorance, greed, poverty, hypocrisy, and all the poisonous elements that corrupt the natures of the closed-minded, the closefisted, and the hard-hearted. On the flip side of that equation, Serling would have heartily seconded the Dickens decree: "No one is useless in this world who lightens the burden of it to anyone else."

In Donlin, we have the personification of that ideal. In Corey, even though he believes they're stranded on a world with only four living beings, we hear Scrooge's awful pronouncement on those who would rather die than go to a workhouse: "If they would rather die, they had better do it, and decrease the surplus population." To Corey, the navigator is nothing more than surplus population. Today, the unreformed Scrooge could be the poster boy for those who can't get enough of having enough.

In the closing narration to "I Shot an Arrow into the Air," Serling calls the episode a "practical joke wearing the trappings of nightmare, of terror, of desperation." One wonders how his Dickens-style anger would have been channeled if he had seen the nightmarish, terrible, and desperate conditions in much of today's world.

Still, if adversity brings out the monstrous side of human nature, as it does with Corey, it can also show us at our best, sharing what we can, when we can. Observing how his fellow citizens responded to the Great Depression, John Steinbeck put these words into the mouth of Ma Joad in *The Grapes of Wrath*: "'I'm learning one thing good . . . Learnin' it all the time, ever' day. If you're in trouble or hurt or need—go to the poor people. They're the only ones that'll help—the only ones.'"

Steinbeck's view of sharing seems to be a Depression-era reworking of Mark's New Testament account of the widow who makes the greatest temple offering with two small coins—because the rich people gave out of their wealth while she gave out of her poverty. That's not to say there isn't generosity among the rich and selfishness among the poor. Ma's observation, however, is indicative of how adversity can drive home the need for sharing, even among people who have lost their homes.

Donlin tries to tell Corey that the desert around them is, for better or worse, home. They need to share that idea as well as the water. The irony is that Donlin is speaking a greater truth and doesn't even realize it. They *are* home. For rich and poor, blessed and underprivileged, the quality of sharing should be the same. No matter how far we travel, we are home. And our concept of sharing shouldn't be limited to money and resources.

The concept should be expansive enough to encompass time and sympathy and understanding. In that spirit, the closing argument will be made by legendary lawyer Clarence Darrow: "When we fully understand the brevity of life, its fleeting joys and unavoidable pains; when we accept the facts that all men and women are approaching an inevitable doom: the consciousness of it should make us more kindly and considerate of each other. This feeling should make men and women use their best efforts to help their fellow travelers on the road, to make the path brighter and easier as we journey on. It should bring a closer kinship, a better understanding, and a deeper sympathy for the wayfarers who must live a common life and die a common death."

GUEST LESSON: DAVID CHASE

Long before he created The Sopranos *for HBO, David Chase was the story editor and a writer on ABC's* Kolchak: The Night Stalker *(1974–1975). He then wrote and produced episodes of* The Rockford Files *and* Northern Exposure. *He has won seven Emmy awards: one for writing an episode of* The Rockford Files, *one for writing the TV movie* Off the Minnesota Strip, *and five for* The Sopranos. The Twilight Zone *is his favorite show of all time, and favorite episodes include "A Stop at Willoughby," "The Monsters Are Due on Maple Street," "Walking Distance," and "Nick of Time" (nothing wrong with this guy's tastes).*

Well, there were many of them, but I guess the one that I would consider having the strongest message for me was "I Shot an Arrow into the Air," the one where the astronauts were lost on this planet. They behave terribly to each other and then it turns out they were in Nevada, near a superhighway. They've been on Earth the entire time. And I guess the lesson I learned, that you learn, from this is, you know, paranoia is not a good thing and don't take things as they seem. Which is the whole lesson of *The Twilight Zone*, I guess: don't take things as what they seem.

IMAGINE A BETTER WORLD
"A WORLD OF HIS OWN"
(ORIGINAL AIRDATE: JULY 1, 1960)

You unlock this door with the key of imagination . . . a wondrous land whose boundaries are that of imagination . . . This is the dimension of imagination." Even before a *Twilight Zone* tale begins, we are reminded of the key word shaping the series, the concept, the storytelling terrain. *The Twilight Zone* stands for a lot of things, but a constant throughout all the 156 episodes is the incredible power of imagination. One of Serling's familiar introductions to the show told us that *The Twilight Zone* was situated "between science and superstition," but what bridges that gap is imagination. Both science and mythology require great imagination. It doesn't take an Einstein to figure that out. In fact, it was Albert Einstein who declared, "Imagination is more important than knowledge."

"To raise new questions, new possibilities, to regard old problems from a new angle, requires creative imagination and marks real advance in science," he said. "Logic will get you from A to B. Imagination will take you anywhere." Carl Sagan phrased it in a slightly different way: "Imagination will often carry us to worlds that never were. But without it we go nowhere."

John Lennon wrote an entire song challenging us to imagine a better world. Kris Kringle urges all of us to take regular trips to the Imagine nation in *Miracle on 34th Street*. And Napoléon decreed that, "Imagination rules the world." Are you going to ignore John Lennon, Santa Claus, and Napoleon?

Fiction writers live by imagination, particularly attuned to how restorative, how redemptive, how insightful, how salubrious, how necessary it is. Few shows embraced and celebrated imagination to the glorious extent that *The Twilight Zone* did. And that's one reason Richard Matheson was an ideal contributor. He keenly understood that the literary imagination is at its most visceral when dealing with humor or horror. He understood that there are two emotions you can't fake: what makes you scream in terror and what makes you scream with laughter. Every imagination is different, of course, so we respond in vastly different ways to the funny and the frightening; but, make no mistake, humor and horror are flip sides of the same coin. They are words that even seem to mirror each other: two-syllable words beginning with *h* and ending in *r*.

They also are forms that tend to get relegated to the subbasement of literature. Imagine that. If you're dealing with mirth or monsters, you don't stand much of a chance of being classified with the "serious" literature. But no less an authority than mystery writer John D. MacDonald rose to the defense of these forms in his introduction to Stephen King's first collection of short stories, *Night Shift*. "Note this," MacDonald wrote. "Two of the most difficult areas to write in are humor and the occult. In clumsy hands the humor turns to dirge and the occult turns funny." Or, to put it another way, the horror becomes humorous and the humor becomes horrible. "But once you know how," MacDonald said of the high degree of difficulty in humor and horror, "you can write in any area."

Matheson was able to imaginatively examine the human condition in a terror tale, yet, he also could tickle our fancy with a story that was as funny as it was fanciful. Case in point: "A World of His Own," the comedy that put a perfect punctuation point on the first season of *The Twilight Zone*. It also happens to be a whimsical tribute to imagination in general and the writer's imagination in particular. What better way to wrap up that first season?

Keenan Wynn, who had pivotal roles in such Serling golden-age dramas as *The Rack* and *Requiem for a Heavyweight,* stars as successful playwright Gregory West. When his wife, Victoria (Phyllis Kirk), catches him with another woman, Gregory explains that the beautiful blonde, Mary (Mary La Roche), was a figment of his imagination. He tells her that when he describes something or someone while talking into his dictation machine, that person or thing materializes before him. If he burns the portion of the tape with the description, the person or thing disappears. She doesn't believe him, so he demonstrates how it works. Despite this proof, Victoria believes Gregory is insane and must be committed. His response is to remove an envelope from a wall safe hidden in the bookcase. It has her name on it. He tells her it contains the section of tape with her description. He tells her that she, too, is a product of his imagination. Refusing to accept a word of it, she impulsively tosses the envelope in the fire . . . and promptly disappears. Gregory rushes to the dictation machine and begins to describe her back into existence, but then has a better idea. He decides to imagine a better world for himself. He instead describes Mary, who now has a last name—his last name. The new wife appears, mixing Gregory a drink.

But the fun isn't quite over. Making his first on-camera appearance in an episode (we only heard his opening narrations during that first season), Rod Serling tells the audience, "We hope you enjoyed tonight's romantic story on *The Twilight Zone*. At the same time, we want you to realize that it was, of course, purely fictional. In real life, such ridiculous nonsense could never—" Here an indignant Gregory interrupts him. "Rod, you shouldn't. I mean, you shouldn't say such things as 'nonsense' and 'ridiculous.' " Out from the wall safe comes another envelope, this one bearing the name Rod Serling. Gregory tosses it on the fire. Rod looks at the audience and philosophically says, "Well, that's the way it goes," and disappears. Gregory goes back to Mary as the closing narration assures us that he is very happy and "apparently in complete control of *The Twilight Zone.*"

And it's all due to his imagination. As you pull back from that final scene, it grows in perspective. Gregory represents the writers on *The Twilight Zone,* using their imaginations to shape a better world, but he also represents all fantasy writers. Pull back a little more and you see that Gregory represents all writers, who realize that storytelling is, in itself, an act of hope and optimism. Pull back a little more and you see that Gregory represents all the dreamers, from poets and inventors to scientists and songwriters. Pull back a bit more and you see that Gregory represents us, using our imaginations as starting points to reach for something perhaps wondrous and wonderful. Many of us feel that the door to something better is locked, but *The Twilight Zone* is always there to remind us that you unlock this door with the key of imagination.

LESSON 33:

TO THINE OWN SELF BE TRUE
"THE FOUR OF US ARE DYING"
(ORIGINAL AIRDATE: JANUARY 1, 1960)

"MR. BEVIS"
(ORIGINAL AIRDATE: JUNE 3, 1960)

"THE AFTER HOURS"
(ORIGINAL AIRDATE: JUNE 10, 1960)

"NERVOUS MAN IN A FOUR DOLLAR ROOM"
(ORIGINAL AIRDATE: OCTOBER 14, 1960)

"THE LATENESS OF THE HOUR"
(ORIGINAL AIRDATE: DECEMBER 2, 1960)

"IN HIS IMAGE"
(ORIGINAL AIRDATE: JANUARY 3, 1963)

"NUMBER 12 LOOKS JUST LIKE YOU"
(ORIGINAL AIRDATE: JANUARY 24, 1964)

This above all else," goes the advice of windy Polonius to his son, Laertes, in Shakespeare's *Hamlet,* "to thine own self be true." It's an idea that gets a constant going-over in *The Twilight Zone,* yet with radically different results. As with almost any famous Shakespeare line of dialogue, this one is open to many interpretations. It can be read as the father stressing the value of self-awareness. That's good. It can be read as a handy catchall excuse for abhorrent behavior ("Hey, just being true to myself here, and this guy Shakespeare said it was the way to go."). That's bad. It can be read as a call for fidelity to all things virtuous. That's good. It can be read as single-minded

Anne Francis and James Millhollin star in "The After Hours," an eerie episode written by Rod Serling.

Courtesy CBS Photo Archive

refusal to consider opposite points of view. That's bad. Scholars even debate whether we're supposed to take Polonius seriously. He is, after all, depicted as somewhat pompous and foolish. Is this, at bottom, meant to be nothing more than a lesson taught by an idiot—sound and fury, signifying nothing (if you'll pardon the smuggling of *Macbeth* into *Hamlet* territory)?

The Twilight Zone clearly argues for the more positive interpretations, but, even allowing for this, the stories stress how tricky this advice is to follow. While there's nothing in the land of shadow and substance that suggests this is easy to figure out, we are told the search for a strong sense of self-identity is important, even if the search leads to the revelation that you are a robot. Well, that happened a couple of times. In Serling's second-season episode "The Lateness of the Hour," Jana (Inger Stevens) keeps rebelling against her parents' reliance on robots, until, too late, she realizes she is a robot. She has discovered her true self, and it costs Jana her place in the household as a daughter. She is reprogrammed as a maid. In Charles Beaumont's fourth-season episode "In His Image," Alan Talbot (George Grizzard) tracks down a scientist named Walter Ryder Jr. (also George Grizzard). They are twins but not brothers. Walter made Alan, a robot, in his image. When Alan turns violent, Walter deactivates him. Instead of working on a better robot, Walter decides to work on being a better Walter. Alan had gone looking for answers to what seem to be a human past, and, of course, like Jana, it brought him to a sad realization and a sadder end. There is a more hopeful ending to "In His Image," however, because Walter is human and can get in touch with his true self. "There may be easier ways to self-improvement," Serling tells us, "but sometimes it happens that the shortest distance between two points is a crooked line—through the Twilight Zone."

Similarly, Marsha White (Anne Francis) is faced with the truth about her identity in Serling's first-season episode "The After Hours." Marsha ultimately learns that she is a department store mannequin, each of whom gets a turn to spend a month among humans. Marsha lost touch with her true identity. To thine own self be true? She is forced by the other mannequins to accept her true nature, and it puts Marsha back into an inanimate form modeling clothes in the store.

Humans have more possibilities in the "to thine own self be true" realm, yet, here, too, the results aren't always entirely cheerful. We get object lessons from both sides of the equation. In "The Four of Us Are Dying," Serling's first-season adaptation of a story by George Clayton Johnson, small-time crook Arch Hammer (Harry Townes) is doomed because his defining characteristic is cheapness—"a cheapness of mind, a cheapness of taste." He's also doomed because he can't even stay true to that identity. He has the ability to change his face. He assumes the identity of deceased trumpet player Johnny Foster (Ross Martin) in order to persuade Foster's girl, singer Maggie (Beverly Garland), to run away with him. He assumes the identity of murdered gangster Virgil Sterig (Philip Pine) in order to get money from mob boss Penell (Bernard Fein). He assumes the identity of punch-drunk boxer Andy Marshak (Don Gordon) in order to escape Penell's gunmen, then the police. His run of luck reaches a dead end when Andy Marshak's father (Peter Brocco) sees the son who caused so much misery. Thinking Hammer is the real Andy, he shoots him. If Hammer, like Walter Ryder Jr., could have realized that the wiser course was some self-improvement on his actual identity, he wouldn't have ended in the the Twilight Zone gun sights. To thine own self he was false, many times over, and that left him on a sidewalk in a pool of irony.

Still, the reverse happens for Jackie Rhoades (Joe Mantell) in Serling's second-season episode "Nervous Man in a Four Dollar Room." Like Hammer, Jackie is a cheap crook. Unlike Hammer, he looks deep inside himself and finds he does have the courage to be true to more admirable character traits. When he lets that Jackie out, he's not only being true to himself, he is giving himself a fighting chance.

Orson Bean's ever-hopeful title character in Serling's first-season episode "Mr. Bevis" is given a chance for professional and financial security, but he learns that this kind of life makes him miserable. The free-spirited Bevis isn't being true to himself. When he goes back to being broke and unemployed, he is again happy and contented with life. Everybody loves him again, and he likes himself. Bevis is smart to realize what works for him, and he refuses to accept any substitutes. Here is one of Serling's strongest endorsements of "to thine own self be true." Bevis learns that he simply can't be someone else's vision of him. He takes the road less traveled, and he marches down that path to the beat of his own drummer. He is told this won't be easy. And he doesn't care.

Finally, in John Tomerlin's fifth-season episode "Number 12 Looks Just Like You" (based on a Beaumont story), we get an entire futuristic society where everyone is told to be true to state-mandated notions of identity. Marilyn Cuberle (Collin Wilcox) puts up a fight to stay true to her sense of self. She finally gives in and accepts society's standards of beauty and behavior. "Mr. Bevis" is a life-affirming tale because the main character battles to hold on to his identity and wins. "Number 12 Looks Just Like You" is a chilling story because the main character battles to hold on to her identity and loses. The loss is devastating, disturbing, and incalculable.

Unswerving fidelity to a sense of self-identity isn't sufficient. Here is where Polonius, for once, doesn't go far enough. What *The Twilight Zone* advises is not only staying true to yourself but making sure that your sense of identity is rooted in self-sustaining strengths. Without that, you might as well be lumbering through life as a robot or a mannequin.

GUEST LESSON: GREG NICOTERO

The special makeup effects supervisor, coexecutive producer, and occasional director on AMC's The Walking Dead, *Greg Nicotero has been a leading special makeup effects creator for more than thirty years. His first major job as a makeup artist was on director George A. Romero's* Day of the Dead. *Nicotero's many films as a special makeup effects supervisor include* Misery *(1990),* The People Under the Stairs *(1991),* Army of Darkness *(1992),* From Dusk Till Dawn *(1996),* Scream *(1996),* Boogie Nights *(1997),* Vampires *(1998),* The Green Mile *(1999),* Ray *(2004),* Sin City *(2005), and* The Chronicle of Narnia: The Lion, the Witch and the Wardrobe *(2005).*

The lesson I always took away from *The Twilight Zone* was that science was an uncontrollable factor and human beings must realize and accept that they don't know everything. I particularly liked the episodes where characters think they're smarter or better than anyone else. *The Twilight Zone* could be a wonderfully sharp and insightful indictment of man's arrogance. Man often thinks he knows everything, and *The Twilight Zone* constantly reminded him that he did not.

LESSON 34:

SUFFER THE LITTLE CHILDREN

"ONE FOR THE ANGELS"
(ORIGINAL AIRDATE: OCTOBER 9, 1959)

"THE BIG TALL WISH"
(ORIGINAL AIRDATE: APRIL 8, 1960)

"LONG DISTANCE CALL"
(ORIGINAL AIRDATE: MARCH 31, 1961)

"IT'S A GOOD LIFE"
(ORIGINAL AIRDATE: NOVEMBER 3, 1961)

"THE FUGITIVE"
(ORIGINAL AIRDATE: MARCH 9, 1962)

"LITTLE GIRL LOST"
(ORIGINAL AIRDATE: MARCH 16, 1962)

"IN PRAISE OF PIP"
(ORIGINAL AIRDATE: SEPTEMBER 27, 1963)

"THE BEWITCHIN' POOL"
(ORIGINAL AIRDATE: JUNE 19, 1964)

The biblical phrase "suffer the little children to come unto me" often suffers in translation. In this context, *suffer* means "allow" or "permit." In modern vernacular, it might be, "Hey, make way for the kids." And kids were a constant on *The Twilight Zone*. There is a general rule when it comes to how youngsters are treated in this world. If you treat children lovingly and well, or you feel a special kinship with them, it's your ticket to a happy ending, or at least a better place. One of the first characters we meet in the series is sidewalk salesman Lew

Bookman (Ed Wynn) in Rod Serling's early first-season episode "One for the Angels." He adores the neighborhood children, and they love him. Before the episode is a few minutes old, we know he's a great guy. His devotion to the children leads him to accept his own mortality, making certain Mr. Death (Murray Hamilton) takes him instead of a little girl. I'm telling you—a great guy. So he dies? Happy ending? Yes, indeed, because Death informs Lew that he's heading "up there." Was there ever a doubt? Children are our future, and *The Twilight*

Anthony Fremont (Billy Mumy) looks as if he's about to send someone to the cornfield in "It's a Good Life," Rod Serling's adaptation of Jerome Bixby's short story. *Courtesy CBS Photo Archive*

Zone teaches us that the best way to take care of the future is to take care of the children.

Serling returns to this theme with the fifth-season episode "In Praise of Pip," which features Jack Klugman in his fourth *Twilight Zone* tale and Billy Mumy in his third. Klugman plays Max Phillips, a small-time bookie who learns that his beloved son, Pip, has been wounded in South Vietnam. Max, too, is wounded, after committing an act of kindness. Staggering to an amusement park once a favorite for him and his son, he finds Pip as a boy. After a joyful reunion, Pip tells Max that he's dying. Max makes a deal with God: take him instead of Pip. His sacrifice is accepted, and Max dies. But, as with Lew, do we harbor any doubts about the redemptive nature of his act? Serling offers us the reminder that "the capacity to live is a vital, rich, and all-consuming function of the human animal, and that you can find nobility and sacrifice and love wherever you may seek it out—down the block, in the heart, or in the Twilight Zone." Pip not only represents the best of Max, he represents the future, and Max is fighting so the future can have a chance.

Similarly, our best wishes are riding with Bolie Jackson (Ivan Dixon), the aging boxer so devoted to young Henry (Steven Perry) in Serling's first-season episode "The Big Tall Wish." We're also rooting for Old Ben (J. Pat O'Malley), the elderly fellow who is a fun-loving favorite with the neighborhood kids, particularly little Jenny (Susan Gordon), in Charles Beaumont's third-season episode "The Fugitive." As the title suggests, Ben is a fugitive, and he walks into the hands of his pursuers because of his love for Jenny. But Old Ben is so sweet and caring, we're delighted when the aliens searching for him reveal that he's a real prince of a guy. In fact, he's a king. He's the shape-shifting monarch of a faraway planet. And, someday, Jenny will become the planet's queen. It's a heartwarming science-fiction take on a traditional fairy-tale theme.

Bolie, we believe, will know real magic in his life because he returns the love and devotion of a child. Lew, Max, and Ben move in the right direction, guided by their love and devotion to a child. It is the moral compass that tells them what to do. Each of them puts the life of a child before his own. Bolie unquestionably would do the same if placed at a similar crossroad. And such love and devotion save children's lives in the second season's "Long Distance Call," written by William Idelson and Beaumont, and Matheson's third-season episode "Little Girl Lost."

Making the first of three memorable *Twilight Zone* appearances, Billy Mumy stars as young Billy Bayles in "Long Distance Call." His devoted grandmother (Lili Darvas) gave Billy a toy telephone for his fifth birthday, and after she dies Grandma uses the toy to communicate with him. Gradually, Grandma tries to lure Billy to be with her. She nearly succeeds, until her son Chris (Philip Abbott) pleads for the life of his son. He tells the spirit of his mother that, if she really loves Billy, she'll let him live, she'll let him grow up, she'll let him go. She'll give him back to his parents. That's what does it. The love of a grandmother and the love of a father combine to make lifesaving magic.

In "Little Girl Lost," Chris Miller (Robert Sampson) ventures into another dimension to save his young daughter. This other dimension is a chaotic, confusing place, yet his way is clear. He must rescue his daughter, and, with the help of the family dog, he does.

Still, not all children are perfect angels on *The Twilight Zone*, and not all parents are models of love and devotion. When this equation goes out of whack, the consequences can be extreme. Mumy returned for a third-season episode, playing a much different child in "It's a Good Life," Serling's adaptation of the Jerome Bixby short story. You can alter the meaning of "suffer the little children," putting the accent on real suffering. Anthony Fremont, after all, is a real little monster. No, really. Serling tells us so in his opening narration: "He's six years old, with a cute little-boy face, and blue guileless eyes. But when those eyes look at you, you'd better start thinking happy thoughts, because the mind behind them is absolutely in charge."

Absolutely right. Little Anthony has a monster's powers and a child's view of the world. With his mind, he can control the weather, strike someone mute, or turn a drunken neighbor into a grotesque jack-in-the-box. Again and again, Anthony wishes the grotesqueries he creates into the cornfield. Every person in Peaksville, Ohio, lives in terror of the monster. No matter how awful his impulsive actions might be, his fearful parents (John Larch and Cloris Leachman) assure him, "It's a good thing you did that. It's a *real* good thing."

Bixby told *Twilight Zone* historian Marc Scott Zicree that he couldn't remember what inspired the story. It's always best when an author doesn't explain. Still, "It's a Good Life" could be viewed as an indictment of parents who relentlessly indulge, excuse, and spoil their children. No matter how terrible the behavior, it is met with a variation on "It's a good thing you did that." If even a little of that informs the story, then it's a caution against the kind of love that blinds us to greater responsibilities. The Fremonts are so pathetic, however, they have our sympathy, especially since the only option presented to them (which they do not take) is to kill Anthony. There's more of a sense that the Fremonts are trapped.

A more direct indictment of bad parenting is "The Bewitchin' Pool," a fifth-season episode by Earl Hamner Jr. Bickering, self-centered, petty parents treat their two children so callously, they lose them to a never-never land sanctuary presided over by kindly Aunt T (Georgia Simmons). Here, it's the little children who are suffering. They get a happy ending. The parents are left with each other and an empty house. These parents, by failing to show their children the love they need, have doomed themselves to a private Hell. Both paths go through the Twilight Zone.

GUEST LESSON: BILL MUMY

As a child actor, Billy Mumy was (and is) best known for playing brave and resourceful Will Robinson on Lost in Space *(CBS, 1965–1968), sharing a great deal of screen time with the actor playing cowardly Dr. Zachary Smith, Jonathan Harris (in two second-season* Twilight Zone *episodes, "Twenty Two" and "The Silence"). But his many 1960s TV credits include two episodes of* Alfred Hitchcock Presents *("The Door Without a Key" and "Bang! You're Dead"), as well as episodes of* The Munsters, Perry Mason, The Fugitive, Bewitched, *and* I Dream of Jeannie. *His films include* Dear Brigitte *(1965),* Disney's Rascal *(1969),* Bless the Beasts & Children *(1971),* Papillon *(1973), and* Twilight Zone: The Movie *(1983). From 1994 to 1998, he played Lennier on* Babylon 5. *He's also an accomplished musician and voice actor.* Twilight Zone *fans know him for three episodes: "Long Distance Call," "It's a Good Life," and "In Praise of Pip." Each is powerful in its own way, but his portrayal of Anthony in "It's a Good Life" had the greatest impact (and abilities). His lesson is drawn from that story.*

The biggest lesson I learned from *The Twilight Zone*? Think real good thoughts.

MAKE THE MOST OF THE TIME YOU'VE GOT

"ESCAPE CLAUSE"
(ORIGINAL AIRDATE: NOVEMBER 6, 1959)

"THE TRADE-INS"
(ORIGINAL AIRDATE: APRIL 20, 1962)

"NINETY YEARS WITHOUT SLUMBERING"
(ORIGINAL AIRDATE: DECEMBER 20, 1963)

There might be at least enough fodder for a doctoral dissertation with the title "Dead at Forty-four." Anton Chekhov, a medical doctor, became the master of the short story and the theatrical play before dying at (you guessed it) forty-four. Robert Louis Stevenson produced an impressive shelf of literature, before dying at (uh-huh) forty-four. F. Scott Fitzgerald penned such novels as *The Great Gatsby* and *Tender Is the Night* before a heart attack claimed him at (take a stab at it) forty-four. Stephen Vincent Benét's poetry won a Pulitzer Prize and his short stories "The Devil and Daniel Webster," "King of the Cats," and "By the Waters of Babylon" won acclaim before he died, also of a heart attack, at (say it with me now) forty-four. Satirist and songwriter Tom Lehrer once noted that it is people like this that make you realize how little you have accomplished. "It is a sobering thought, for example," Lehrer said when he was thirty-seven, "that when Mozart was my age, he had been dead for two years."

Yes, Chekhov lived to a ripe old age compared to Mozart.

Back on the literary front, consider that both Edgar Allan Poe and Jack London died at forty. Flannery O'Connor died at thirty-nine, Emily Brontë at thirty, Stephen Crane died at twenty-nine. These were writers who, like Rod Serling, made the most of the time they got. Also in this august company is regular *Twilight Zone* contributor Charles Beaumont, who died at thirty-eight.

We have become a generation obsessed with living as long as possible. Not that there's anything wrong with that. We are given the tools to add many years to the life span but not the understanding of how to seize the day, enjoy the day, appreciate the day. It's a matter of quality of life, not quantity. If you get both, swell, but where is the triumph of making it to ninety with a lifetime of regrets, bitterness, and unrealized dreams? Walter Bedeker, the unpleasant hypochondriac in "Escape Clause," is given all the time he desires—eternity, in fact, through his deal with the Devil. But all Bedeker is doing is prolonging the misery. He has done everything to make certain he goes on living. He has done nothing to improve his approach to life.

In his nonfiction book *On Writing: A Memoir of the Craft*, Stephen King talks about the importance of a writer not feeling guilty or inferior in matters of vocabulary: "As the whore said to the bashful sailor, 'It ain't how much you've got, honey, it's how you use it.'" A bit crude, perhaps, but effective . . . and true. The same philosophy applies to life. It ain't how many years you get, it's how you use them.

Elderly Sam Forstmann (Ed Wynn) learns this in the fifth-season episode written by Richard deRoy (based on a story by George Clayton Johnson), "Ninety Years Without Slumbering." Sam believes that, like the old song, he will die if his grandfather clock stops running. He becomes obsessed with prolonging his life by making sure the clock doesn't wind down or break. Finally, Sam realizes that living under these conditions means dying a little bit each day. He can go on living, even if the clock does run down, and, by giving up this constant worry, he can again make the most of life—make the most of whatever time he has left. "Clocks are made by men," Serling reminds us at the conclusion. "God creates time. No man can prolong his allotted hours. He can only live them to the fullest—in this world or in the Twilight Zone."

Another elderly resident of the Twilight Zone grasps this in Serling's touching third-season episode "The Trade-Ins." Aging and arthritic John and Marie Holt (Joseph Schildkraut and Alma Platt) turn to the New Life Corporation, hoping to transfer their consciousnesses into artificial bodies that will literally give them a new lease on life. It's an extremely expensive procedure, and they have enough money only for one artificial body. Since John is in constant pain, Marie begs him to go through with the operation. He does, but then realizes that his youthful appearance and energy will create a distance between them. It is a greater pain than any physical ailment he knew in the worn-out body that was his true self. He returns to that body, determined to make the most of the time he has left . . . with Marie. Here, too, is a splendidly romantic variation on an earlier lesson: to thine own self be true and to your true love be true. John and Marie can make the most of whatever time they have left only if they are together.

On a far less sentimental note, one of my favorite exchanges in any movie occurs in that sublime 1948 mix of horror and comedy, *Abbott and Costello Meet Frankenstein.* Wilbur, played by Lou Costello, has been introduced to the aristocratic Doctor Latos, an alias being used by none other than Count Dracula (Bela Lugosi playing the role for only the second time on film). Wilbur says that he is on his way to a masquerade ball. "Ah, you young people," Dracula says with a smile, "making the most of life." There's a pause, then he ominously adds three words: ". . . while it lasts." To which a clueless Wilbur responds with an appreciative, "Thank you!" But count on Dracula to provide the perfect expression of the lesson. Make the most of life . . . while it lasts.

GUEST LESSON: CARL REINER

A funny thing happened to Carl Reiner during his sixty-seven-year (and counting) career in television. He became a legend by being very good at being very funny—as a performer, a producer, a director, and a writer. The ten-time Emmy winner hasn't stopped since making his TV debut as comic photographer on ABC's The Fashion Story *in (ready?) November 1948. Less than two years later, he was both performing and writing for Sid Caesar on NBC's acclaimed comedy-variety series* Your Show of Shows. *Also in that amazing writers room was a young lunatic named Mel Brooks. Reiner again did double duty for* Caesar's Hour, *sitting in a writers room that included future Oscar, Emmy, Grammy, Tony, and Pulitzer Prize winners Brooks, Neil Simon, and Larry Gelbart. Reiner took that experience and turned it into* The Dick Van Dyke Show, *writing forty of the first sixty episodes. He also has directed such films as* Enter Laughing, The Comic, The Jerk, *and* All of Me. *A constant throughout the decades is the Grammy-winning "2,000 Year Old Man" routine he regularly revisited with Brooks. He also is the author of many books. One of his best-loved episodes of* The Dick Van Dyke Show *is a* Twilight Zone *parody titled "It May Look Like a Walnut."*

The lesson is to be grateful for the Rod Serlings for as long as we have them. I always was. Let me tell you, one of the best times I had on *The Dick Van Dyke Show* was when I was able to do a satire based on *The Twilight Zone*. Another wonderful time in my life was when I was honored to meet with Rod Serling when he asked me to appear in an episode of *Night Gallery*.

NOBODY LIVES FOREVER
"LONG LIVE WALTER JAMESON"
(ORIGINAL AIRDATE: MARCH 18, 1960)

A corollary lesson to "make the most of the time you've got" is the reminder that "nobody lives forever." Few of us are comfortable with the notion that, yep, our ticket is stamped. We just don't know the day and time. One day, this planet will go on spinning its merry old way and we won't be on it. Make peace with it. Horror stories, like their ancient-myth ancestors, are often used to wrap our minds around unpleasant realities we don't like to think about as we go through our days. Mortality zooms near the top of that list. We keep the very idea of it at arm's length. We try not to think about it. But death is, as Harlan Ellison once said, hovering there, right out of view, near your shoulder, "like a salivating fan boy at a *Star Trek* convention." We're all going to die, so an episode like "Ninety Years Without Slumbering" reminds us to live rather than obsess about the inevitable. An episode like "Long Live Walter Jameson" reminds us that nobody lives forever. But, as the episode suggests, nobody should.

A first-season episode written by Charles Beaumont, "Long Live Walter Jameson" stars Kevin McCarthy as a college professor who is "popular beyond words." He has a startling firsthand grasp of his subject. He makes history come alive, talking to his students as if he actually had been there. And you guessed it. He was. An elderly colleague, Samuel Kittridge (Edgar Stehli), guesses the truth. He realizes that, in Serling's words, "Walter Jameson has access to knowledge that couldn't come out of a volume of history but rather from a book on black magic." When Kittridge finds a photograph of a Civil War officer who looks exactly like Jameson, the handsome professor reveals his dark secret. He was given the gift of immortality more than two thousand years ago by an alchemist. Jameson was one of those trying to keep death at arm's length, and he believed the trick could be pulled off on a permanent basis. "I was like you, Sam, afraid of death," Jameson tells Kittridge. "And when I thought of all the things there were to know, and the miserable few years that a man had to know them, it seemed senseless. . . . Only if a man lived forever, I thought, could there be any point in living at all."

He paid dearly for the gift, and he's still paying for it. Like Walter Bedeker in "Escape Clause," he quickly discovered that immortality was more of a curse than a gift. Over the centuries, he has outlived wives, children, and friends. Death, as Wanda Dunn learns in George Clayton Johnson's "Nothing in the Dark," can come as a friend, not an enemy to be feared. Walter knows this now. "It's death that gives this world its point. . . . I'm tired of living," he says. "I want to die." But he lacks the courage to kill himself with the revolver he keeps in his desk drawer.

Also, he has fallen in love with Kittridge's daughter, Susanna (Dody Heath), and intends to marry her. Kittridge threatens to tell Susanna the truth, but Jameson correctly points out that the truth will sound like madness. Yet the past has a way of catching up with you, particularly if your past spans centuries. Laurette Bowen (Estelle Winwood) shows up at Jameson's home. An old woman, she is a wife abandoned by him long ago. She does not lack the courage to use the revolver. She shoots Jameson, and Kittridge arrives on the scene in time to see his colleague rapidly age and turn to dust.

Beaumont, as previously noted, valiantly tried to make the most of his talents and time before his death on February 21, 1967. By 1963, most of Beaumont's friends knew something was terribly wrong. The incredibly prolific and imaginative writer suddenly looked much older. Never in robust health, this twentieth-century master of the horror story was trapped in a nightmare, diagnosed with having Alzheimer's or Pick's disease (maybe both). His symptoms included an acceleration of the aging process, with progressive loss of memory and coordination. His dear friend William F. Nolan told *Twilight Zone* historian Marc Scott Zicree that, "Like his character Walter Jameson, he just dusted away."

Writers, though, do get to prolong their lives through the alchemy of storytelling. They get to live on, if they can write stories that never get old—stories as powerful and enduring as "Long Live Walter Jameson." The story certainly remained a special memory for the man who played Walter Jameson.

"People associate me with the fantasy and science-fiction genre," McCarthy told me during a 1996 interview, "but that really comes down to two roles: Miles Bennell in *Invasion of the Body Snatchers* and Walter Jameson on *The Twilight Zone*. They always remember that I was the guy who lived to be more than two thousand years old and then vanished into dust when I was finally accosted and shot by the wonderful Estelle Winwood."

When McCarthy filmed a cameo appearance for the 1978 remake of *Invasion of the Body Snatchers* (with Donald Sutherland and Leonard Nimoy), the cast and crew marveled at how little the actor had changed since the 1956 original. They wondered if the Walter Jameson story was merely a story.

In 1983, McCarthy was tapped by director Joe Dante to appear in his reworking of Jerome Bixby's "It's a Good Life" for *Twilight Zone: The Movie* (the segment also featured *Twilight*

Zone veterans Bill Mumy, Patricia Barry, and William Schallert). Dante had already used McCarthy in the 1981 werewolf film *The Howling*.

"I don't know if my character's name is on the screen or not, but it's supposed to be Walter Jameson," McCarthy said. "That was Joe Dante's idea. He said, 'Let's call him Walter Jameson.' And there was a scene that actually got lost because of a technical problem with the film exposure. But I had a scene, just as I am about to be blown away by the kid's powers. I fling myself into a chair and dig out of the chair a big bottle of booze. I take a last drink, because I know I'm going, and then I say, 'Well, this *is* the last of Walter Jameson!' That never got into the movie. They said it was because of a chemical problem with the film processing, but maybe they just had it with me."

REMEMBER YOUR HAPPY PLACE

"THE SIXTEEN-MILLIMETER SHRINE"

(ORIGINAL AIRDATE: OCTOBER 23, 1959)

"A WORLD OF DIFFERENCE"

(ORIGINAL AIRDATE: MARCH 11, 1960)

"A STOP AT WILLOUGHBY"

(ORIGINAL AIRDATE: MAY 6, 1960)

"MR. BEVIS"

(ORIGINAL AIRDATE: JUNE 3, 1960)

"KICK THE CAN"

(ORIGINAL AIRDATE: FEBRUARY 9, 1962)

"ON THURSDAY WE LEAVE FOR HOME"

(ORIGINAL AIRDATE: MAY 2, 1963)

Harried advertising executive Gart Williams (James Daly) is unhappy at work and unhappy at home. His relentless boss at the agency has driven him to the point of collapse. Gart's self-centered wife is oblivious to the strain on him, callously replying with nothing but soul-withering contempt. There's no place he can find peace . . . except Willoughby. And here he is happy. Here he is serene.

But where is Willoughby? Going home on the train, Gart falls asleep and dreams that he's on an old-fashion train making a stop at Willoughby. The small town is a restful spot "where a man can slow down to a walk and live his life full measure." It is July 1880. It is Gart's happy place. And he escapes there in his sleep. Or is it a dream? He's not so sure, and neither are we. When he awakes, the conductor assures him that there is no town named Willoughby. As his life continues to spiral out of control, the increasingly weary Gart is determined to find his way back to Willoughby and stay there. And we're rooting for just that.

Gart, of course, is the main character in one of Rod Serling's finest episodes, "A Stop at Willoughby." Whatever Willoughby is, and wherever it is, it represents that place we all need to escape to now and then. When stress and pressure wear us down, making it difficult to laugh or even smile, we need that place of

Weary businessman Gart Williams (James Daly) longs for different kind of life in "A Stop at Willoughby."
Courtesy CBS Photo Archive

refuge. We need a happy place. We need our Willoughby. If you don't have one, then get one.

Metaphorically, Serling's classic first-season story zeroes in on a yearning deep inside all of us. Gart is not alone, either in real life or on *The Twilight Zone*. Many an episode follows a sympathetic character like Gart, searching for his or her happy place. Each, like Gart, feels trapped. They might be trapped by the rat race or age or loneliness or circumstances or bad luck or a relationship or environment. They are very different people from different walks of life. Yet they share that aching for the sanctuary where they can be happy.

For faded film star Barbara Jean Trenton (Ida Lupino), in "The Sixteen-Millimeter Shrine," it's a matter of age. Her happy place is the Hollywood of her youth, and she tries to recapture that time by constantly running her old movies in the screening room of her mansion. Yes, we just arrived at the intersection of *Sunset Boulevard* and *The Twilight Zone*. The world has changed and passed her by, as happens to so many characters in Serling stories and *Twilight Zone* episodes. She was big; it's her world that got small. She's ready for her close-up, Mr. Serling. She's ready to escape to her happy place. And she does. She is drawn onto the screen and into the past, surrounded by the forever-young stars of her halcyon Hollywood days. Realizing what has happened, Barbara Jean's friend and agent, Danny Weiss (Martin Balsam), remarks, "To wishes, Barbie. To the ones that come true."

Serling adds a tribute: "to the strange, mystic strength of the human animal, who can take a wishful dream and give it a dimension of its own." This is precisely what elderly Charles Whitley does in George Clayton Johnson's third-season episode "Kick the Can." He remembers his happy place—an eternal summer place where the days and nights are filled with games of kick the can. But he, too, is trapped. He, too, will make a clean break of it. Arthur Curtis takes a different route in

Richard Matheson's first-season episode "A World of Differ-ence," escaping . . . where? Into a film role or back to reality? We're not quite sure if Arthur has slipped into a parallel dimen-sion where he is known as Jerry Raigan, an actor hired to play Arthur Curtis, or if Jerry is having a psychotic break and yearns to be Arthur. It doesn't matter, because the movie set that rep-resents the office of businessman Arthur Curtis is the only means of escape. It is the only link to his happy place. And he must get to that set before it is torn down.

The solutions for Gart, Barbara Jean, Charles, and Arthur are extreme, no doubt, and they have both a dreamlike and night-mare quality to them. Yet we feel happy for them because they have made it . . . all the way to their happy places. Our solution does not need to be anywhere near this drastic. It can be just a momentary escape: a few balance-restoring moments that per-mit us to breathe easier, smile more readily, and think more clearly. Sometimes, all it takes is a meditative moment on what truly makes us happy.

Case in point, someone we've encountered a couple of times before, Mr. James B. W. Bevis. Many closely related lessons ap-ply to the story of "Mr. Bevis," another of Serling's first-season episodes. He's a useful fellow, this James B. W. Bevis. We've used him for "be your own person" and "to thine own self be true." Bevis realizes the importance of these lessons because he re-members his happy place. And what makes James B. W. Bevis happy is not money, success, or security. It's putting a smile on the faces of other inhabitants of this globe. He can't have both. He opts for happiness. He joyfully rejects the corrosive pursuit of the almighty dollar, returning to a happy place filled with zither music, stuffed animals, and the works of Charles Dickens.

Again and again, *The Twilight Zone* shows us that we are re-warded for cherishing our happy places and keeping them alive. But one of the most heartrending of all the episodes, Ser-ling's "On Thursday We Leave for Home," poignantly drives

James Whitmore delivers a stunning performance as William Benteen in Rod Serling's "On Thursday We Leave for Home." *Courtesy CBS Photo Archive*

home the lesson from the opposite direction. Thanks to Serling's writing and a towering performance by James Whitmore, this fourth-season episode is a pain-etched reminder of what can happen if we forget our happy place.

Whitmore is brilliant as William Benteen, the leader of a colony on a desolate planet with two suns. The unforgiving terrain is rocky and barren in this isolated settlement where hope is battered by meteor showers, forever day, and scorching heat. Benteen manages to keep hope alive among the 187 survivors. He does this by telling them stories of the Earth, a blue world where the sun disappears at night, wrapping its occupants in quiet, coolness, and darkness. He tells them of snow and clouds. He tells them of autumn colors. He takes them to a happy place, and, for one more day, they have the strength to go on . . . barely. Benteen was just a boy when the colony began thirty ago, yet he hasn't forgotten home. It is his happy place, and he shares memories of it as a kind of daily psychological sustenance. When a rescue ship arrives, however, Benteen's memories are overrun by the unnerving realization that his people no longer need him. He has been their captain. He has been the absolute authority on this planet. Now he sees it all slipping away from him. Unable to cope with this, he tells his people that he made up the stories about Earth. It isn't a happy place, at all. All his caring has been replaced by megalomaniacal anger. When they unanimously vote against him, Benteen determines to stay on the planet. They plead with him to go with them. They search for him, but he hides until it's too late. Stranded and alone, he suddenly remembers the Earth as it truly is. He has remembered his happy place . . . too late. The hope he gave others he has denied himself.

GUEST LESSON: CHRIS CARTER

Drawing inspiration from teenage memories of the TV movie and short-lived series starring Darren McGavin as supernatural sleuth Carl Kolchak, Chris Carter created The X-Files *(Fox, 1993–2002), the horror–science-fiction series starring David Duchovny and Gillian Anderson as FBI agents Fox Mulder and Dana Scully.* The Twilight Zone *and* Night Gallery *were other influences on Carter's landmark show. He also created three other series for Fox:* Millennium, Harsh Realm, *and* The Lone Gunmen. *There also have been two big-screen* X-Files *movies and a 2016 miniseries. His lesson references "A Penny for Your Thoughts," George Clayton Johnson's second-season episode with Dick York as a man who receives a special power after tossing a coin that lands on its edge.*

I always toss a coin into the box of a beggar, on the off chance it'll land on edge and I'll become a mind reader.

LESSON 38:

FILL YOUR LIFE WITH SOMETHING OTHER THAN HATE

"TWO"
(ORIGINAL AIRDATE: SEPTEMBER 15, 1961)

"ONE MORE PALLBEARER"
(ORIGINAL AIRDATE: JANUARY 12, 1962)

"FOUR O'CLOCK"
(ORIGINAL AIRDATE: APRIL 6, 1962)

"HE'S ALIVE"
(ORIGINAL AIRDATE: JANUARY 24, 1963)

Had it been common currency in the pop culture during the early sixties, the phrase "don't be a hater" would have been enthusiastically endorsed by *The Twilight Zone*. Again and again, the series cautioned against giving into hatred of other people and groups of people. You want to give into hate? Be my guest. There are plenty of worthy and deserving targets for your hatred. Go ahead, by all means, and hate prejudice, ignorance, poverty, injustice, war, famine, and illness. But hating people . . . uh-uh . . . big no-no as far as the show's writers were concerned. They lined up with a fifth-century line written by Saint Augustine, rendered by Gandhi as, "Hate the sin, but love the sinner."

This isn't so much about saving others as it about saving yourself. Those consumed *with* hate will be consumed *by* hate. This message rings out loud and clear across the wide imaginative expanse that is *The Twilight Zone*. In Rod Serling's fourth-season episode "He's Alive," Dennis Hopper plays a young man who is part of a neo-Nazi group. Adolf Hitler literally is alive to him because he follows the path of hate, and is destroyed by it. "Anyplace, everyplace, where's there's hate, where there's prejudice, where there's bigotry, he's alive," Serling warns us. There's a similar warning in "Four O'Clock," his third-season episode about hate-mongering Oliver Crangle (Theodore Bikel), intent on destroying all those he declares evil. His hate rebounds on him, and the fate Crangle has selected for his enemies is visited on him. Much the same thing happens to Paul Radin (Joseph Wiseman) in Serling's third-season episode "One More Pallbearer." The elaborately cruel joke he plays on the objects of his hatred backfires. His hate leaves him a wreck, sitting in the ruins of his own twisted view of the world.

In each of these stories, Serling is demonstrating how hate destroys when it is aimed at people who are, as Dickens put it, "fellow-passengers to the grave, and not another race of creatures. . . ." His stories also underscore how much hate is powered by the twin engines of fear and ignorance. Behind this you can hear the echo of another master of the English language, Shakespeare: "In time we hate that which we often fear." A later English writer, Graham Greene, added, "Hate is an automatic response to fear, for fear humiliates."

Yet how easy it is to slip down this dark back alley of human nature. Hate is a strong emotion, and, I hate to tell you, but, like any strong emotion, it can be incredibly addictive. There is a short-term rush to an explosion of hatred. What you have to remember is that you are always at the center of the explosion. Hatred is an insidious little ogre. Before it destroys you, it delights in weighing you down. This isn't just some malevolent monkey on your back. It's an eight-hundred-pound psychological gorilla. Martin Luther King Jr. had it exactly right when he said, "Hate is too great a burden to bear. I have decided to love."

So hate is destructive and self-destructive. It is corrosive and consuming. It is sneaky and cunning. It is the Devil that takes many forms, making it extremely challenging to be on your guard against it. Therefore, if you need some more reasons, courtesy of *The Twilight Zone* (and others), here are a few more items to consider.

Hate is giving people who don't matter power over you. Let Booker T. Washington field this one: "I will permit no man . . . to narrow and degrade my soul by making me hate him."

Hatred is a lack of understanding and imagination, as Greene observed. So, on top of (or below) everything else, hatred is stupid.

The Twilight Zone works this lesson the other way by showing what happens when characters understand their hatred and let it go. In the episode that opened the third season, Montgomery Pittman's "Two," Charles Bronson and Elizabeth Montgomery played the only occupants of a war-ravaged village. They are soldiers on opposite sides of a presumably apocalyptic conflict (although Pittman keeps things on the most general terms, never even telling us the two characters' names). Only when they can put aside their hatred can they truly see each other. Then there is reason to hope. Then there is the possibility of love. It is a moment that recalls another observation by Martin Luther King Jr.: "Darkness cannot drive out darkness; only light can do that. Hate cannot drive out hate; only love can do that."

"Two" does not suggest that letting go of hate is easy. Indeed, Pittman is an insightful observer who keenly understands that it's exceedingly hard to find that road and stay on it. He shows how difficult it is to get past fear, mistrust, and ignorance. Pittman is in no way saying it's easy, but he *is* cautioning that, for individuals and for the human race, it is the only way to go. Love may not conquer all, but it is preferable to hate, which has a nasty tendency to destroy all—everything in its path, then double-backing on the hater.

TO FORGIVE IS DIVINE

"DUST"

(ORIGINAL AIRDATE: JANUARY 6, 1961)

The redemptive nature of forgiveness is a gospel teaching that finds great resonance on *The Twilight Zone*. And as commandments go, they don't come any tougher than the one about how to treat your enemies. We're supposed to forgive them. More than that, we're supposed to *love* them. You find this monumentally challenging mandate in both the gospels of Matthew and Luke. If you love only those who love you, we are asked, well, where's the challenge in that?

Many a modern psychiatrist will say that when we judge others, we're really judging ourselves; when we forgive others, we're forgiving ourselves. Back in Matthew, we find the promise that if we forgive, we'll be forgiven. Whether the reasoning comes from psychiatry or religion, philosophy or *The Twilight Zone*, forgiveness is something highly prized—difficult to achieve but something to work toward.

Errare humanum est. For those of you not up on your Latin, that is the ancient proverb you know as "To err is human." And that's how it stood for many centuries, until in 1711, English poet Alexander Pope added the familiar second line, "to forgive, divine." Ah, that's what was missing. The first half is basically Latin for, "Hey, lighten up, we all make mistakes." It's a reminder that we're all human and therefore prone to error. Go a little easy on the neighbor, teammate, coworker, or relative who goofs up today. There's a good chance you'll be cast in the role of the goofball tomorrow. Pope takes this a step further. Nothing special about making mistakes. But to forgive, now that's something special. In fact, you know what it is? It's downright divine. Yet in this acknowledgment that forgiveness is a divine virtue, there is the realization of how hard it is for mere mortals. It is something to aim for, even though we know how often we will fall woefully short of the target. There are moments, however, that show what we're capable of as individuals and as a species. Rod Serling explores this in his second-season episode "Dust."

Set in a shabby little windswept town, the Western tale opens on the day when young Luis Gallegos (John Alonso) is to be hanged. He got drunk and ran over a little girl with his wagon, killing her. He didn't mean to do it, of course, but the townspeople are not in a forgiving mood. A village of "crumbling clay and rotting wood," as Serling tells us, it has a virus. This virus is a collective loss of faith and hope. And without faith and hope, there is no possibility of forgiveness. Sykes (Thomas Gomez), a cynical and mean-spirited peddler, delights in taunting the conscience-stricken Luis. He even boasts about the rope he sold the town for the execution. He also accuses Sheriff Koch (John Larch) of being partial to "foreigners." "When this day is over, which one will you weep for, Koch?" Sykes asks. Koch answers, "I have tears enough for both."

Playing on the desperation of the condemned man's father (Vladimir Sokoloff), Sykes sells him a bag of "magic dust" for a hundred pesos. He says the dust "makes people love and forgive." It is, of course, only dirt, but the father believes in the magic. As his son is about to be hanged, the old man throws the dust over the crowd in front of the gallows. "You must pay heed to the magic!" he shouts. "It is for love." He is stopped by the terrible sound of the trapdoor of the gallows being released. To the amazement of all, Luis is alive. The rope broke. The most amazed of all is Sykes, who says it was a brand-new five-strand hemp rope: "Nobody could have broken it. It couldn't have gotten broken!"

The parents of the dead girl decide there might be another hand in such a startling turn of events. They give Luis back to his father. The magic, which is forgiveness, has worked. "One victim is enough," the girl's father says. After the crowd has dispersed, three young children approach Sykes, who tosses them the money he received for the "magic dust." They look doubtful until he tells them to take it. The magic even works on him.

Most of the episode shows human beings as we typically are, forgetting that to err is so distinctly human. Some of the episode shows us at our worst, circling around death and misery in an approximation of a vulture dance. The conclusion, though, is what we're capable of at those rare moments when the magic works. Nobody is confusing us with anything divine. We're simply not that forgiving. But, yes, we have our moments. And sometimes, moments are enough.

LESSON 40:

PAYBACK IS A . . . OR, WHAT GOES AROUND COMES AROUND

"JUDGMENT NIGHT"
(ORIGINAL AIRDATE: DECEMBER 4, 1959)

"DEATHS-HEAD REVISITED"
(ORIGINAL AIRDATE: NOVEMBER 10, 1961)

"FOUR O'CLOCK"
(ORIGINAL AIRDATE: APRIL 6, 1962)

"HE'S ALIVE"
(ORIGINAL AIRDATE: JANUARY 24, 1963)

"A SHORT DRINK FROM A CERTAIN FOUNTAIN"
(ORIGINAL AIRDATE: DECEMBER 13, 1963)

"THE BRAIN CENTER AT WHIPPLE'S"
(ORIGINAL AIRDATE: MAY 15, 1964)

Poetic payback. Righteous reciprocity. Just deserts. A dose of one's own medicine. Repaid in kind. Reaping what one sows. However you define it, cosmic karma is a house specialty on *The Twilight Zone*. We might subtitle this entry, "Taking it in the shorts in the land of superstition and knowledge." What goes around, comes around; and if you throw around evil, hateful, petty stuff in this realm, expect providence's boomerang to be swishing its way toward the back of your skull. When an eminently worthy target gets clobbered in a *Twilight Zone* tale, you almost can hear the repeated refrain of "he had it coming" in the "Cell Block Tango" number from *Chicago*.

Members of the Third Reich were number-one comeuppance

Rod Serling welcomes Robby the Robot to *The Twilight Zone.* *Courtesy CBS Photo Archive*

targets in this fifth dimension. Serling's passion burned hot in the episodes he wrote about the Nazis, including the powerful "Judgment Night" and the even more powerful "Deaths-head Revisited." Still, the dramatist knew that the punishments must fit the crimes. In the first season's "Judgment Night," a German named Carl Lanser (Nehemiah Persoff) finds himself on a British freighter that has lost its convoy. It is 1942, you see, when any British ship in the North Atlantic might be stalked by German U-boats. Yet Lanser has no memory of boarding the S.S. *Queen of Glasgow* or booking passage. He has no idea how he got on board. He seems at first nervous, then fearful. He tells those on board that a U-boat is stalking the *Glasgow* and that something will happen at 1:15 a.m. At that precise time, a U-boat does indeed surface. Lanser grabs binoculars and spots the German commander. He is looking at himself. The *Glasgow* is sunk and the survivors are wiped out by machine guns. A lieutenant aboard the sub wonders if their actions court damnation. His captain brushes aside the suggestion, but what's awaiting him is a Flying Dutchmen kind of Hell. He will be sailing on the *Glasgow* forever, experiencing the terror of its sinking again and again and again. "This is what is meant by 'paying the fiddler,'" Serling tells us about this exercise in payback. "This is the comeuppance awaiting every man when the ledger of his life is opened and examined, the tally made, and then the reward or the penalty paid. And in the case of Carl Lanser . . . this is the penalty. This is the justice meted out. This is judgment night in the Twilight Zone."

Justice is also awaiting Gunther Lutze, the former SS captain played by Oscar Beregi in Serling's third-season episode "Deaths-head Revisited." "He was a black-uniformed, strutting animal whose function in life was to give pain," Serling says, "and, like his colleagues of the time, he shared the one affliction most common amongst that breed known as Nazis: he walked the Earth without a heart." Lutze is happily reliving his SS days during a visit to Dachau. He is not haunted by any sense of re-gret, guilt, or self-recrimination. Indeed, for Lutze, this trip is an exercise in nostalgia. Strolling through the concentration camp, he encounters Becker (Joseph Schildkraut), a former in-mate. Becker is a ghost, a spokesman for the rest of the camp's victims. These specters from the past put Lutze on trial. Found guilty, he is sentenced to suffer the misery and agonies of those who died under his brutal command. The pain drives Lutze insane. An attending doctor can't imagine what could have caused such a quick breakdown. Then, looking at what sur-rounds him, he wonders why Dachau is kept standing. Serling provides the answer with a few moving sentences: "All the Dachaus must remain standing. The Dachaus, the Belsens, the Buchenwalds, the Auschwitzes, all of them. They must remain standing because they are a monument to a moment in time when some men decided to turn the Earth into a graveyard. Into it they shoveled all of their reason, their logic, their knowl-edge, but, worst of all, their conscience. And the moment we forget this, the moment we cease to be haunted by its remem-brance, then we become the gravediggers. Something to dwell on and remember, not only in the Twilight Zone, but wherever men walk God's Earth."

Not all those on the receiving end of karma are guilty of crimes as heinous as those listed on the ledger sheets for Lanser and Lutze. There are lesser monsters populating the five seasons of *The Twilight Zone*, but, in each case, you can be sure that the punishment will fit the crime. In Serling's "Four O'Clock," for instance, hate-mongering Oliver Crangle (Theodore Bikel) shrinks to a height of two feet, the fate he had selected for those he considered evil. That swishing sound you hear is a boomerang making its way through the Twilight Zone, back toward Oliver. In Serling's fifth-season episode "The Brain Center at Whip-ple's," coldhearted factory owner Wallace V. Whipple (Richard Deacon) uses automation to throw thousands of employees out of work, only to be ultimately replaced by a robot. In another of Serling's fifth-season episodes, "A Short Drink from a Certain Fountain," a gold digger wife (Ruta Lee) is pleased when her much older husband (Patrick O'Neal) uses an experimental youth serum in a desperate bid to keep up with her. It works . . . too well. He gets younger and younger, until left an infant. The wife is ready to walk out, but her brother-in-law tells her she will stay and take care of the child. She will see to his every need. And if she doesn't consent, she will be cut off without a cent.

Each of these is a case of poetic justice. Yet even Oliver Crangle's fate seems like a light sentence compared to what is waiting for Lanser and Lutze in the Twilight Zone. The hate-mongering fanatic, the coldhearted factory owner, and the gold-digger wife are not condemned to death or to a living death or to reliving death. Serling was making a statement with those extreme types of payoffs and paybacks. He reserved that kind of karma for the most deserving. For instance, Serling again put the Nazi hate machine in his story sights for his fourth-season episode "He's Alive" (just as he would for "The Escape Route," one of three stories that make up his 1969 TV movie, *Night Gallery*). The main character in "He's Alive," neo-Nazi Peter Vollmer (Dennis Hopper), having shot a concentration camp survivor, is shot down by the police. Like Lanser and Lutz, he is on the receiving end of a punishment he visited on others. The ledger sheet shows each has been paid in kind.

DON'T FEAR THE UNKNOWN

"NOTHING IN THE DARK"

(ORIGINAL AIRDATE: JANUARY 5, 1962)

"THE GIFT"

(ORIGINAL AIRDATE: APRIL 27, 1962)

You're sitting in an ultramodern movie theater, surrounded by friends who, like you, are rhythmically swallowing popcorn morsels bathed in an oily substance that is some distant cousin to butter. You're watching a scary movie, and all is right with the world. Then a character on the screen ventures into a dimly lit basement. The one ancient, flickering lightbulb providing any illumination suddenly goes out. The music, already unnervingly eerie, grows in intensity. There is a rustling noise from the other side of the basement. You want to look away but you can't. You hear the figure enveloped by darkness breathing harder, faster. You have no idea what's going to happen next, and you're scared. Intellectually, you know you're safe in the company of dear friends and junk food. Emotionally, you are the character on that screen. You are alone in the dark with your fear. And you're scared . . . scared . . . scared of what? Well, you're scared of what might happen next. What *is* going to happen next? You don't know, and that, ladies and gentlemen, is why you're scared.

I think we can all agree that H. P. Lovecraft, whatever his

failings, knew something about fear. The horror master decreed that, "The oldest and strongest emotion of mankind is fear, and the oldest and strongest kind of fear is fear of the unknown." So fearing the unknown is deeply imprinted on our DNA. It's what we do. It's natural . . . didn't say it was smart, but it is natural. When we're young enough to possess all our baby teeth, we fear the unknown thing lurking in a dark closet or underneath the bed. When we're old enough to understand that there's nothing lurking in the closet or under the bed, the fear shrivels up and dies. See, that's what fear is afraid of. It can't stand the light of a little knowledge, a little wisdom, or a little understanding. What do you know? That Franklin Roosevelt quote hits another bull's-eye. Truly, the only thing we have to fear is fear itself. We have the tools to vanquish fear. They are called knowledge and understanding.

"Nothing in life is to be feared, it is only to be understood," said Marie Curie, who I think we can all agree knew something about vanquishing fear. "Now is the time to understand more, so that we may fear less."

We fear what we do not understand. That idea has been expressed many times in many ways in many cultures. And even people who understand it can fall into the fear trap. It could be argued, for instance, that the racist and elitist Lovecraft himself fell prey to fearing things (and people) he did not understand. "The enemy is fear," Gandhi told us. "We think it is hate; but it is fear."

Now, if I have this right, moving the ball around the philosophical infield, understanding eliminates fear, and fear eliminates hate. Fear: if we do not battle it back with knowledge and understanding, we go on fearing what might be lurking in the closet or under the bed. Instead of looking for monsters in the dark corners of our room, however, we go looking in corners of the globe we don't understand—people of different cultures, races, ethnicities, religions, nationalities, beliefs, and political views. Sometimes, to be sure, there are things to fear out there. Too often, though, we let our fear run away with us. How many times in your life have you turned on the light and found nothing at all lurking in the closet?

As the title of one of George Clayton Johnson's episodes suggests, fearful Wanda Dunn (Gladys Cooper) discovers there is nothing in the dark. When she gets to know Mr. Death, the light of knowledge conquers fear. She can leave the dark and move toward the sunlight. And all she's leaving behind in the dark is her fear.

In Rod Serling's third-season episode "The Gift," an alien calling himself Mr. Williams (Geoffrey Horne) befriends a young Mexican orphan named Pedro (Edmund Vargas). He gives Pedro a gift, but before Williams can tell anybody what it is, he is surrounded by soldiers and villagers. He asks Pedro to show them the gift. It is viewed with alarm and suspicion, much as Williams is. They set fire to the gift and kill Williams. The village doctor (Nico Minardos) then reads the unburned fragment of the gift: "Greetings to the people of Earth. . . . We bring you this gift. The following chemical formula is a vaccine against all forms of cancer. . . ." The rest has been lost to the fire—a fire sparked by fear.

"The subject: fear," Serling says in his closing narration. "The cure: a little more faith." Yes, and a little more knowledge and understanding.

> **GUEST LESSON: FRANK SPOTNITZ**
> *Perhaps best known for the eight years he spent as a writer and producer on* The X-Files, *Frank Spotnitz also was a writer-producer on such series as Fox's* Millennium, The Lone Gunmen, *and* Harsh Realm, *as well as Cinemax's* Hunted *and* Strike Back. *He developed* The Man in the High Castle, *an adaptation of the acclaimed 1962 alternate history novel by Philip K. Dick,*

penning the first two episodes of the Amazon series that pre-miered in 2015. His fellow executive producers include Blade Runner *director Ridley Scott and David W. Zucker* (The Good Wife). *He then went to work on* Medici: Masters of Florence, *an eight-part series starring Dustin Hoffman and Richard Madden* (Game of Thrones) *He focuses on an episode written by Charles Beaumont.*

This is a tough one because I could easily cite a dozen episodes that have stayed with me for decades, "Eye of the Beholder" and "Time Enough at Last" being particular favorites. But the episode that I have returned to most often is "Shadow Play." Dennis Weaver's desperate pleas showed the truth in the old adage "Just because you're paranoid doesn't mean they're not out to get you." And the episode's ending was a haunting reminder that happy endings are far from inevitable.

LESSON 42:

PLAY NICE WITH OTHERS
"I SHOT AN ARROW INTO THE AIR"
(ORIGINAL AIRDATE: JANUARY 15, 1960)

"A MOST UNUSUAL CAMERA"
(ORIGINAL AIRDATE: DECEMBER 16, 1960)

"THE RIP VAN WINKLE CAPER"
(ORIGINAL AIRDATE: APRIL 21, 1961)

"THE MIND AND THE MATTER"
(ORIGINAL AIRDATE: MAY 12, 1961)

"THE MASKS"
(ORIGINAL AIRDATE: MARCH 20, 1964)

It sounds so simple and basic and benign. Play nice with others. We not only ask it of our children, we expect it of them. Yet we, meaning adults, rarely set a good example in this regard. Look at what passes for political, religious, or cultural discussion these days. Consider the lack of civility and common courtesy to be found on daytime talk shows, twenty-four-hour news channels, or the comments section of most news articles posted online. Think of the road rage you routinely encounter on the nation's highways or crowded city streets. Think of the rude, angry, and churlish behavior you're bound to encounter everywhere from a movie theater to a line at the supermarket. Think of the ugly, obnoxious, anything-but-sporting outbursts actually cheered and celebrated at "sporting" events. The hypocrisy is simply staggering. Play nice with others?

Why should children listen to adults on this one when adults act so childish (and that designation might be an insult to children, by the way)? The perfectly reasonable kid response to "play nice with others" could be "you first." Do the people to whom we entrust the reins of government play nice with each other? Has "play nice with others" been trampled underfoot by such cynical expressions as "nice guys finish last" and "I got mine"? As a people, a nation, and as a race, we clearly need some remedial work on this one at almost every level. Yes, it sounds fundamental, but it may be the most daunting challenge facing our planet. Where do we start? We start with individual human behavior—yours and mine. And several *Twilight Zone* episodes look at the consequences of not playing nice with others.

In Rod Serling's first-season episode "I Shot an Arrow into the Air," selfish, narcissistic, and opportunistic Corey (Dewey Martin) thinks he can get away with murder because he and his fellow astronauts are on an uninhabited asteroid. They are on Earth, where the law will judge him severely for not playing nice with others. He believes, of course, that he is prolonging his own survival and there will be no consequences for his actions. He has lost his way in the Twilight Zone, however, and he actually is hurting his odds for survival—and there will be consequences.

You see this again with the petty thieves in Serling's second-season episode "A Most Unusual Camera." They also are petty people. They can't even play nice with each other. And it leads to their downfall—figuratively and literally, since each of them falls out of a hotel window. You see it again in another of Serling's second-season episodes, "The Rip Van Winkle Caper." Thieves again fall out, this time over gold. And the wages of sin (and not playing nice with others) is death. And you see it in Serling's fifth-season episode "The Masks," in which we get a family of four that has perfected the art of not playing nice with others. Their penalty is that they must show the world their true faces—ugly, grotesque, distorted visages of vice.

Each of these Serling stories follow characters who must live (or die) with the consequences of their actions. One character gets to learn a valuable lesson and profit by it: Archibald Beechcroft (comedian Shelley Berman) in Serling's "The Mind and the Matter." When we first encounter the bilious Beechcroft in this second-season episode, he is annoyed by . . . well, just about everything. He hates his coworkers at the insurance company. He hates crowds. He hates sharing the planet with other bipedal beings (and the four-legged pets, too). He hates people. It's not exactly that he fails at playing nice with others. It's more like he doesn't even try. Channeling his inner Scrooge, the misanthropic Beechcroft tells his boss, "If I had my way, here's how I'd fix the universe. I'd eliminate the people. I mean, cross 'em off, get rid of them, destroy them, decimate them. And there'd be only one man left—me, Archibald Beechcroft, esquire." He gets his wish, sort of, when Henry (Jack Grinnage), a clumsy coworker gives him a book to make up for spilling coffee on him. The title of this tantalizing tome is *The Mind and the Matter: How You Can Achieve the Ultimate Power of Concentration.* Intrigued, Archibald uses mind control to shut out the world around . . . or, more specifically, the people around him. He starts with his landlady. "Today the landlady," he declares triumphantly, "tomorrow, the world." Through the powers of concentration, he rids his world of everyone but himself. It is his dream come true, but this is *The Twilight Zone,* so it is only a matter of time before the dream turns a trifle sour. It isn't long before solitude turns to boredom and loneliness. So he decides to populate the world with people who look, think, and sound exactly like him. It is at this point that Archibald Beechcroft realizes what an unpleasant, miserable, dyspeptic person he is. He puts the world back the way it was, but, perhaps, with a little more patience, understanding, and enjoyment of his fellow beings. He has discovered, as Serling tells us, "that with all its faults, it may well be that this is the best of all possible worlds." To make the best of it, learn to play nice with others. Fail to do this, and, like Archibald Beechcroft, you're making the worst of it. "People notwithstanding," Serling says of this world, "it has much to offer." It's a lesson Beechcroft learns "through trial and error—mostly error." Beechcroft isn't alone on that, as much as he thinks he wants to be alone.

LESSON 43:

BE CAREFUL WHAT YOU WISH FOR

"TIME ENOUGH AT LAST"
(ORIGINAL AIRDATE: NOVEMBER 10, 1959)

"THE CHASER"
(ORIGINAL AIRDATE: MAY 13, 1960)

"THE MAN IN THE BOTTLE"
(ORIGINAL AIRDATE: OCTOBER 7, 1960)

"THE MIND AND THE MATTER"
(ORIGINAL AIRDATE: MAY 12, 1961)

"ONCE UPON A TIME"
(ORIGINAL AIRDATE: DECEMBER 15, 1961)

"I DREAM OF GENIE"
(ORIGINAL AIRDATE: MARCH 21, 1963)

"THE LAST NIGHT OF A JOCKEY"
(ORIGINAL AIRDATE: OCTOBER 25, 1963)

In addition to the "play nice with others" rule, Shelley Berman's Archibald Beechcroft learns another lesson in Rod Serling's "The Mind and the Matter." He learns one of the most basic rules of life and *The Twilight Zone:* be careful what you wish for. This goes hand in hand with the one about reading contracts correctly and phrasing terms as carefully as possible. Remember, the universe is listening to your wish and the universe has a sense of humor. Rod Serling is listening, and he really has a sense of humor . . . and irony. Archibald wishes that all the people in the world would vanish, and he gets his wish. Be careful what you wish for. Then he is lonely and bored. So he wishes all the people back, but they must look and act like him. Be careful what you wish for. He has placed himself in a world of sour people.

In the Disney world, if you wish upon a star, your dreams come true. In the realm of the Twilight Zone, you can wish upon all the glittering stars that open each trip to this wondrous land, and your dream might come true . . . and it might turn into a nightmare. Fate isn't always kind in this realm. You may get what your heart desires, only to discover that, like a bolt out of the blue, irony steps in and leaves you black and blue. We here in the fifth dimension aren't saying don't make wishes. Often enough, as in "Kick the Can" or "Night of the Meek," there's a good heart and true magic in that wish. But we are stressing caution. Be careful what you wish for.

Henry Bemis wishes he had all the time in the world to read. We know how that works out in Serling's "Time Enough at Last." Arthur Castle wishes for money and to be the ruler of a country. Both wishes take him down dead-end alleys in Serling's "The Man in the Bottle." Roger Shackleforth wishes that the beautiful Leila would return his affections in Robert Presnell Jr.'s "The Chaser." He ends up with a clinging, obsessive wife, and he is miserable. Woodrow Mulligan wishes to escape 1890 for the future in Richard Matheson's "Once Upon a Time." He gets his wish and is desperately unhappy.

The instant gratification of a granted wish is typically a glittering facade with nothing much behind it. It's an empty thing. It's a shimmering soap bubble that bursts soon after being bestowed on those requiring a good lesson more than a quick wish. Two diminutive fellows are on the receiving end of very different lessons in the fourth and fifth seasons of *The Twilight Zone*. "I Dream of Genie," a fourth-season episode by John Furia Jr. features Howard Morris as George P. Haley, a bookkeeper granted one wish by a genie played by Jack Albertson.

"The Last Night of a Jockey," a fifth-season episode by Serling, stars Mickey Rooney as Grady, a crooked jockey who wishes to be big.

For George, it's all about being careful with the wish. He works through possible wishes in his mind, pondering what could go wrong. Smart fellow. You don't meet many of his type on *The Twilight Zone*. Instinctively, he knows it's important to be careful what you wish for. At first, he dreams about wishing for his lady love, Ann (Patricia Barry), but, in his dream, she not only has no time for him, she's cheating on him. He dreams about wishing for great wealth, but this dream merely brings home the adage about money not being able to buy happiness. He then dreams about wishing for power, but this dream collapses under the weight of awesome responsibility. Finally, he has thought it through and makes his wish. The next time someone rubs the lamp, the genie who shows up is George. And he grants three wishes. This is his real heart's desire. It's a happy ending because George has been careful about his wish and because it is a true reflection of his heart and the best of his generous nature. Life didn't treat George with "deference, honor, or success," Serling tells us, yet he is "wise enough to decide on a most extraordinary wish that makes him the contented permanent master of his own altruistic Twilight Zone."

A far different fate awaits the corrupt Grady in "The Last Night of a Jockey." What's in his heart is not so nice, so there will be no genuine caring behind his wish. He's a small man who doesn't realize that standing tall has nothing to do with height. He is, in Serling's words, "one of the rotten apples, bruised and yellowed by dealing in dirt." Banned for life from racing for doping horses, the angry and bitter Grady stews in his shabby hotel room. A voice inside his head—his alter ego—asks him what he wants. Grady is so shortsighted, he can't see this is a trap, and a trap of his own devising. He wants to be big. That's his wish. And the five-foot Grady wakes up eight feet tall. His alter ego tells him his dreams are small. He realizes this, tragically, when the phone call comes from the racing commission, telling him that he has been reinstated as a jockey. But he got what he wished for, and that will prevent him from riding. He begs to be made small again, and his alter ego tells him, "You *are* small." He has learned, too late, as Serling says, "that you don't measure size with a ruler, you don't figure height with a yardstick." You do measure wishes by what's in the heart.

I'm not sure when I first spotted the bumper sticker that declared, "Mean people suck." I *am* sure you can plaster it on any vehicle that might be driving toward that signpost up ahead—the one that says, your next stop, the Twilight Zone. It's a sentiment expressed many times in many ways throughout the show's five-season run. And you can be certain that metaphoric justice will be swift and frightening for a particular classification of mean people: bullies. Perhaps nowhere since the works of Charles Dickens has a bully been so detested as on *The Twilight Zone*. Since its 1959 to 1964 run, the scale and scope of bullying has been better studied, documented, and understood.

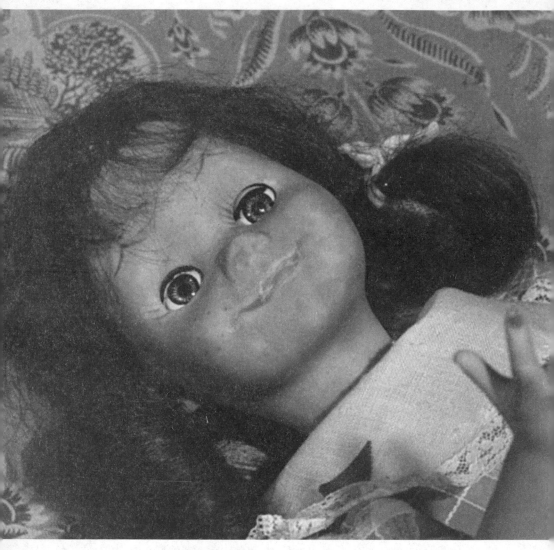

Her name is Talky Tina, and she doesn't like bullies, as we find out in "Living Doll."
Courtesy CBS Photo Archive

We know that, with children, it can cause concentration problems, a loss of interest in school, low self-esteem, anxiety, depression, humiliation, headaches, stomachaches, fear, and alienation. We also know that bullies are not confined to school buses and junior high hallways.

Playgrounds have bullies. Relationships have bullies. The Internet has bullies. Nations have bullies. Families have bullies. Companies have bullies. Neighborhoods have bullies. Religions have bullies. Even nursing homes can have bullies. The awareness that has grown since 1964 is that we all have a part to play in breaking the cycle of bullying, wherever and whenever it occurs. "If you are neutral in situations of injustice, you have chosen the side of the oppressor," said Archbishop Desmond Tutu. "If an elephant has its foot on the tail of a mouse, and you say that you are neutral, the mouse will not appreciate your neutrality."

No such neutrality exists in the Twilight Zone, and the punishment for bullies tends to be extreme. Most pay the ultimate price for their bullying behavior. Bullies get slapped down with the same viciousness they have visited on others. The message, while certainly rudimentary in its approach, pushed us to today's greater awareness concerning bullies and the bullied and the people who observe bullying. Silence, in this case, does amount to consent, and the Twilight Zone is anything but silent when it comes to bullies. Bullying is never okay. That's the message ringing through the wondrous land. Don't be a person who sucks the hope and happiness out of life and replaces it with fear and torment. Don't be a person who watches this and says . . . nothing.

In the flip-the-script world of *The Twilight Zone,* a bully is either facing a death sentence or humiliation. In Rod Serling's first-season episode "What You Need," for instance, the bullying of an elderly man puts Fred Renard into the path of a speeding car. Exit Fred Renard. In Serling's second-season episode "A Thing About Machines," gourmet writer Bartlett Finchley (Richard Haydn) takes out his wrath on machines . . . until the machines fight back and Finchley is found dead at the bottom of his swimming pool. Metaphorically, Finchley is a machine-mangling stand-in for the bully who lashes out at people he believes are helpless to fight back. In Serling's third-season episode "The Little People," astronaut Peter Craig (Joe Maross) finds an alien race of people about the size of insects. He terrorizes them and proclaims himself their god. His bullying comes to an abrupt end when a spaceship lands with two astronauts that make him seem the size of an insect. Craig is crushed to death.

And then there's Erich Streator (Telly Savalas), the bullying stepfather and husband who becomes the victim of Talky Tina, a talking doll that makes good on her threat: "My name is Talky Tina, and you'll be sorry. . . . My name is Talky Tina, and I'm going to kill you." Dolls, like clowns (or clown dolls), can be magnificently unnerving fright figures in the horror realm, and Talky Tina makes the all-scare team in "Living Doll," a fifth-season episode written by Jerry Sohl (although credited to Charles Beaumont, who plotted it with Sohl). Talky Tina, with June Foray providing the creepily cute voice, becomes a little girl's "friend, defender, guardian," as Serling puts it. Streator is heading for a fall, and this one ends at the bottom of a flight of stairs. Renard, Finchley, Craig, and Streator take separate roads that lead to the same dead-end destination in the Twilight Zone.

Sometimes, though, humiliation is the retribution visited on a bully. We've already seen this in Serling's "Four O'Clock," when bullying fanatic Oliver Crangle becomes the victim of the fate he wanted to visit on others: being shrunk to a height of two feet. Another malicious and mean-spirited misanthrope, theater critic Fitzgerald Fortune (Barry Morse), delights in bullying party guests in "A Piano in the House," a third-season episode written by Earl Hamner Jr. He buys a player piano that magically reveals the true nature and innermost secrets people keep hidden. The cynical, sadistic Fortune takes great enjoyment in the humiliation this causes, until fortunes are reversed and he must face the music. The tables are turned by his disgusted wife (Joan Hackett) and the piano reveals that behind the monster is nothing more than a desperately insecure and frightened child who doesn't know how to return love or embrace people.

Humiliation is also visited on the lead character in Serling's fourth-season episode based on a story by Malcolm Jameson, "Of Late I Think of Cliffordville." Ruthless businessman William Feathersmith (Albert Salmi) takes over the company built by a man named Deidrich (John Anderson). Bored with success, Feathersmith makes a deal with devilish Miss Devlin (Julie Newmar) to go back to 1910 and start all over. When he returns to his own time, he is no longer the owner of the company. He is the janitor. The man who was the janitor, Hecate (Wright King), is now the owner. The lesson, Serling tells us, is "that nice guys don't always finish last." And the bullied person who survives and thrives sometimes comes out on top. It's a hopeful message from a dimension where bullying will not be tolerated, the Twilight Zone.

GUEST LESSON: SCOTT SKELTON

Rod Serling scholar Scott Skelton coauthored Rod Serling's Night Gallery: An After-Hours Tour *(1998), with Jim Benson. He and Benson were historical consultants for Universal Studios Home Entertainment's season-two DVD box set for* Night Gallery. *Members of the Rod Serling Books editorial board, they produced a "lost episode" of* Night Gallery *for the season-three box set.*

I was born on October 2, 1959, the very day *The Twilight Zone* premiered, so it seems entirely apt that this particular television series has had much to teach me over the years. As a youngster, sitting in front of that flickering black-and-white screen, the *Zone*'s crackerjack yarns drew me in—the suspense, the twists, the ingenious speculations on "what if?"—tales that sparked my imagination as I watched ordinary, everyday citizens slip through a crack in reality to find themselves immersed in a nightmare world, sometimes of their own making. As I got older, though, the series' strong ethical undercurrents surfaced in my consciousness: its indignant stance on social injustice, its rage at the too often petty nature of our species—prejudice, mob rule, the ever-present threat of fascism, the shadow of superstition and ignorance that has, throughout history, halted the progress of our species. From these bite-size morality plays I drew an unshakable belief in the basic dignity of man—that despite our individual mistakes, our foibles, our follies, and our general bad behavior, we all have a right to respect, to a collective esteem based on the actions and sacrifices of a few of our more noble representatives. In discussing this with my wife, I find she has drawn more succinct lessons: that it's spectacularly satisfying to see the cruel and the malicious punished—in the *Zone*, an often cosmic event. In the world of Rod Serling and his fellow scribes, you can always depend on harsh justice for those among us who choose to live without conscience, compassion, or humanity.

LESSON 45:

REMEMBER THE PEOPLE WHO GOT YOU WHERE YOU ARE

"RING-A-DING GIRL"

(ORIGINAL AIRDATE: DECEMBER 27, 1963)

Somebody on Facebook recently posted an intriguing question to *Twilight Zone* fans: Which episode was the scariest to you? Now, remember, you're not being asked which episode you think is the pinnacle of quality, the most memorable, the best written, or the one with the strongest payoff. No, this question comes with very specific parameters. Which one scared you the most? I liked the question a lot, because it's sort of a Rorschach test that tells you more about the respondent than the episode that gets chosen.

Every semester in my Vampires on Film and Television class at Kent State University, I ask my students to look deep within and tell me what scares them. It's a simple bonding exercise that elicits an amazing array of responses. You get some of the common ones: heights, snakes, drowning, enclosed places, the dark. You get some profound ones: loneliness, eternity, annihilation. One student simply replied, with a shudder, "Octopus." Well, it's their individual fears, and they can't lie to themselves. The first thing I ask them to notice is how different the responses are. Nobody repeats an already admitted fear (I also point out how fears change over time). Then I ask them to name the scariest movie they've ever seen and the scariest book they've ever read. Again, no repeats in the arena of fear. The responses are all over the terror map. What barely raises a goose bump with one student terrorizes another. So I was interested to see how people would respond to the *Twilight Zone* question. Among the episodes mentioned were "The Invaders," "Nightmare at 20,000 Feet," "The After Hours," "Mirror Image," "Long Distance Call," "Eye of the Beholder," "Living Doll," "It's a Good Life," "The Dummy," "Shadow Play," "The Hitch-hiker," and "Night Call." My answer was a tie between episodes: "Twenty Two" and "Ring-a-Ding Girl." What can I say? They were that ones that "did it" to me. They're the ones that got under my skin.

Both episodes culminate with plane crashes, but I've never suffered from even a hint of flight anxiety, so that doesn't fly as a reason (at least, not with me). Besides, the really eerie stuff in Serling's "Twenty Two" occurs before you even know there's a plane in the story. When Liz Powell (Barbara Nichols) leaves her hospital bed at night and finds her way down to the morgue (room twenty-two), well, my frazzled senses were ordered to a state of heightened alert. But then that creepy nurse (Arline Sax) emerged from the depths of the morgue to ominously announce, "Room for one more, honey." And that did it for me.

I found something similarly unnerving about "Ring-a-Ding Girl," a fifth-season episode written by Earl Hamner Jr. I realize that neither of these episodes would make most *Twilight Zone* fans' top-ten list (or top-twenty, for that matter). Doesn't matter. Each got under my skin in ways that more acclaimed episodes never did. Hamner also slipped a message into "Ring-a-Ding Girl" that meant something to him, and increasingly, the older I get, something to me: remember the people who got you where you are. Don't forget where you came from. No matter how high you climb in the world, don't forget you got there by first standing on other people's shoulders.

You sense an appreciation of this running through all of Hamner's work, from the 1963 film *Spencer's Mountain,* with Henry Fonda and Maureen O'Hara, to his long-running semi-autobiographical series *The Waltons.* There is no such thing as a self-made man or woman, although it's human nature to give ourselves way too much credit for our achievements. When we first meet Bunny Blake (Maggie McNamara), she comes across like a Hollywood celebrity who has gone Hollywood in every sense of the term. A film star known as "the ring-a-ding girl," Bunny is about to leave for a flight from Los Angeles to New York. She receives a gift from the fan club in her hometown, Howardville. She is particularly grateful to these fans because the folks of Howardville took up a collection to send her to Hollywood. The present is a ring with an enormous gem, but in that gem she can see the worried faces of people from Howardville. They're telling her she's needed at home. She drops by on the day of the annual Founder's Day picnic. It is her first visit home in five years, and her sister, Hildy (Mary Munday), tells her everybody in town chipped in a dollar for the ring. She's only there for a day, Bunny says, explaining that she should be on her way to location filming in Rome. Bunny asks that the picnic be postponed, but her request is refused. Doctor Floyd (George Mitchell) sees this as the capricious whim of a spoiled star. So Bunny goes on local television and announces she will be performing her one-woman show at the high school auditorium that day only. That will draw most of the people away from the picnic, and Hildy can't believe Bunny could be that selfish and self-centered. But Bunny never shows up at the performance. A plane has crashed into the picnic grounds. Most of Howardville's citizens have been saved because they headed for the auditorium. They are stunned to learn that Bunny is dead.

She was a passenger on the plane. Drawn by the gift of the ring and her love for Howardville, Bunny magically came home long enough to keep loved ones out of harm's way.

If you're looking for a sentiment that captures the spirit of Hamner's episode, you will find it in a novel started one hundred and twenty years before this episode aired. You'll find it in *Martin Chuzzlewit* by Charles Dickens: "Home is a name, a word, it is a strong one; stronger than magician ever spoke, or spirit ever answered to, in the strongest conjuration."

THE CIVILIZATION THAT DOES NOT VALUE THE PRINTED WORD AND THE INDIVIDUAL IS NOT CIVILIZED
"THE OBSOLETE MAN"
(ORIGINAL AIRDATE: JUNE 2, 1961)

In Rod Serling's first-season episode "Time Enough at Last," Burgess Meredith plays a banker who loves to read, even though everyone in his life views him as a foolish little man. In Serling's second-season episode "The Obsolete Man," Meredith plays a librarian who insists on reading, even though a futuristic totalitarian state has banned books and views him as an obsolete little man. Indeed, the state has banned books and religion, libraries and churches. Both a book-loving and God-fearing man, Meredith's aptly named Romney Wordsworth emerges as one of the most heroic individuals in all five seasons of *The Twilight Zone*.

Through Wordsworth's heroism, Serling celebrates the value of the individual and the printed word. As the book and the printed word in our modern world increasingly come under fire, not by the state but by an Internet culture that devours everything in its path, "The Obsolete Man" seems all the more relevant. Its message about the worth of the individual, however, is timeless. "This is not a new world," Serling cautions us. "It is simply an extension that began in the old one." This future "has

Librarian Romney Wordsworth (Burgess Meredith) has the title role in "The Obsolete Man," Rod Serling's cautionary tale about a futuristic society that bans books. *Courtesy CBS Photo Archive*

refinement, technological advances, and a more sophisticated approach to the destruction of human freedom." Lurking in there, do you hear something that perhaps sounds vaguely and disturbingly familiar?

Wordsworth proudly declares his occupation as librarian, even though the state decrees that this profession no longer exists. So he has been called before the chancellor (Fritz Weaver), charged with obsolescence.

"You are obsolete, Mr. Wordsworth," the chancellor declares.

"A lie," he responds. "No man is obsolete. . . . I am nothing more than a reminder to you that you cannot destroy truth by burning pages."

Wordsworth is sentenced to death within forty-eight hours, yet he can choose the time and method of execution. Little does the chancellor suspect that the seemingly powerless Wordsworth has the ideological upper hand. Wordsworth asks that he be assigned an executioner and that only he and the assassin will know the chosen method. He also asks that his death be televised. Believing that executions have an educative effect on the population, the chancellor grants these requests. And the trap has been set. The chancellor asks that Wordsworth set the time and place for execution, and the librarian chooses his room at midnight the next day.

The next evening, the chancellor is at the door of Wordsworth's book-packed room. The condemned man has invited him there, an hour before midnight. The chancellor tells him that, very soon, he will be cringing and pleading for his life. "We'll see then which is the stronger, the state or the librarian," he says. The cocky chancellor doesn't know how right he is. Wordsworth has chosen to die by a bomb hidden in his room. The cameras are rolling. The door is locked. And the chancellor is locked inside with him and the bomb and the great equalizer of death.

Wordsworth calmly reads from his forbidden Bible: "'Yea, though I walk through the valley of the shadow of death, I will fear no evil, for thou art with me. Thy rod and thy staff they comfort me. Thou preparest a table before me in the presence of mine enemies.'" The chancellor grows increasingly nervous. The librarian faces death with grace and courage and conviction. The steely representative of the state begins to crumble. Finally, with seconds left, the Chancellor screams: "Please! Please! Let me out! In the name of God, let me out! Let me out!" In the name of God, Wordsworth does let him out. The bomb goes off just as he gets safely outside. Wordsworth is dead, but the victory is his. The next day, it is the chancellor who has been declared obsolete, and representatives of the state tear him apart.

Meredith and Weaver are sensational in what is essentially a two-person play. Here we have two incredibly fine actors digging deep into a script that speaks to the dignity of the individual and the importance of the printed word. That which fails to recognize these, no matter how strong it might appear, is weak. That which fails to embrace these, no matter how powerful it becomes, is a model of failure.

It is a point underscored by Serling in his closing narration: "Any state, any entity, any ideology that fails to recognize the worth, the dignity, the rights of man, that state is obsolete. A case to be filed under *M* for mankind in the Twilight Zone."

GUEST LESSON: FRITZ WEAVER

I interviewed Tony winner Fritz Weaver for my first book, a history of Virginia's Barter Theatre, which was published in 1982. About thirty-five years after that first conversation, the star of the Twilight Zone episodes "Third from the Sun" and "The Obsolete Man" graciously contributed these lessons for this book:

For "The Obsolete Man": In a world in which everything is, or becomes, obsolete, humanity must never be regarded in that light.

For "Third from the Sun": Imagine the despair of a civilization that, itself collapsing, has targeted the Earth as its "last best hope"!

LESSON 47:
EVERYBODY NEEDS SOMEBODY SOMETIME

"WHERE IS EVERYBODY?"
(ORIGINAL AIRDATE: OCTOBER 2, 1959)

"THE LONELY"
(ORIGINAL AIRDATE: NOVEMBER 13, 1959)

"TWO"
(ORIGINAL AIRDATE: SEPTEMBER 15, 1961)

"THE TRADE-INS"
(ORIGINAL AIRDATE: APRIL 20, 1962)

"MINIATURE"
(ORIGINAL AIRDATE: FEBRUARY 21, 1963)

That great American philosopher Dean Martin had it exactly right. Dino's theme song, "Everybody Loves Somebody Sometime," conveys in mellow tones a theme you find in some of the most poignant and profoundly moving episodes of *The Twilight Zone*. And this goes beyond romantic love, as important as that is in and out of *The Twilight Zone*. Remember, one of the lyrics recorded by Dino in 1964 stresses that everybody finds somebody someplace and to find you must search. And the search for somebody can be out of a need for friendship or simple companionship, as well as for romance. Broaden the scope of this a bit, and we realize that everybody needs somebody sometime. The musical rebuttal might be Paul Simon's "I Am a Rock," first recorded and released a year after "Everybody Loves Somebody Sometime." In Simon's bitter song, the

Charles Bronson is one of the two in writer-director Montgomery Pittman's "Two."

Courtesy CBS Photo Archive

narrator defiantly declares he doesn't need anybody. He has built a fortress of walls around himself, with no need of love or friendship. He is an island unto himself, isolated and beyond the touch of companionship of any kind. And he's convincing precisely no one. It is a song about a person lying to himself. We feel the pain he claims not to feel. We know his way doesn't work—can't work. We know because, in 1624, English poet John Donne told us, "No man is an island, entire of itself." We know because we've been to the Twilight Zone.

Indeed, the very first *Twilight Zone* episode explores that basic human need for other humans. Earl Holliman plays Mike Ferris, the character who asks the desperate question that becomes the episode's title, "Where Is Everybody?" Ferris, suffering from amnesia, finds himself in a small town that has everything but people. He doesn't know who he is. He doesn't know how he got there. His only clue is the air force jumpsuit he's wearing. He's air force, but nothing else makes any sense to him.

We've all dreamed about having the world to ourselves, or at least a corner of it. But, for Ferris, the dream takes on the dimensions of a nightmare. The loneliness continues to build, until he's crushed beneath its awful burden. It's then we learn that Ferris is an astronaut in training. He has spent 484 hours in an isolation booth, and his wanderings through this empty town have been a hallucination. Serling tells us that "up there is an enemy known as isolation." Down here, too.

Issues of loneliness, alienation, and isolation are probed to great dramatic effect in many episodes of *The Twilight Zone*. Serling immediately returned to this theme with another early first-season episode, "The Lonely," starring Jack Warden as James A. Corry, a convicted murderer sentenced to solitary confinement on an asteroid nine million miles from Earth. "Witness, if you will, a dungeon made out of mountains, salt flats, and sand that stretch to infinity," Serling tells us. "Now witness, if you will, a man's mind and body shriveling in the sun—a man dying of loneliness." Four years into his fifty-year sentence, Corry knows he is innocent. He killed in self-defense. He also knows his sanity is on the line. His only respite from boredom and isolation is the supply ship that visits his desert dungeon four times a year. Taking pity on Corry, supply ship captain Allenby (John Dehner) leaves behind a box containing Alicia (Jean Marsh), a robot programmed with emotions and a memory track. She can reason, think, and speak. Corry at first views her as an illusion—a lie that mocks his loneliness. Gradually, though, he falls in love with her. He's not lonely anymore. But then the supply ship arrives with the news of his pardon. Allenby tells Corry he can only take fifteen pounds of gear with him. Corry refuses to leave Alicia behind, claiming she is a woman. Allenby finally must shoot Alicia directly in the face to reveal the wires and circuitry of a robot. "All you're leaving behind is loneliness," Allenby tells him. "I must remember that," Corry responds. "I must remember to keep that in mind."

The episode that launched the third season, writer-director Montgomery Pittman's "Two" is set in the ruins of a village. "It's been five years since a human being walked these streets," Serling says. "This is the first day of the sixth year." War has devastated the village and, we assume, the planet. We follow two survivors—a man and a woman—around the streets They were soldiers on opposite sides of the conflict. They are first suspicious and antagonistic, but the man (Charles Bronson) has had his fill of killing. The woman (Elizabeth Montgomery), who is warming up to him, sees old propaganda posters and, well, old habits die hard. She takes a few shots at him. Humans, huh? Can't live with 'em, can't live without 'em. Never fear. Love conquers all. The need for romance and companionship trumps hatred and mistrust. The man takes off his uniform and dons civilian duds. The woman puts on a dress they spotted in a store window. "This has been a love story about two lonely people who found each other," Serling says.

Another third-season episode, "The Trade-Ins," shows how lonely elderly John Holt (Joseph Schildkraut) would be if there was any distance at all between himself and his beloved wife, Marie (Alma Platt). John has the chance to rid himself of crippling pain by transplanting his mind and personality into an artificial body. The Holts have the money for only one operation. John realizes the loneliness of going on without Marie would be more painful than any physical ailments. He doesn't need a new body. He needs Marie.

And then there is "Miniature," Charles Beaumont's beautifully crafted fourth-season episode starring Robert Duvall as Charley Parkes, a lonely and shy bachelor who becomes fascinated by a museum display with a nineteenth-century dollhouse. To his delight, a wooden doll comes to life, playing a Mozart sonata on a miniature harpsichord. He thinks this is part of the display and asks a museum employee how it all works. The guard thinks he's joking. He points to a sign that says this nineteenth-century townhouse is a model of the Boston residence of Mr. and Mrs. Copley Summers. The figure represents their daughter, Alice. The artist used wood from the original balcony to carve this remarkable likeness. Again and again, this lifeless figure of the beautiful Alice seems very much alive in his presence. To everyone else, she is just an inanimate doll. Finally, he finds the doll crying. She is lonely. He is, too. Charley tells her he understands. "There's always loneliness and suffering and heartache," Charley says. "Look at you. Crying because you're alone. Well, I've been alone all my life. . . . We could understand each other and help each other and love each other. If only . . ."

That's as far as he gets. His family and doctor come looking for him. He is nowhere to be found. The museum guard is astonished to see Charley sitting happily with Alice in the dollhouse.

Everybody needs somebody sometime. And their sometime is now . . . in the Twilight Zone.

THE UNIVERSE DOES NOT REVOLVE AROUND YOU

"THE MIND AND THE MATTER"
(ORIGINAL AIRDATE: MAY 12, 1961)

"SHOWDOWN WITH RANCE McGREW"
(ORIGINAL AIRDATE: FEBRUARY 2, 1962)

"A PIANO IN THE HOUSE"
(ORIGINAL AIRDATE: FEBRUARY 16, 1962)

"A KIND OF STOPWATCH"
(ORIGINAL AIRDATE: OCTOBER 18, 1963)

"SOUNDS AND SILENCES"
(ORIGINAL AIRDATE: APRIL 3, 1964)

The 6.7 magnitude Northridge earthquake rumbled through Southern California at 4:31 a.m. on January 17, 1994. It was one heck of a wake-up call for the television critics gathered at Pasadena's Ritz-Carlton Huntington Hotel for their semiannual press tour. Those critics included one of my closest friends, Tom Feran, representing Cleveland's *Plain Dealer,* and me, then with the *Akron Beacon Journal.* You know, I'd read somewhere that you can hear a major earthquake before you feel it—and what you hear sounds like a freight train bearing down on you. An editor once told me that this description had entered the realm of cliché, but I assure you there's nothing cliché about it when that's what jars you from a sound sleep. After the hotel's violently rattling windows helped announce the earthquake's imminent arrival, the ground liquefied under that grand old hotel, temporarily turning beds into surfboards. There was an enormous dresser to the left of my bed, and the top half housed a television set behind two highly polished wooden doors. Like something out of a horror movie, those doors swung open and that TV set started to emerge from its cave, trundling down the sliding track on which it was mounted. I watched in morbid fascination as the set continued its journey, realizing that, if it reached the end of that track, it might well tip over and fall directly on my head. "Oh, great," I remember thinking, "I'm going to be killed by my beat. They'll be identifying me through dental records. And I'm pretty certain they won't let you into Heaven if you arrive wearing a TV set. And what the heck was I watching when I fell asleep a few hours ago?" But the set stopped short of committing criticide. Jolted awake and jostled out of bed, badly shaken hotel guests gathered on the lawn. Hastily grabbed jackets and robes offered some protection against the morning chill. But nothing could keep off the chilling questions hanging in the predawn air. Was it safe to go back in the hotel? Was another, perhaps bigger, quake on the way? What did the greater Los Angeles area look like out there? The expressions on the faces I encountered ranged from apprehensive to terrified . . . until . . . wandering through the shivering crowd, I spotted the calm, determined figure of Tom Feran. He was a man with a purpose. I wondered what that purpose could be. Stopping directly in front of me, he said in a conspiratorial yet completely matter-of-fact way, "Hey, let's go loot the Starbucks." That's Tom. The editor of the *Harvard Lampoon* in his college days, he has the gift of not taking himself too seriously.

Still, you simply haven't experienced an earthquake until you've gone through one with a hotel full of self-absorbed, whiny critics, who are, after all, professional complainers. Tom and I soon realized that many (though hardly all) of our colleagues viewed the earthquake as something staged for their personal annoyance. If one of these critics had been asked to cover this as a breaking story, the headline would have read, "Massive earthquake rocks Los Angeles, critics inconvenienced." Look, folks, we rode out that earthquake in a luxury hotel without loss of electricity or phone service, and the ultimate privation? What, no melon balls on the morning buffet? At this point, I fully expected to see Rod Serling standing behind us.

We're all guilty of this kind of thinking now and then. We all have moments when we think the universe revolves around us. If this becomes a pattern, however, expect a visit to that universe known as the Twilight Zone. This is what happens to Archibald Beechcroft, Shelley Berman's character in Serling's "The Mind and the Matter." He knows the universe was made for him, and these annoying creatures called human beings are there to bother him. He needs some perspective. He needs a good lesson. And he gets one.

So does egotistical, temperamental, demanding cowboy star Rance McGrew (Larry Blyden) in Serling's third-season episode "Showdown with Rance McGrew." His lesson arrives from the Twilight Zone courtesy of the real Jesse James (Arch Johnson). Straight-shooting Jesse punctures the phony-baloney windbag, completely deflating Rance's oversize ego. This is played as the stuff of comedy, but another third-season episode, "A Piano in the House," is a tragedy of sorts by Earl Hamner Jr. Theater critic Fitzgerald Fortune (Barry Morse) has Beechcroft's sour disposition and McGrew's self-centered nature. It's an ugly combination, and the egotist who presents himself as a giant is revealed to be a pathetic and frightened child.

Two fifth-season episodes also result in hard lessons for windy individuals who fail to realize that the universe does not revolve around them. Serling's "A Kind of a Stopwatch" (based on a story by Michael D. Rosenthal) introduces us to Patrick Thomas McNulty (Richard Erdman), "a dull, argumentative, bigmouth." He is given the gift of a stopwatch that freezes time and everything in the world, except the person who possesses it. When McNulty decides to use the watch to rob a bank, it gets broken. The world around him is frozen, and, when he talks, no one can hear him.

Roswell G. Flemington (John McGiver) is also in love with sound—the sound of his own voice when shouting commands and very loud nautical sounds (horns, whistles, naval battles, you name it). The owner of a model-ship company and the lead character in "Sounds and Silences," he bellows orders in the manner of a captain on the deck. When his wife leaves him, he is pleased. He no longer needs to share the center of his noisy universe. Then, of course, he is put on the receiving end of po-etic justice. The slightest sound, even a dripping faucet, is ear-splitting to him. For the first time, he wants quiet. A psychiatrist convinces him to use mind control to reduce the noise. It works, but then everything sounds like the merest whisper or squeak. The S.S. *Roswell G. Flemington* has run aground because he charted an unsound course that took him directly into the Twi-light Zone. With all that self-generated noise, he couldn't hear the alarm bells. Did you really think the likes of Flemington, McNulty, Fortune, and McGrew would be allowed to quietly get a pass? Wouldn't hear of it. They are at the center of a uni-verse, all right. They are the bull's-eye on a target, and the darts heading their way have been dipped in an acidic substance known as comeuppance.

NEVER CRY WOLF
"HOCUS-POCUS AND FRISBY"
(ORIGINAL AIRDATE: APRIL 13, 1962)

To my mind, the best retelling of Aesop's the Boy Who Cried Wolf can be found in the "Foney Fables" cartoon released by Warner Bros. in 1942. With the marvelous Mel Blanc providing many of the voices, the eight-minute animated romp presents the boy who cried wolf as an obnoxious practical joker who enjoys seeing people rush to his rescue, then, between derisive laughter, exclaim in distinctly Noo Yawk tones, "What a jerk! What a dope!" "There's a lad who could stand some discipline," the narrator observes. "He'll learn his lesson someday." He repeats the gag again and again, until, in the final scene, it's the wolf cackling away while happily picking his teeth.

Twenty years after this Merrie Melodies cartoon, *The Twilight Zone* presented its own variation on the Boy Who Cried Wolf. Based on an unpublished story by Frederic Louis Fox, Serling's lighthearted third-season episode was titled "Hocus-Pocus and Frisby." Veteran character actor Andy Devine, known for his raspy-whiny voice, plays Somerset Frisby, a lazy shopkeeper and a relentless spinner of tall tales. He has an endless supply of stories, and each one is about some grand exploit. The hero of the exploit always is Somerset Frisby. He claims to be an expert on everything, from computers and automobile design to military maneuvers and meteorology. "I just can't take anymore, Frisby," says Scanlan (Dabbs Greer), one of the shop regulars. "The way you tell it, you'd have to be a hundred different people living in two hundred places during twelve periods of American history." The locals roll their eyes as each claim gets more and more ridiculous. "The only industrious thing about Frisby's whole body is his mouth," observes Mitchell (Howard McNear).

But then two strangers pull up in front of Frisby's general store in Pitchville Flats. They are "from quite a way off." They are aliens who have had their eyes (and ears) on Frisby's tall tales. They believe every word. They believe he is the most important person on the planet. "An incredible specimen," one of them says. "Done everything, knows everything, studied in most of their major universities, holds a doctorate in at least eight fields. Obviously a key man."

It's not the wolf of the fable Frisby needs to fear. These wolves are aliens in human clothing.

The aliens take Frisby to their spacecraft, telling him that he will be taken to their planet and displayed as an example of a superior human being. Frisby tries to tell them that he's only "a country boy with a big mouth," but they know all about his accomplishments. They've heard all about them—from him. He's finally telling the truth, and they don't believe him. As they are about to leave, he decides to relax by playing his harmonica. The sound causes the aliens to collapse. He manages to escape, and the now frightened aliens flee. When he makes it back to the store, his friends are waiting for him. They've assembled for a surprise birthday party. They present him with a cup engraved with "World's Greatest Liar." He tries to tell them about being abducted by aliens. For the second time that night, he's telling the truth. For the second time that night, he isn't believed. "This is the truth, honest," Frisby tells them. They take it as just another of his tall tales.

"Mr. Somerset Frisby, who might have profited by reading an Aesop fable about a boy who cried wolf," Serling says in his closing narration. The fable is about twenty-six-hundred years old, but the moral remains the same, even when the lesson lands in the Twilight Zone: "A liar will not be believed, even telling the truth." Of course, he could always go into politics, where his wind power, his penchant for prevarication, and his positive fondness of self-aggrandizement would carry him far . . . maybe not into outer space but certainly to Congress.

ANGELS ARE ALL AROUND YOU
"A PASSAGE FOR TRUMPET"
(ORIGINAL AIRDATE: MAY 20, 1960)
"MR. BEVIS"
(ORIGINAL AIRDATE: JUNE 3, 1960)
"CAVENDER IS COMING"
(ORIGINAL AIRDATE: MAY 25, 1962)

If you look around, you might notice an angel or two in your life. Many of us have them. Many of us have been blessed by their presence over the years. You don't need to be sentimental or spiritual to acknowledge this. With most of us, it's just the plain truth. They certainly don't look like angels as pictured in stained-glass windows or Sunday school books. They don't have the wings and halos and beatific faces. "I'm beginning to believe that there are angels disguised as men who pass themselves off as such and who inhabit the earth for a while to console and lift up with them toward Heaven the poor, exhausted, and saddened souls who were ready to perish below." Was writer George Sand speaking metaphorically or literally? Does it matter?

There are those who believe in actual angels. There are those without a shred of religious belief who act the role of angels, every day in many ways. You can be on either side of this equation and be on the side of the angels. And, yes, you'll encounter actual angels on the metaphoric landscape known as the Twilight Zone.

An angel named Cavender (Jesse White) tries to help Agnes Grep (Carol Burnett), who is suffering the unwanted attentions of an amorous partygoer (Albert Carrier) in Rod Serling's "Cavender Is Coming." *Courtesy CBS Photo Archive*

A great fan of director Frank Capra's *It's a Wonderful Life*, Rod Serling was fond of using angels in his stories. Following George Sand's lead, he preferred angels disguised as men. Following Capra's lead and his angel (second class) Clarence Oddbody, he preferred heavenly helpers with the down-to-Earth touch. That's just the type of angel you're bound to find in the Twilight Zone (or real life). So, as the immortal bard put it in *Hamlet,* let flights of angels sing thee to *The Twilight Zone.*

Now, to be sure, there's another type of angel we regularly run into over in the fifth dimension: the angel of death. We first meet him as Mr. Death, played by Murray Hamilton in Serling's "One for the Angels." He makes return appearances played by Leonard Strong in Serling's "The Hitch-hiker" and by Robert Redford in George Clayton Johnson's "Nothing in the Dark." But then there are the angels intent on changing people's lives, rather than claiming them.

The first of these is a celestial superstar. Gabriel (John Anderson), looking like one hep horn player, puts troubled musician Joey Crown (Jack Klugman) back on a righteous path in Serling's "A Passage for Trumpet." One trumpet player to another, he gets through, and the suicidal Joey decides to give life another chance. The moment hits a soaring high note for the first season of *The Twilight Zone,* reminding us that you don't need to be Gabriel to be there for a troubled soul.

Almost immediately during the show's first season, Serling trotted out an angel who looked like veteran character actor Henry Jones. Named J. Hardy Hempstead, he is the guardian angel of the title character played by Orson Bean in "Mr. Bevis." Then Serling reworked the "Bevis" idea as the third-season episode "Cavender Is Coming." Intended as the pilot episode for a spin-off series, it stars Carol Burnett as klutzy Agnes Grep, "put on Earth with two left feet, an overabundance of thumbs, and a propensity for falling down manholes." She has lost her job as a theater usher, but help is winging its way to her in the form of Harmon Cavender (Jesse White), a cigar-smoking apprentice angel intent on winning his wings. His superior, Polk (Howard Smith), considers him a clod. Can the clod help the klutz . . . in twenty-four hours? He bestows on her fabulous wealth and a mansion, but of course we know money won't buy happiness. Agnes not only is unhappy, she's miserable. She's bored in high society. Even worse, her old friends and the neighborhood kids no longer recognize her. She wants her old life back. "That's for me," she tells him. Cavender at first thinks she's making a mistake, but then realizes Agnes is the richest woman he has ever met. Agnes goes back to being happy, and Cavender goes back to Heaven to face the empyreal music. His supervisor believes he has failed, until he sees how happy Agnes is. He decides there are other deserving people on Earth Cavender can help.

An angel who looked like Harmon Cavender would, indeed, be difficult to recognize as an angel. He loves cigars and gin. He has the elocution of a racetrack tout. Cavender brings to mind the George Bernard Shaw line, "In heaven an angel is nobody in particular." But if an angel can look, sound, and act like Harmon Cavender, maybe, sometimes, all of us have the power to be an angel to others. Can't happen? It does happen, all the time. And you don't need to be looking for that kind of power in *The Twilight Zone*. Just look inside yourself.

GUEST LESSON: CAROL BURNETT
Rod Serling was a great fan of Carol Burnett. She was wrapping up her three-year run on The Garry Moore Show *when Serling asked her about appearing on an episode of* The Twilight Zone. *The year 1962 was an auspicious one for the Texas native. She won an Emmy that year (for* The Garry Moore Show). *She starred with Julie Andrews in the special* Julie and Carol at Carnegie Hall *(which brought her another Emmy in 1963). And she*

appeared in that Twilight Zone *episode. Five years after "Cavender Is Coming" aired, her long-running variety show began its* CBS *run. Burnett, a great fan of* The Twilight Zone *and Rod Serling, sent this lesson for this book:*

I learned that there are no limits to the imagination.

Rod Serling, during his tenure as host of *Night Gallery*, about the time he gave his talk in Akron, Ohio. NBC

ONE FINAL LESSON

Consider this the book's last guest lesson, and it's from Rod Serling himself. The following are his closing comments from a March 1971 speech delivered to an audience largely made up of University of Akron students. After cautioning against name-calling and "the polarization of viewpoints," he said:

Think before we act, but listen before we shout, ponder before we strike, and care damn much before we commit. In closing, one last apocryphal story. The German philosopher Goethe lay dying. He was supposed to have opened his eyes in that last moment before death and plaintively whispered, "Light. Please, let me have light. I must have more light." And a hundred years later, the Spanish philosopher [Miguel de] Unamuno, upon hearing what was reported to be Goethe's deathbed statement, was supposed to have responded, "Impossible. Goethe would not have asked for light. Not light. He would have asked for warmth. He would have said, 'Warmth. Let there be warmth.' Men do not die of the darkness. They die of the cold. It is the frost that kills." I wish you'd think about that, young friends, because I believe

"Remember that your salvation is in your capacity for human warmth—in that remarkable propensity for love." *Courtesy Anne Serling*

that's what it really is all about. Light candles if the darkness warrants it, but remember that your salvation is in your capacity for human warmth—in that remarkable propensity for love.

A LIST OF ALL 156 ORIGINAL EPISODES OF *THE TWILIGHT ZONE,* WITH AIRDATES AND WRITING CREDITS

SEASON ONE

1. "Where Is Everybody?"(October 2, 1959), by Rod Serling.

2. "One for the Angels" (October 9, 1959), by Rod Serling.

3. "Mr. Denton on Doomsday" (October 16, 1959), by Rod Serling.

4. "The Sixteen-Millimeter Shrine" (October 23, 1959), by Rod Serling.

5. "Walking Distance" (October 30, 1959), by Rod Serling.

6. "Escape Clause" (November 6, 1959), by Rod Serling.

7. "The Lonely" (November 13, 1959), by Rod Serling.

8. "Time Enough at Last" (November 20, 1959), by Rod Serling.

9. "Perchance to Dream" (November 27, 1959), by Charles Beaumont (based on his short story).

10. "Judgment Night" (December 4, 1959), by Rod Serling.

11. "And When the Sky Was Opened" (December 11, 1959), by Rod Serling (based on the short story "Disappearing Act," by Richard Matheson).

12. "What You Need" (December 25, 1959), by Rod Serling (based on the short story "What You Need," by Henry Kuttner and C. L. Moore, writing as Lewis Padgett).

13. "The Four of Us Are Dying" (January 1, 1960), by Rod Serling (based on an unpublished story by George Clayton Johnson).

14. "Third from the Sun" (January 8, 1960), by Rod Serling (based on the short story "Third from the Sun," by Richard Matheson).

15. "I Shot an Arrow into the Air" (January 15, 1960), by Rod Serling (based on an idea by Madelon Champion).

16. "The Hitch-hiker" (January 22, 1960), by Rod Serling (based on the radio play "The Hitch-hiker," by Lucille Fletcher).

17. "The Fever" (January 29, 1960), by Rod Serling.

18. "The Last Flight" (February 5, 1960), by Richard Matheson.

19. "The Purple Testament" (February 12, 1960), by Rod Serling.

20. "Elegy" (February 19, 1960), by Charles Beaumont (based on his short story).

21. "Mirror Image" (February 26, 1960), by Rod Serling.

22. "The Monsters Are Due on Maple Street" (March 4, 1960), by Rod Serling.

23. "A World of Difference" (March 11, 1960), by Richard Matheson.

24. "Long Live Walter Jameson" (March 18, 1960), by Charles Beaumont.

25. "People Are Alike All Over" (March 25, 1960), by Rod Serling (based on the short story "Brothers Beyond the Void," by Paul Fairman).

26. "Execution" (April 1, 1960), by Rod Serling, (based on an unpublished story by George Clayton Johnson).

27. "The Big Tall Wish" (April 8, 1960), by Rod Serling.

28. "A Nice Place to Visit" (April 15, 1960), by Charles Beaumont.

29. "Nightmare as a Child" (April 29, 1960), by Rod Serling.

30. "A Stop at Willoughby" (May 6, 1960), by Rod Serling.

31. "The Chaser" (May 13, 1960), by Robert Presnell Jr. (based on the short story "The Chaser," by John Collier).

32. "A Passage for Trumpet" (May 20, 1960), by Rod Serling.

33. "Mr. Bevis" (June 3, 1960), by Rod Serling.

34. "The After Hours" (June 10, 1960), by Rod Serling.

35. "The Mighty Casey" (June 17, 1960), by Rod Serling.

36. "A World of His Own" (July 1, 1960), by Richard Matheson.

SEASON TWO

37. "*King Nine* Will Not Return" (September 30, 1960), by Rod Serling.

38. "The Man in the Bottle" (October 7, 1960), by Rod Serling.

39. "Nervous Man in a Four Dollar Room" (October 14, 1960), by Rod Serling.

40. "A Thing About Machines" (October 28, 1960), by Rod Serling.

41. "The Howling Man" (November 4, 1960), by Charles Beaumont (based on his short story).

42. "Eye of the Beholder" (November 11, 1960), by Rod Serling.

43. "Nick of Time" (November 18, 1960), by Richard Matheson.

44. "The Lateness of the Hour" (December 2, 1960), by Rod Serling.

45. "The Trouble with Templeton" (December 9, 1960), by E. Jack Neuman.

46. "A Most Unusual Camera" (December 16, 1960), by Rod Serling.

47. "The Night of the Meek" (December 23, 1960), by Rod Serling.

48. "Dust" (January 6, 1961), by Rod Serling.

49. "Back There" (January 13, 1961), by Rod Serling.

50. "The Whole Truth" (January 20, 1961), by Rod Serling.

51. "The Invaders" (January 27, 1961), by Richard Matheson.

52. "A Penny for Your Thoughts" (February 3, 1961), by George Clayton Johnson.

53. "Twenty Two" (February 10, 1961), by Rod Serling (based on an anecdote in *Famous Ghost Stories,* edited by Bennett Cerf).

54. "The Odyssey of Flight 33" (February 24, 1961), by Rod Serling.

55. "Mr. Dingle, the Strong" (March 3, 1961), by Rod Serling.

56. "Static" (March 10, 1961), by Charles Beaumont (based on an unpublished story by Oceo Ritch).

57. "The Prime Mover" (March 24, 1961), by Charles Beaumont (based on an unpublished story by George Clayton Johnson).

58. "Long Distance Call" (March 31, 1961), by William Idelson and Charles Beaumont.

59. "A Hundred Yards Over the Rim" (April 7, 1961), by Rod Serling.

60. "The Rip Van Winkle Caper" (April 21, 1961), by Rod Serling.

61. "The Silence" (April 28, 1961), by Rod Serling.

62. "Shadow Play" (May 5, 1961), by Charles Beaumont.

63. "The Mind and the Matter" (May 12, 1961), by Rod Serling.

64. "Will the Real Martian Please Stand Up" (May 26, 1961), by Rod Serling.

65. "The Obsolete Man" (June 2, 1961), by Rod Serling.

SEASON THREE

66. "Two" (September 15, 1961), by Montgomery Pittman.

67. "The Arrival" (September 22, 1961), by Rod Serling.

68. "The Shelter" (September 29, 1961), by Rod Serling.

69. "The Passersby" (October 6, 1961), by Rod Serling.

70. "A Game of Pool" (October 13, 1961), by George Clayton Johnson.

71. "The Mirror" (October 20, 1961), by Rod Serling.

72. "The Grave" (October 27, 1961), by Montgomery Pittman.

73. "It's a Good Life" (November 3, 1961), by Rod Serling (based on the short story "It's a *Good* Life," by Jerome Bixby).

74. "Deaths-head Revisited" (November 10, 1961), by Rod Serling.

75. "The Midnight Sun" (November 17, 1961), by Rod Serling.

76. "Still Valley" (November 24, 1961), by Rod Serling (based on the short story "The Valley Was Still," by Manly Wade Wellman).

77. "The Jungle" (December 1, 1961), by Charles Beaumont (based on his short story).

78. "Once Upon a Time" (December 15, 1961), by Richard Matheson.

79. "Five Characters in Search of an Exit" (December 22, 1961), by Rod Serling (based on the short story "The Depository," by Marvin Petal).

80. "A Quality of Mercy" (December 29, 1961), by Rod Serling (based on an idea by Sam Rolfe).

81. "Nothing in the Dark" (January 5, 1962), by George Clayton Johnson.

82. "One More Pallbearer" (January 12, 1962), by Rod Serling.

83. "Dead Man's Shoes" (January 19, 1962), by Charles Beaumont and Oceo Ritch.

84. "The Hunt" (January 26, 1962), by Earl Hamner Jr.

85. "Showdown with Rance McGrew" (February 2, 1962), by Rod Serling (based on an idea by Frederic Louis Fox).

86. "Kick the Can" (February 9, 1962), by George Clayton Johnson.

87. "A Piano in the House" (February 16, 1962), by Earl Hamner Jr.

88. "The Last Rites of Jeff Myrtlebank" (February 23, 1962), by Montgomery Pittman.

89. "To Serve Man" (March 2, 1962), by Rod Serling (based on the short story "To Serve Man," by Damon Knight).

90. "The Fugitive" (March 9, 1962), by Charles Beaumont.

91. "Little Girl Lost" (March 16, 1962), by Richard Matheson (based on his short story).

92. "Person or Persons Unknown" (March 23, 1962), by Charles Beaumont.

93. "The Little People" (March 30, 1962), by Rod Serling.

94. "Four O'Clock" (April 6, 1962), by Rod Serling (based on the short story "Four O'Clock," by Price Day).

95. "Hocus-Pocus and Frisby" (April 13, 1962), by Rod Serling (based on an unpublished story by Frederic Louis Fox).

96. "The Trade-Ins" (April 20, 1962), by Rod Serling.

97. "The Gift" (April 27, 1962), by Rod Serling.

98. "The Dummy" (May 4, 1962), by Rod Serling (based on an unpublished short story by Lee Polk).

99. "Young Man's Fancy" (May 11, 1962), by Richard Matheson.

100. "I Sing the Body Electric" (May 18, 1962), by Ray Bradbury (based on his short story).

101. "Cavender Is Coming" (May 25, 1962), by Rod Serling.

102. "The Changing of the Guard" (June 1, 1962), by Rod Serling.

SEASON FOUR

103. "In His Image" (January 3, 1963), by Charles Beaumont (based on his short story).

104. "The Thirty-Fathom Grave" (January 10, 1963), by Rod Serling.

105. "Valley of the Shadow" (January 17, 1963), by Charles Beaumont.

106. "He's Alive" (January 24, 1963), by Rod Serling.

107. "Mute" (January 31, 1963), by Richard Matheson (based on his short story).

108. "Death Ship" (February 7, 1963), by Richard Matheson (based on his short story).

109. "Jess-Belle" (February 14, 1963), by Earl Hamner Jr.

110. "Miniature" (February 21, 1963), by Charles Beaumont.

111. "Printer's Devil" (February 28, 1963), by Charles Beaumont (based on his short story "The Devil, You Say?").

112. "No Time Like the Past" (March 7, 1963), by Rod Serling.

113. "The Parallel" (March 14, 1963), by Rod Serling.

114. "I Dream of Genie" (March 21, 1963), by John Furia Jr.

115. "The New Exhibit" (April 4, 1963), by Jerry Sohl (credited to Charles Beaumont, from an idea developed by Sohl and Beaumont).

116. "Of Late I Think of Cliffordville" (April 11, 1963), by Rod Serling (based on the short story "Blind Alley," by Malcolm Jameson).

117. "The Incredible World of Horace Ford" (April 18, 1963), by Reginald Rose.

118. "On Thursday We Leave for Home" (May 2, 1963), by Rod Serling.

119. "Passage on the *Lady Anne*" (May 9, 1963), by Charles Beaumont (based on his short story "Song for a Lady").

120. "The Bard" (May 23, 1963), by Rod Serling.

SEASON FIVE

121. "In Praise of Pip" (September 27, 1963), by Rod Serling.

122. "Steel" (October 4, 1963), by Richard Matheson (based on his short story).

123. "Nightmare at 20,000 Feet" (October 11, 1963), by Richard Matheson (based on his short story).

124. "A Kind of a Stopwatch" (October 18, 1963), by Rod Serling (based on an unpublished story by Michael D. Rosenthal).

125. "The Last Night of a Jockey" (October 25, 1963), by Rod Serling.

126. "Living Doll" (November 1, 1963), by Jerry Sohl (credited to Charles Beaumont, from an idea developed by Sohl and Beaumont).

127. "The Old Man in the Cave" (November 8, 1963), by Rod Serling (based on the short story "The Old Man," by Henry Slesar).

128. "Uncle Simon" (November 15, 1963), by Rod Serling.

129. "Probe 7, Over and Out" (November 29, 1963), by Rod Serling.

130. "The 7th Is Made Up of Phantoms" (December 6, 1963), by Rod Serling.

131. "A Short Drink from a Certain Fountain" (December 13, 1963), by Rod Serling (based on an idea by Lou Holtz).

132. "Ninety Years Without Slumbering" (December 20, 1963), by Richard deRoy (based on an unpublished story by George Clayton Johnson).

133. "Ring-a-Ding Girl" (December 27, 1963), by Earl Hamner Jr.

134. "You Drive" (January 3, 1964), by Earl Hamner Jr.

135. "The Long Morrow" (January 10, 1964), by Rod Serling.

136. "The Self-Improvement of Salvadore Ross" (January 17, 1964), by Jerry McNeely (based on the short story by Henry Slesar).

137. "Number 12 Looks Just Like You" (January 24, 1964), by John Tomerlin (credited to Charles Beaumont, based on Beaumont's short story "The Beautiful People").

138. "Black Leather Jackets" (January 31, 1964), by Earl Hamner Jr.

139. "Night Call" (February 7, 1964), by Richard Matheson (based on his short story "Long Distance Call").

140. "From Agnes—with Love" (February 14, 1964), by Bernard C. Schoenfeld.

141. "Spur of the Moment" (February 21, 1964), by Richard Matheson.

142. "An Occurrence at Owl Creek Bridge" (February 28, 1964), by Robert Enrico (based on the short story by Ambrose Bierce).

143. "Queen of the Nile" (March 6, 1964), by Jerry Sohl (credited to Charles Beaumont, from an idea developed by Sohl and Beaumont).

144. "What's in the Box" (March 13, 1964), by Martin M. Goldsmith.

145. "The Masks" (March 20, 1964), by Rod Serling.

146. "I Am the Night—Color Me Black" (March 27, 1964), by Rod Serling.

147. "Sounds and Silences" (April 3, 1964), by Rod Serling.

148. "Caesar and Me" (April 10, 1964), by Adele T. Strassfield.

149. "The Jeopardy Room" (April 17, 1964), by Rod Serling.

150. "Stopover in a Quiet Town" (April 24, 1964), by Earl Hamner Jr.

151. "The Encounter" (May 1, 1964), by Martin M. Goldsmith.

152. "Mr. Garrity and the Graves" (May 8, 1964), by Rod Serling (from an unpublished story by Mike Korologos).

153. "The Brain Center at Whipple's" (May 15, 1964), by Rod Serling.

154. "Come Wander with Me" (May 22, 1964), by Anthony Wilson.

155. "The Fear" (May 29, 1964), by Rod Serling.

156. "The Bewitchin' Pool" (June 19, 1964), by Earl Hamner Jr.

MARK DAWIDZIAK

Mark Dawidziak has been a regular visitor to *The Twilight Zone* since glimpsing images beamed from the fifth dimension to the television set in the living room of the Long Island home where he grew up (if, indeed, he ever did). The television critic at the Cleveland *Plain Dealer* since July 1999, he will tell anyone who asks (and many who don't) that *The Twilight Zone* is his all-time favorite TV show.

Before moving to Ohio in 1983, the New York native worked as a theater, film, and TV critic at newspapers in Tennessee and Virginia. He began his journalism career in the late 1970s at the Associated Press and Knight-Ridder bureaus in Washington, D.C. During his sixteen years at the *Akron Beacon Journal,* he held such posts as TV columnist, movie critic, and critic-at-large.

Also an author and playwright, his many books include the 1994 horror novel *Grave Secrets* and two histories of landmark TV series: *The Columbo Phile: A Casebook* (1989) and *The Night Stalker Companion* (1997). A recognized Mark Twain scholar, he frequently is invited to lecture on Twain or television history at universities, libraries, and museums (he has three times been the guest lecturer at Elmira College's Center for Mark Twain Studies). His acclaimed Twain-centric books include *Mark My Words: Mark Twain on Writing* (1996), *Horton Foote's The Shape of the River: The Lost Teleplay About Mark Twain* (2003), *Mark Twain in Ohio* (2015), *Mark Twain's Guide to Diet, Exercise, Beauty, Fashion, Investment, Romance, Health and Happiness* (2015), and *Mark Twain for Cat Lovers: True and Imaginary Adventures with Feline Friends* (2016). He also has portrayed Mark Twain on stage for more than thirty-five years. His study of the writer born Samuel Clemens has prompted no less than Ken Burns to observe, "Nobody gets Mark Twain the way Mark Dawidziak does."

In addition to two histories of the Carl Kolchak character, *Night Staking* and *The Night Stalker Companion*, his work on the horror side of the street also includes *The Bedside, Bathtub & Armchair Companion to Dracula* (2008), a play (*The Tell-Tale Play*), short stories, and comic-book scripts. Several of his essays and introductions appear in *Richard Matheson's Kolchak Scripts* (2003), *Bloodlines: Richard Matheson's Dracula, I Am Legend, and Other Vampire Stories* (2006), and *Richard Matheson's Censored and Unproduced I Am Legend Screen-play* (2012), three books he edited for Gauntlet Press. He contributed the career appreciation and overview to *Produced and Directed by Dan Curtis* (2004) and he is the creative consultant to Moonstone's comic book series *Kolchak: The Night Stalker*. He also is on the editorial board for Rod Serling Books.

The biography *Jim Tully: American Writer, Irish Rover, Hollywood Brawler,* written with Paul J. Bauer, was published by the Kent State University Press in 2011 with a foreword by Ken Burns. It's the first full-length biography of "hobo writer" Jim Tully, a forgotten author hailed as "America's Gorky" and as a literary superstar in the 1920s and 1930s. He and Bauer edited and wrote introductions for four reprints of books by Tully: *Beggars of Life, Circus Parade, Shanty Irish,* and *The Bruiser.*

Dawidziak and his wife, actress Sara Showman, founded the Largely Literary Theater Company in 2002. Dedicated to promoting literacy and literature, the company has staged his three-person version of Charles Dickens's *A Christmas Carol* and his two-act play based on sketches by Mark Twain, *The Reports of My Death Are Greatly Exaggerated.* He and Showman regularly appear in their two-person plays *Twain By Two, Shades of Blue and Gray: Ghosts of the Civil War, Ghosts by the Tale,* and *Force of Nature* (about the founding of the National Park Service).

An adjunct professor at Kent State University, he has taught classes each semester since 2009: Reviewing Film and Television and Vampires on Film and Television. Dawidziak also has been a regular contributor to such magazines as *TV Guide, Commonwealth, Cinefantastique, Scarlet Street, Mystery Scene, Sci-Fi Universe, Not of This Earth, Ohio Magazine,* and *Parents' Choice.* A member of the Television Critics Association's board of directors for five years, he has won many Cleveland Press Club awards for entertainment writing, as well as a Society of Professional Journalists award for coverage of minority issues. In 2015, he was inducted into the Press Club of Cleveland Journalism Hall of Fame.

A journalism graduate of George Washington University, he was born in Huntington, New York. He lives in Cuyahoga Falls, Ohio, with his wife and their daughter, Rebecca "Becky" Claire.

INDEX